FOUR HUNDR
LUGUS PUBLI(

"The Home served its purpose for those times, when there was no mothers' allowance, no baby-sitters, no subsidized housing, no free medical care, very little assistance of any kind. There was a need for a home like that, and it served its purpose well.

Many of the children, like myself, had one parent, but in those days of great need, it was not possible for a single parent to survive. The Home was the best possible solution—which is hard for today's generation of plenty to understand. Very different times.

But we all went on to make lives for ourselves and in most cases, rich and rewarding ones, with a special love for family."

Earl Greenberg, Alumnus, Montefiore Home.

"We believe this is the first such history and we are pleased to aid in seeing that the book comes to the attention of the Jewish community."

Emanuel Weiner, The Jewish Community Foundation of Montreal.

FOUR HUNDRED
BROTHERS AND SISTERS

TWO JEWISH ORPHANAGES
IN
MONTREAL, QUEBEC 1909-1942

Dear Rose-
Thanks for your interest.
Enjoy the read-
Judy Gordon
Oct. 10, 2002

BY

JUDY GORDON

LUGUS

Published by
Lugus Publications
48 Falcon Street
Toronto
Ontario
Canada
M4S 2P5

Canadian Cataloguing in Publication Data

Gordon, Judy, 1935-
Four Hundred Brothers and Sisters: Two Jewish Orphanages in Montreal, Quebec 1909-1942 / Judy Gordon
Includes Index
ISBN: 1-896266-97-5
1. Montefiore Hebrew Orphans' Home—History. 2. Montreal Hebrew Orphans' Home
—History. 1. Title
HV1010.M6G67 2002 362.73'2 C2002-903854-5

The Publisher would like to acknowledge the use of Images provided by The National Archives of The Canadian Jewish Congress, Montreal.

Dedicated

to

my dear parents, the late Mae and Al Gold
who would have been so proud that their daughter's creative ability
was finally recognized...

to my dear Myer, who is still moved to tears (of happiness)
—after more than sixty years—
reminiscing about his years with his 'brothers and sisters'

and

to all the MHOH Alumni,
whose shared experiences, stories and coping mechanisms
are awe-inspiring and treasured.

CONTENTS

ILLUSTRATIONS

LISTS AND TABLES

FOREWORDS

I

We live in an age which tempts us to become incurably cynical. Our politicians and religious leaders seem incapable of putting aside age-old causes that serve only to divide us. Our historians fail us too. In their determination to "connect all the dots" of the past, too often they manipulate facts to suit their individual agendas. We are constantly warned that those who ignore history are doomed to repeat it, and yet the question remains: Whose version of history?

There is no arguing with the proposition that, to understand the present and prepare for the future, we must know the past. But whom should we trust to illuminate the past for us?

My response is this: let us put our trust in scribes like Judy Gordon to "get it right." With the assistance of her husband Myer Gordon—an alumnus of Montreal's Montefiore Home—and inspired by other alumni, many of whom went on to distinguished careers after childhoods spent at one or other of Montreal's two homes for Jewish orphans, Judy Gordon has recorded Jewish life in that city as it existed during the most difficult decades of the Twentieth Century.

And it is no ordinary record!

Four Hundred Brothers and Sisters brims with personal recollections that best describe an important era because the people who speak of those times were there. These chapters stem from first-hand knowledge and experience, and offer unadorned, straightforward, and honest remembrances, enhanced by reproduced documents and photographs that tell all the truth one could wish for. The stories are at once touching, sad, joyful, and above all life-affirming.

Isaac Bashevis once wrote that Jews suffer from many diseases, but amnesia is not one of them. To which I would add—bearing Judy Gordon's fine work in mind—Thank God!

Morley Torgov, Toronto

II

Although I grew up in Montreal in the 1940s, and have a special interest in the history of the city, I was never aware of the existence of Jewish orphanages here—at least not until reading this excellent book. If the word orphanage ever came to mind, it was only to evoke a picture of a hungry Oliver Twist pleading for more porridge in that dreadful institution where he was confined. Closer to home—and in real-life Quebec, not Dickensian fiction—we had those miserable human warehouses where the so-called Duplessis Orphans were kept, in the 1940s and '50s, and where they suffered abuse and deprivation.

But Judy Gordon's book shows us two very different institutions, two Jewish orphanages, where the children were very well treated, so as to be launched into happy, productive lives. There were a few dark shadows in these orphanages, such as that cast by Mr. Ogulnick, a cruel supervisor, but by and large the people who ran these institutions were kind, caring and efficient. The children adored many of them, especially Matt Max, the supervisor who was so reluctant to punish children who misbehaved that he advised boys who had to be spanked to conceal a telephone book in the seat of their pants so as to lessen the pain (telephone books were much thinner in those days).

It is details such as this that make this book such a pleasure to read, and make it so revealing about life in the bygone days it deals with, an era that began in 1909 and ended in 1942. Readers who enjoy glimpses of a largely forgotten past will value reminders of things like the *Montreal Maroons,* the *Golden Gloves* and tag days. Realities like bagels that cost one cent each in the 1930s, and men's suits that could be bought for $9.99, enliven these pages.

Life for the children in the orphanages is well described, and we hear about the Mandolin Club; about the romance between Earl and Sarah, who were on dish-washing duty and were holding hands under the dirty dish water; and the weekly battle against head lice, when the children lined up to be combed and examined.

The research that went into the making of this book is impressive. The author has unearthed much documentation about these institutions and thus we are able to see a list of what a month's supply of food for one of the orphanages consisted of, including two cases of sardines, 24 pounds of matzo meal and 24 quarts of sour cream. Documents that survive include memos about where supplies may be purchased most economically and reports by attending physicians.

Perhaps most revealing of all are the detailed memories of many of the former residents of the two orphanages. They write not only of the happy times they had there as children but also about the lives they led in later years, long after "graduating" at the obligatory age of 16.

And it is most gratifying to read about how much good was done, how many fruitful lives were fostered by the generosity of Jewish philanthropy, even in the lean years of the Great Depression of the 1930s.

William Weintraub, Montreal

PROLOGUE

The question may fittingly be asked: what is there specifically Jewish in the care received by our orphaned children, or stated in another way: does the Jewish way of living produce a communal care that differs from the treatment received by other dependent children? This may quite frankly be answered in the affirmative. The Jew does take a distinctive attitude toward the unfortunate among his people.

Jewish life, since its beginning, has been marked by uncertainty and precariousness. A wealthy land-owner in Judaea became a slave in Babylon. A merchant prince in Spain became a mendicant in Holland. And even today, a boycott in one country or some silly edict in another may force whole masses of Jews to the verge of ruin.

For centuries the great majority of our people have had little opportunity to become rooted anywhere and as a result, their fortunes have ever been an unknown quantity from year to year. This fact has served strongly to enforce one of the grandest ideas ever evolved by a people, *Zedokoh.* Instead of condescending charity, the handing out of alms by the salt of the earth to the pitiable, we have *Zedokoh,* the aid extended by brother to brother on the plane of equality.

The spirit of *Zedokoh*, justice flavoured with benevolence, pervades the Jewish Orphan Home. The children are not mere receivers of charity, they are the sons and daughters of the Jewish community, which regards them as its very own flesh of its flesh and blood of its blood.

The support of a federation plays an important part in the bringing up of orphaned children in spirit of *Zedokoh.* Where there is a federation, the children are far removed from the open *schnorring* that is the bane of benevolent enterprises. Children in a Home should receive new clothing just as their schoolmates do and just when they need them. The supply of food must be regular as the meals must be planned in advance...the effects of irregular food, donations, etc. has a bad effect on the children. They cannot be like little beggars dependent on the whim of a passer-by. With the aid of a federation, they can be brought up as they should be. The children know their clothes come from a place of business, their groceries from a grocer, their meat from a butcher, and so on.

This sort of a system should appeal to every Jew who has the real welfare of orphan children to heart, for a Home which is under a federation can closer approach that ideal of normal living, which is the real spirit of *Zedokoh.*

In addition to this general atmosphere we need a very practical system of Jewish education in order to make the children of the community worthy and able to carry on the torch of Jewish life. In the Home's kitchen the girls, and boys as well, learn the rudiments of the Jewish laws regarding the preparation and serving of food. This is the only way to inculcate a knowledge of *Kashruth,* teaching by example...the basis of Jewish education can be found in the laws, methods, tastes and smells of the kitchen. When the meal is prepared and the table set with the appropriate dishes, the children learn to thank Him who sends forth the bread from the earth. When the meal is done even the little ones learn to say the *B'rochoh.* Since "early to bed and early to rise" is the rule in the orphans' home, just about the time that the first *minyon* is gathering in the *shul,* the boys are davening. In a small home, there is often enough to make a *minyon.*

...the formal part of the education is Hebrew School...conducted in the Home on modern lines...no rapping of knuckles...no droning...the *Siddur* loses its terrors and when the children go to the synagogue Saturday morning, they do not find it difficult to find the place or know what is said next...Even those little jackanapes, who formerly had a *Magnet Library* or a *Sexton Blake* surreptitiously hidden where they could read while no one could tell from their angelic countenance exactly what they were doing, begin to sit up and take notice because they know what it is all about.

On Sunday morning, there is the religious school...Jewish history and ethics. The most colourful part of Jewish education lies in the observance of Friday night, the Holy days and festivals...how one cries if she has not a pretty dress to put on. And if there is something that makes the girls jealous, it is when some poor innocuous male child reaches the dizzy heights of 13 and becomes Bar Mitzvah. Why the boys strut about so, singing their parts at all hours and getting excused to go to the Rabbi is something that surpasseth girlish understanding. Then the Great Day itself, and the party and the presents. The boys, always the boys.

Life has its little joys...and its woes where the orphan is concerned. Every now and then a child receives a *Yahrzeit* candle and the other children pass by silently when it is lit by the little mourner, for the meaning of this they understand well, too well.

...the place of religious education in an orphan home...involves the thoughts and feelings of little Jewish hearts and minds to whom this training is given...for what is education if it does not reach right down into the deepest recesses of a child's mind. Their faith is simple and it can be made full of Jewish colour and feeling.

In an orphan home life is intense because the children have all had sad experiences and this intensity must not be sacrificed to an institutional routine. They can receive an impress that will remain with them throughout the days of their lives and this impress it is our duty to give.

The Jewish Orphan by Irving Gerdy,
Superintendent, Montreal Hebrew Orphans' Home
with excerpts from *The Canadian Jewish Chronicle,* Dec. 15, 1922.

Arthur Daniel Hart wrote about two other Canadian orphanages in his book, *The Jew in Canada,* in 1926. These homes were formed for the same purposes as the two Montreal Homes...to ensure that poor Jewish children/orphans were not placed, as before, in Christian facilities to receive shelter and education. Toronto's Jewish Children's Home first opened in 1909 on the corner of Elizabeth and Dundas Streets—the impetus to open this home was to assist a poor widow and her two children. Not only did her family gain a place to live, but she was also appointed the first superintendent! In 1910, improved quarters were found on Simcoe Street; a final move to Annette Street was made in 1921 to a building accommodating 35 residents, an addition being added in 1926.

In Winnipeg, the Canadian Jewish Orphanage opened in July 1913. Because there were two factions at the time, a second was opened almost simultaneously, financed by Mr. R.S. Robinson and named to commemorate his mother—the Esther Robinson Orphans' Home and Children's Aid of Western Canada. By the end of 1916, it was decided to amalgamate the two homes. The new facility opened in February

1920 and cared for about 110 children.

ACKNOWLEDGEMENTS

Janice Rosen, Director, Archives, Canadian Jewish Congress (CJC) National Archives, Montreal and Eiran Harris, Jewish Public Library Archives, Montreal for their valuable time, patience, guidance, proof-reading, suggestions and support throughout the writing/compilation of this book.
Leslie Lutsky, Producer of "Jewish Digest" on Radio Centre-Ville, Montreal, for his in-depth taping about the book, pre-publication, for radio.
Allan Raymond, Jewish Historian for Montreal and Lachine.
Rafi Aaron, Toronto, for promotion and ongoing support.

Benefactors

Harry Baker, Montreal, (MHOH Alumnus)
Firm Capital Corporation, Toronto, *per* Rubin and Betty Sugar.
Judge Irving Pfeffer, San Francisco, CA (MHOH)
Jewish Family Services of the Baron de Hirsch Institute, Montreal
Max & Wanda Matt, Bloomfield, CT (MHOH Supervisor)
Nettie & Al Shragie, Montreal, (MHOH)
The Jewish Community Foundation of Montreal
Upper Canada Lodge, No. 1615, Toronto
Jack Zukerman, Montreal, (MHOH)

Patrons

Dr. Murray & Jodi Asch
Randy, Marshall & Jordana Asch, Toronto
Hilda Brownstone, Edgewater, NJ (MHOH)
Norman & Sandy Burns, Toronto
Edic Bye, Montreal (MHOH)
Lola & Larry Caplan, Toronto
Manny & Mary Cohen, Montreal (MHOH)

Nathan & Hannah Cohen, Montreal (MHOH)
Sara Frenkel, Toronto (MHOH)
Eileen & David Ginberg, Boca Raton, Florida
Edie & Sonny Goldstein, Toronto
Mordy & Frances Gordon, Dollard des Ormeaux, PQ
Earl & Sandy Greenberg, Toronto (MHOH)
Beatrice Hock, Ottawa (MHOH Volunteer)
Peter & Aurora Kashkarian, Toronto (Ararat Int'l Fine Foods Ltd.)
Morris & Marie Claire Letnick, White Rock, BC (MHOH)
Reggie & Gerry Levene, Toronto
Sol & Zelda Mayoff, Montreal (MHOH)
Phyllis & Michael Mendell, Montreal
Bill & Beth Stern, Toronto
Saul Tolmasky, Montreal (MHOH)
Eleanor Wynston, Aurora, ON

Supporters

Moe & Jeannine Adelstein, Montreal (MHOH)
Henry & Frances Albert, Montreal (MHOH)
Charles Asch & Lainie Ritter, New York City
Helen & Sam Chvertkin, Toronto
(In honour of their special birthdays)
Lester & Irma Dick, Kirkland, PQ (MHOH)
Muriel Fishman, Montreal, (MHOH)
Marilyne Gordon & Karl Hennek, Whitby, ON
Leslie Lutsky, Montreal
Tina & Leonard Rosen, Montreal (MHOH)
Vita & Eric Seidler, Toronto (MHOH)
Syd & Roz Ticker, Toronto (MHOH)
Bernice Vader, Toronto
Gordon Vatch & Richard Brown, Deerfield Beach, FL
Saul & Dorothy White, Montreal (MHOH)
(In honour of grandson Joel Chetner's Bar Mitzvah
& granddaughter Tova Chetner's 1st birthday)
Murray L. Wohlmuth, Toronto

The following libraries, archives, books, and individuals were consulted, quoted, excerpted in preparation of this history:

Irving Abella, *A Coat of Many Colours: Two Centuries of Jewish Life in Canada*, 1990.
Barbara Frum Library, Toronto.
Prof. Myron Echenberg, *The Echenberg Story,* 1986, Montreal/ Sherbrooke.
Jewish Public Library, Toronto.
Jewish War Orphans Committee, *The Jews in Canada* p. 513-520
Joe King, *From the Ghetto to the Main: The Story of the Jews of Montreal,* 2000
The Montreal Jewish Publication Society, Montreal, 2001
Israel Medres, *Montreal fun Nekhtn* (Montreal of Yesterday), 1947, Vehicule Press, Montreal translated into English by his granddaughter Vivian Felsen
Sir Moses Montefiore http:/www.montefiorefevercom/montefiore %20 history.htm
Erna Paris, *Jews—An Account of their Experience in Canada,* 1980, MacMillan of Canada
Hélène Vallée, CJC Archives, Montreal
Jerry Waldston, a former Sunshine Camp counsellor, Sketches
Shulamis Yelin, *Shulamis: Stories from a Montreal Childhood,* 1993, Shoreline Press, Ste.-Anne-de-Bellevue.

> In Jewish history, the distant past and distant future merge.
> All characters are linked, eternally involved with one another—eternally responsible for one another.
> No people has been obsessed with history for so long,
> for a Jew redeems himself only within his own history.

Elie Wiesel. (From the 1978 Annual Report of Allied Jewish Community Services, *We Are Our people*.)

INTRODUCTION

Four Hundred Brothers and Sisters

Once upon a time...there were two Jewish orphanages in Montreal. Yes, really! This is not fairy tale.

Yet we find it puzzling that most Montrealers, especially the Jews, are not even aware that Jewish orphanages existed in their city—certainly not Jewish orphanages—in Westmount, the Montreal Hebrew Orphans' Home on Claremont Avenue, and the Jeanne Mance site of the Montefiore Hebrew Orphans Home—both now lovingly referred to as MHOH.

For more than 60 years, the children of the orphanages considered themselves to be brothers and sisters—more than 300 of them! In the Montreal of the 'teens,' 20s and 30s, they were considered orphans, even though many of them had one parent. So, in the modern sense of the word, many really weren't. Some were just poor Jewish children of that era who were sent to live in one of the two orphanages; some were refugees from World War I.

But they were all equally needy...for care and for love.

Times were so different for poor children back then in the years prior to 1940. There was no money, no children's allowance, no foster care, no day care. No government-sponsored medical insurance, no welfare. To be an orphan back then meant that, in most cases, one parent had died, or was ill, and the remaining parent was unable to properly care for his/her child(ren).

"They were tough times," reminisced Sophie Feldman Kazdan. "The only choice was to put the children into an orphanage when there was no extended family willing or able to help out."

The price of admission to an orphanage was family separation.

While it was not a family in the known sense of the word, the Montreal Jewish orphanages fostered care and caring. And its young residents, aged from 3-16, for the most part, felt as though they were part of a larger extended family. One prime example of this was Myer Gordon, who entered the Montefiore Home in 1926 with his brother

Ben. He was 5, Ben 12, when their widowed mother was forced to put them there so she could go back to New York and a job. One year later, she returned to take them both back with her. Orphanage staff told her, "You can take Benny; but leave Myer...he's such a good boy." So she did! He spent ten years in the orphanage!

To this day, Myer harbours no regrets, no bitterness, no animosity, no fears of abandonment, nor complex over being 'left behind.' He remembers the experience as wonderful and is convinced orphanages were far better than the current practice of fostering out children. There, he was happy being surrounded by his brothers and sisters, getting three 'squares' a day, going to camp every summer.

As youngsters, the children bonded well. They were well cared for, schooled, learned manners, religion, values and caring. And when the Homes were closed, the Montefiore in 1936, the Montreal in 1942, they scattered across the city into the homes of family, friends, foster care and the military arenas of WWII.

It is interesting to note that, though both Jewish and with the same goals, the Homes were kept as two completely separate orphanages/organizations. The children never spent any time together nor did they ever meet. Myer remembers some occasional visits to the Montreal Home that he went to on his own by streetcar—he was a real loner in those days—standing outside the gates, peering through the bars (like a true orphan!), never even seeing one child.

And over the years, the two groups stayed apart, virtual strangers, although with a common past. Even when the first reunions were held in the 1950s, they were two quite separate events. It was only when the combined reunions started in 1989, that they began to come together. True, to this day, the two groups mingle mainly with their own, but some are talking, getting to know each other, getting friendly. Myer and I are lucky...we know them all!

Over the years, some kept in touch with others. Some married, and some moved far and wide. Over the years, the Alumni grew in stature as well as age. We count among them such 'brothers' as Judge Irving Pfeffer and Dr. Sydney Shaner of California; Lester Dick, clothing designer, and business man; the late Sam Baker—both of Montreal; and now Torontonians, 'sisters' Annie Reisler Thomas, composer; Judith Stolov Kazdan, now an over-80 marathoner, and her brother

Meyer Stolov, a renowned violinist living in Ithaca, New York.

Almost twenty years passed before the urge to reconnect became strong enough to attempt a first reunion. Former Montefiore Supervisor Max Matt was in Montreal visiting relatives, and a group of his north-end 'kids' were inspired to organize a reunion in 1957. More than 100 congregated for four years in a row to relive their childhoods—the traumas and the pleasures. And to rejoice once again at being with their brothers and sisters. Montreal Home Alumni also met informally in their own group over those few years.

Another 30 years passed before talk of more reunions resurfaced. Interest began again 'in earnest' in 1988, when a group of Alumni, now all living in Toronto, got together for a social evening. As expatriate Montrealers, the sense of family remained strong among youngsters from the Homes.

Two in particular, Sam Rasminsky and Myer Gordon, realized that this bond still existed...bonds formed as youngsters that now extended out over the miles between cities, over the years since the last get-together...the memories forever etched in the minds of young children who had nowhere else to go, but to an orphanage. And, contrary to the images of orphanages as dark places of misery and despair, these Homes were the scenes of the "happiest days of our lives"—a sentiment expressed freely at the ensuing reunions. Says Gordon, "Whatever I became in life, whatever I am today, I owe to my upbringing at the orphanage."

This time, a combined reunion of both Homes was planned. Montreal Alumni, Sylvia Savitsky Rasminsky and Harry Schwartz, worked with Montefiore 'kids' Myer Gordon, Earl Greenberg, Sophie Feldman Kazdan and Vita Shein Seidler and spouses—Sam Rasminsky was in both homes. They met to organize the many details involved, the least of which trying to amass updated names and addresses of the Alumni living across Canada, the U.S. and abroad. Thanks to the Rasminskys, the list of the Montreal Home kids was maintained, increased and corrected. Myer Gordon and some of his group looked after the lists of those from the Montefiore Home.

The catalyst again was Max Matt, now 91, who lives in Bloomfield, Connecticut. An orphan himself from the cruel world of the Romanian orphanage system, he was less than 10 years older than his charges. But he was loved and admired by the majority.

The first combined reunion was held in Toronto in 1989—a Saturday night dinner and Sunday brunch. One hundred came that year. In 1990, the Montreal reunion location attracted 130 happy brothers and sisters. The occasion was filled with tears of joy.

Over the next years, the committee dwindled down to only Myer Gordon and his wife Judy. Reunions were held annually, mainly in Montreal, several times in Toronto. They started a quarterly newsletter, *The Mishpocha,* to keep Alumni in touch, to offer news and tidbits about the former orphans, to advertise the location, activities, costs of the reunions. Donations were initially solicited to cover the cost of the newsletter, edited by Judy, and to help (in confidence) any Alumnus who was in need. The last few years, the donations have been sent in by generous Alumni to cover costs, now including donations in memory of recently departed Alumni...trees planted in Israel or monies given to the individual's favourite charity.

The monies are building up, and plans for the near future involve donating this fund—as a scholarship to perpetuate the name of MHOH—to Montreal's Jewish Family Services, now part of the former Baron de Hirsch Institute (which originally administered the Montreal Home) to help the poorer children go to camp. Our photos, letters, videos and bios, collected since 1989, will eventually be sent to the Canadian Jewish Congress National Archives in Montreal.

In the meantime, the reunions, the condolence donations, and *The Mishpocha* are ongoing.

At this time, I must extend extra thanks to Max Matt, Bloomfield, CT, Montefiore Home Supervisor, and Judge Irving Pfeffer, San Francisco, CA, noted Alumnus of the Montreal Home, who provided advice, proof-reading, and emotional and financial support throughout this entire writing experience, and to Menda Weinstein, Montreal, for her precious photos of some Ladies Auxiliary members of the Montefiore Home. Special thanks as well to Vita Seidler, Earl and Sandy Greenberg and Elva Strom for providing their opinions, proof-reading and 'backbones of support.' And enduring thanks to my dear Myer, whose experiences, empathy, emotional and secretarial support and way with words were invaluable in the gathering of information, writing, proofing, and compilation of this book. I hope he is pleased that, finally, his early years have found a voice.

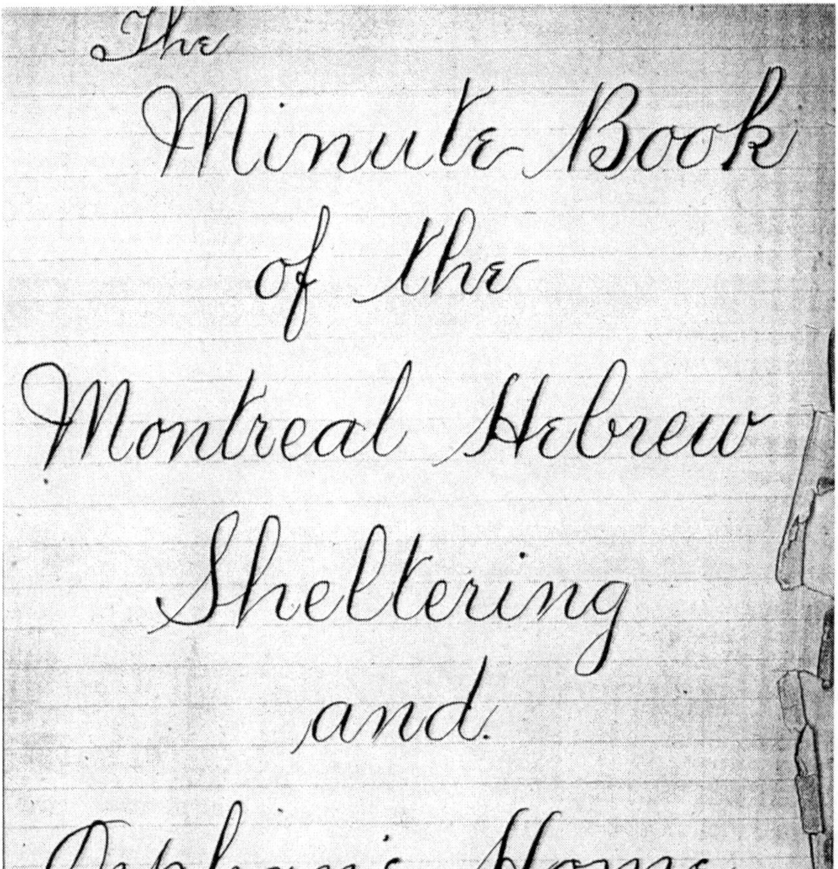

The Minute Book of the Montreal Hebrew Sheltering and Orphan's Home

1914

507 St Urbain St and 16-18 Evans St.

Jewish Refugees arriving 1 Jan. 1928 in Halifax aboard the SS Asia

Lazarus Cohen's son, Lyon Cohen, inherited the leadership of the uptown Jewish community. He was widely respected as a mediator and a diplomat and was the chairman of the first Canadian Jewish Congress in 1919.

S. W. Jacobs represented the mainly Jewish Montreal riding of George Etienne Cartier in the House of Commons from 1917 until his death in 1938. During the 1930s, Jacobs fought desperately (and unsuccessfully) for the admittance of Jewish refugees from Nazi Germany into Canada.

Jewish immigrants in Montreal, circa 1920

Grostern's Deli circa 1920

Hershman's circa 1920

MHOH (Westmount) c. 1920

Berthelet School Group c. 1920

Montefiore Home c. 1920

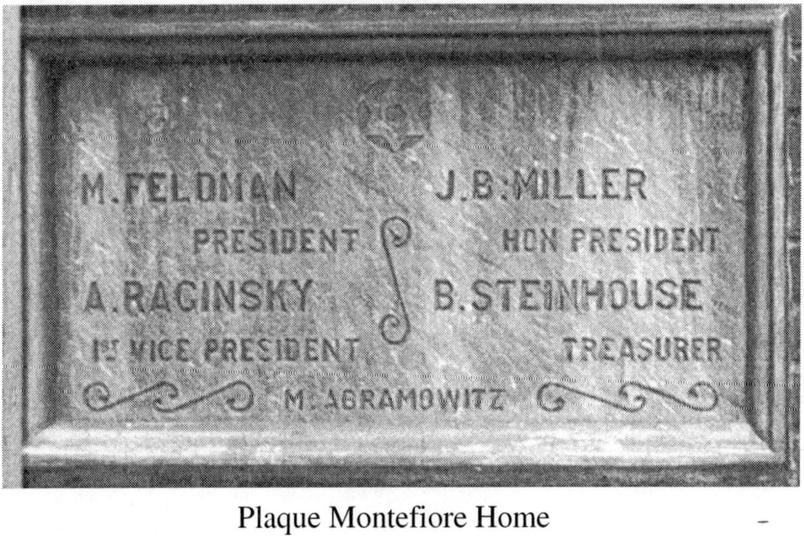

Plaque Montefiore Home

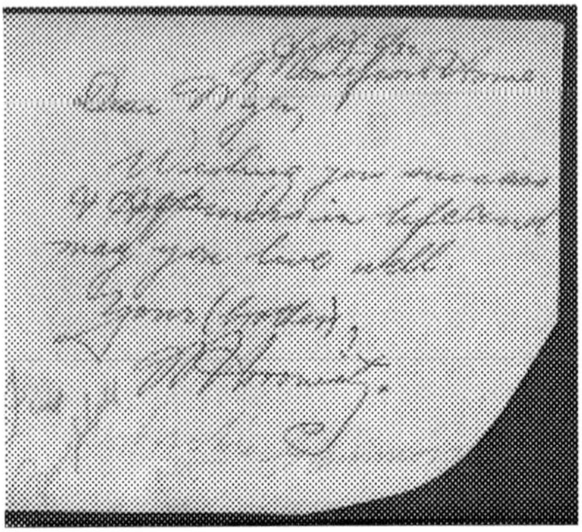

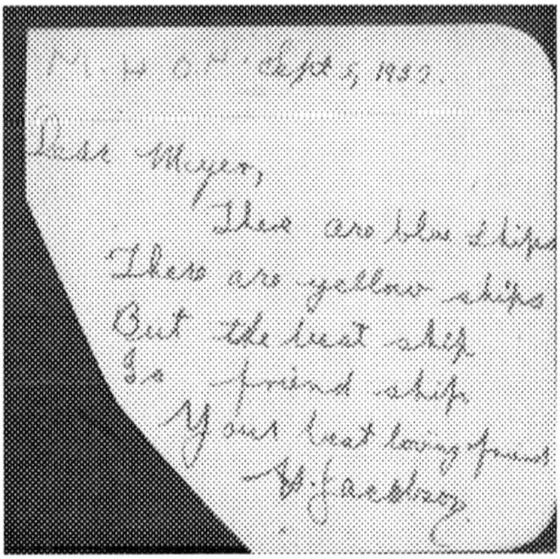

Dear Myer,
There are blue ships
There are yellow ships
But the best ship
Is friend ship
Your best loving friend

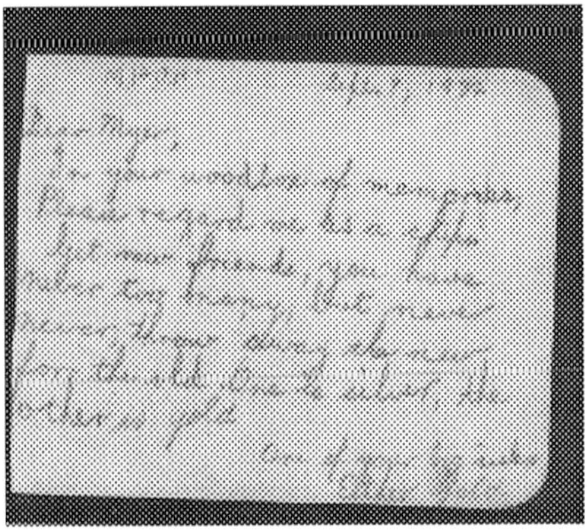

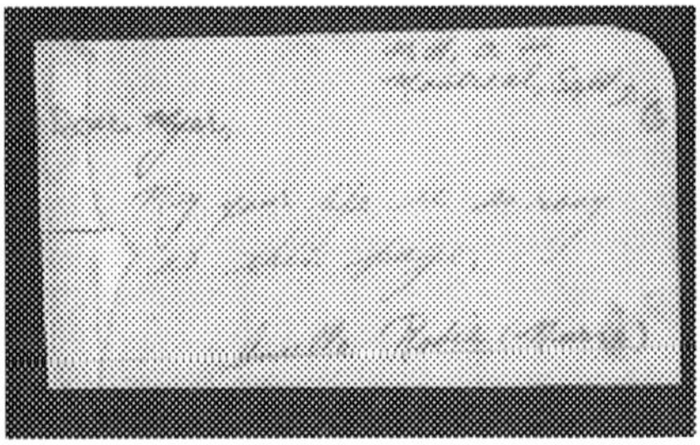

Autographs from Myer Gordon's Book

THE MONTEFIORE
HEBREW
ORPHANS HOME
The Montefiore Hebrew Orphans Home
Ste-Agathe Des Monts 1930

Mrs. Kramer, Cook and Housekeeper,
Montreal Home, 1929

OFFICERS
MONTEFIORE HEBREW ORPHAN'S HOME
M. FELDMAN, President

The Ladies Auxilary of the Montefiore Hebrew Orphans' Home, 1924

THE FLAVOUR OF MONTREAL (1900-1940)
(Just a Taste!)

Chocolate, for the sweet life lived by the 'uptowners'
Lemon, for the bitter pits that life had flung at the 'downtowners'
Chili, for the heated issues dividing the two groups.

A Brief Background

Severe pogroms throughout Europe from 1871 to 1906 killed thousands of Jews. Restrictions resulted in growing economic pressures and poverty. "Pauperization became the general pattern of 19th century (European) Jewish economic life," according to Professor Myron Echenberg of McGill University in his family history.

The Tsars of Russia conscripted Jews into the armed forces. In 1901, they constituted 5.73% of all service men in the Russian army. Between 1880 and 1910, the number of Russian Jews rose from 3,000,000 to 4,200,000. By 1910, there were 1,400,000 in Poland. Warsaw was the largest Jewish city in all of Europe in 1908, with 278,000. The Jewish population everywhere was rising at a faster rate than the general population.

Pressure for Jewish migration from Russia and Europe was part of a complex pattern which saw millions of migrants leave the Old World for the New. This world-wide phenomenon could be traced to three factors—the push of population growth, the push of old and new forms of persecution, and the pull of the New World as the land of opportunity.

The Jewish community in Canada formally began with the British conquest in 1759. Lieutenant Aaron Hart decided to remain, taking up residence in Trois Rivières. For a long time, Sephardic Jews were the only Jews in Montreal—their rites were still popular and prestigious in

England. They came prior to 1800 from Holland, Belgium and England, descendents of the Spanish and Portuguese who left their countries of origin centuries ago. They founded the first Jewish synagogue and congregation on St. James Street.

Apart from the ensuing Hart family, only a handful of Jews settled in Canada until after Confederation in 1867. By 1871, after 111 years in the Province of Quebec, only 518 Jews lived in Montreal, families mainly from Russia and Poland. They became known as the 'uptowners'—about 40 families who had evolved into a Jewish aristocracy—anglicized, established, living mostly in Westmount (alongside the Scottish fur barons), Outremont and other areas west of St. Lawrence Blvd. Lazarus Cohen, the most successful, settled in Montreal in the 1880s.

By 1891, there were only about 6,501 Jews in Canada. German Jews, fleeing political unrest in Germany, Austria and Hungary, started to arrive in Montreal at the beginning of the 20th century, becoming involved in the import and export business and attending the Spanish Synagogue. They soon left to found the *Shaar Hashomayim* whose first building was on Cadieux near Vitre, a fashionable neighbourhood. When their next synagogue, known as the German Synagogue, was built on McGill College Avenue, the old building was taken over by the new *B'nai Jacob* Congregation and was known as the Russian *shul.*

The 'uptowners,' all deeply committed to Jewish life and to community organization, turned the *Shaar Hashomayim* into the rich man's Orthodox synagogue of Canada. As well, the Young Men's Hebrew Benevolent Society was called upon to provide relief to the thousands of immigrants pouring into Canada after the eastern-European pogroms of the 1880s.

Montreal, Canada's largest city, underwent a phenomenal growth in the early 20th century. From 1901 to 1917, a tide of 130,000 immigrant Jews, Russian, Polish and Romanian in origin, surged into Montreal and Toronto (others were sent west to Winnipeg and even to the Rockies to plant their Canadian roots). Initially, almost every aspect of the lives of Montreal's Yiddish speaking Jews was connected to people and events in Russia—they continued to talk and act as though they were still in Russia. The ideas and ideology of the *Bund* (the first Jewish political party in Russia) shaped the Jewish community in Montreal.

The more educated Jews arrived after 1905, becoming the first teachers in the Jewish schools, community activists and writers for the *Keneder Adler*. There were few children—many families were left behind until their men could earn enough money to bring them over.

The variety of cultural influences and backgrounds led them to seek similar others. As more and more arrived, a split became obvious. The poor and middle-class, more steeped in the East European traditions, became known as 'downtowners,' for that is where they lived. They began to found their own social, cultural and charitable organizations, which slowly linked them to Montreal's Jewish community.

Still, their destitution, 'old country' customs and clothing embarrassed many of the wealthy 'old guard.'

> "There was a clash of attitudes between the two groups, the old guard of Westmount—the 'uptowners,' and the new immigrants squashed into slum housing in the streets around St. Lawrence and The Main, the 'downtowners.'"

Nonetheless, the wealthy anglicized Jews were never disloyal to their self-appointed task of aiding refugees and immigrants—dispensing their help and advice

> "with a condescension not untypical of Victorian society; but they dispensed it all the same."

These efforts resulted in the eventual development of the Federation of Jewish Philanthropies—a network of communal and human services as yet unparalled in Canada.

For 40 years, about 20 of these monied families carried the burden for the resettlement and welfare of thousands of Yiddish-speaking immigrants from Eastern Europe. Their wives/women worked in Ladies Auxiliaries as a work force that paralleled the men's. The men agitated to build a hospital; the women visited the sick; men organized charity drives; women made clothing for the poor. The head of women's groups was Mrs. Clarence I. de Sola, whose husband helped found the Canadian Zionist Federation—in 1915 he chaired the Canadian Jewish Conference, a forerunner of Canadian Jewish Congress.

By 1910, Montreal had a Jewish population of approximately 28,000. Following World War 1, the influx of immigrants and orphans continued. By 1931, there were 156,726 Jews in Canada (as opposed to 4,228,029 in the United States)—over 10,000 in Montreal. According to *Canada's Jews* by Louis Rosenberg, 1939, the following denotes the Jewish population in Greater Montreal rising steadily from 1891 to 1931...

1891	2,473
1901	6,941
1911	28,807
1921	45,802
1931	*57,997

*(5.79% of the total—1,000,159)

Origins of the Jewish Community

Jewish community life began at the waterfront as newcomers right off the boats were met by family, friends, established settlers, and manufacturers looking for workers. Narrow streets and lanes sprawled about six blocks on either side of St. Lawrence Boulevard—a square mile of vibrant Jewish life known as The Main.

The corner of St. Urbain and Dorchester was the heart of the Jewish neighbourhood, as was Craig Street (now St. Antoine), running north to Mount Royal. Notre Dame Street was one of the important shopping districts, full of Jewish stores—clothing, furniture, dry goods, second-hand goods and groceries. The junk and rag businesses were concentrated in the Griffintown section (from Notre Dame to the Canal and from McCord to McGill).

Prince Arthur was the street of little Jewish groceries and service stores. Jeanne Mance "wore an aura of elegance" with tall trees... lining its sidewalks and fine two-storey limestone houses with bay windows and little gardens. Long flights of wooden stairs, peculiar to Quebec, stretched from the street up to the top floor, wrought iron railings hanging there for the weary and aged to hang on to...and greatly appreciated during an icy winter.

Nearby, Dufferin Park was filled with immigrants meeting their *landslayt,* reading the papers, looking for work. St. Helen's Island, even then, was a place Jewish families visited on Sundays where... they met friends and discussed their difficulties and adjustments to their new country.

The Baron de Hirsch Institute was the centre of Jewish philanthropic and social activity and responsible for the care of the needy. In its early days, the Institute's night school and library was one of the most important institutions for the Jewish immigrants. Learning English was seen as their key to success, to participation at meetings, social events—and to meeting girls. Many were then able to find work in offices as clerks, salesmen, insurance and news agents on trains—often the first Jewish people immigrants would meet after leaving the ships at Quebec or Halifax.

The Institute was also instrumental in opening and running the first Jewish orphanage, the Montreal Hebrew Orphans' Home, which opened on Evans Street in 1909. It cared for the children of many of the poor, one-parent families so prevalent in the Jewish community in those early years. It also housed the aged.

The biggest adjustment to life in Montreal was made by the religious scholars. In Europe, in near-medieval *shtetls*, they studied and debated the holy writings—maintained by their families. In Canada, in large cities, they were forced to join the modern age and work to care for themselves and their families, sometimes even if it meant working on *Shabbas*. Many became tailors for one reason only—they were not required to work Saturdays. The lucky ones found suitable work in Jewish schools or formed small congregations; the others ended up in the needle trade or whatever employment they could find.

The religious immigrant was resigned to the fact that his traditional values were not relevant in Canada (at that time). He concerned himself with only two religious goals—to have *kosher* meat in the house, and to enable his son(s) to say *kaddish* for him when the time came.

In those early years though, times were tough, rents increased by 36%, and working people were less and less able to pay. Women and children entered the workforce as the men stayed home to study. They were paid less and exploited more. Some children were 'learners,' and paid little or nothing—the promise of a job after training often falling through.

> "Best of all, in Montreal the immigrants were free of fear—free to read, write and say what they wanted. Despite poverty and poor health, for the first time they felt like human beings."

Both Freedom and Poverty

The period of rapid growth and change was both rich and complex. The new immigrants had freedom, but they lived in poverty. They came to escape poverty, but found it waiting for them. In 1901, more than half of Montreal's Jewish population lived in the area south of Pine, east of Park—home to about 7,000 mainly poor and Yiddish-speaking. They lived in tiny flats, shared with more than one family, and used public baths. Some were forced to take in boarders into already crowded conditions. This soon provided the plots of Yiddish stories, movies and plays. And in some instances, the fictional romance became real...the newspapers excelled in printing photos of missing husbands who ran off with the boarder!

Their world was along the congested streets, noisy markets, pushcarts and peddlers. Shops in this district lined the streets, familiar Jewish foods dominated shelves, push-carts offered the best pots and pans, slightly-used clothing and piles of books in every language.

It is interesting to note that, even among this new, young Jewish community, strife reared its head in segments of the food industry. The Jewish bread trade was an important arena of social activism, according to Eve Lerner, M.A. student at Concordia University. She writes that, while it was the responsibility of bakery owners to provide bread at a fair price, it was the expectation of the bakery workers that members of the Jewish working class community would eat union made bread. "Virtually all Jews, assimilated or not, ate 'Jewish' bread." Bread bearing the union-made stamp was promoted as the only 'kosher' alternative to the *trafe* bread produced by 'scab bakeries.'

It was the Jewish women in Montreal and Toronto who led what was probably the first consumer boycott in the country. In 1910, upset by two years of the high price of meat and bread, they organized the Jewish community not to purchase those products until the cost came down. About 1,000 immigrant women protested. They rebelled again in 1917 against the limitations of their lives. They no longer only wanted to marry and have children. They also wanted the chance to play a more important part in Jewish society. They wanted recognition for their contributions.

Disputes in the bakeries led to continued conflicts—the bread boycott of 1925 and the bakery workers' strike of 1927-29. The former resulted when the Hebrew Consumers League, an organization of Jewish housewives, declared another boycott of Jewish bakers to protest a rise in the price of bread to 12 cents per loaf. Women tore the loaves from customers'' hands, broke them over the buyers'' heads and threw them into the streets or back into the shops. However, they were willing to pay up to 14 cents for "Christian" bread until the time their dispute was settled. As you can see, women were both prominent and militant on this issue.

Unionized bread wars continued off and on for three decades, well into the 1930s. Around the same times, another disputed area, more intense but not as visible, was the kosher meat battles, added Prof. Ira Robinson, also of Concordia. The results live on today.

There were choices of work...one could work himself up, from tailor to *klapper* (door-to-door salesman) to custom peddler to proprietor of a dry-goods store to wholesaler/merchant. The Canadian Pacific Railway (CPR) also employed Jews as locksmiths, carpenters and tinsmiths. Living near the ports/dock area, Jews also found work as longshoremen. Most immigrants scraped by as shopkeepers and peddlers. Horses and wagons soon became a common sight on the streets and back alleys as the merchants struggled to provide for their customers, many of whom had large families of 10 or more children, as well as for their own families. Soup kitchens, set up by the somewhat Canadianized East Europeans, helped feed destitute immigrants during the depression of 1907-08.

They worked 60-80 hours a week and still found time to create their own cultural and social world.

> "They flocked to book stores and attended night school, created libraries and amateur theatre groups, and assembled for heated discussions of world affairs."

Yiddish troups, burlesques and movie theatres abounded—the *Atlantic Palace* stood at Prince Arthur and St. Lawrence; the *Royal Theatre* on Cote Street; the *Fairyland* on Notre Dame. The main theatre of Jewish Montreal was the *Monument National.* Yiddish theatre was at its height in the Montreal of the 1920s. The *Standard Theatre* then opened in 1921 in Toronto and became known as the finest Yiddish theatre in North America.

Newcomers felt comfortable with Yiddish theatre because of the warm, friendly atmosphere—as well as the play! They could well relate to the homeliness of the plots, the old-country types and the familiar stars. Yiddish vaudeville, with its varied acts, also had great appeal. For those who could not afford the theatre, a five cent movie filled the bill. It provided important history and geography lessons of the current times.

And at that time, when boy meets girl and dating began, the initial outing would be a movie. If there was a future for the couple, they next went to the theatre—a sure sign that an engagement would soon follow. The weddings took place in a hall. The couple was expected to look sad, until the ceremony was over. Then the dancing began, interrupted by the meal...a long table filled with smoked meat, dill pickles, raisins, nuts, bananas, ginger ale and homemade whiskey—water mixed with gin. The one-day honeymoon was spent around the city, at St. Helen's Island or Dominion Park with its carnival atmosphere, ending with a visit to the Yiddish theatre.

But, in those days, other problems surfaced. In certain areas of the city, Griffintown and Pointe St. Charles, bullies began to harrass the new immigrants—they would bully, insult and beat them. It was thought they learned this behaviour from attending the burlesque shows featuring comedians who mocked the newly arrived Jews. As a result, the Jews began to take an interest in politics, figuring a Jewish alderman sitting on the city council could demand more police protection against this form of anti-semitism. In 1912, Abraham Blumenthal was voted in. This paved the way for future campaigns where Peter Bercovitch and S. W. Jacobs were elected.

The Beginning of Business

The garment industry entered Canada through the U.S. in the late 1870s, and was soon notorious for its sweatshops. Aaron Sanft started his business in 1894, followed a year later by M. Joseph, both on Craig Street. The needle trade was housed in ramshackle buildings between St. Denis in the East, University in the West, but huddled around St. Catherine Street. Immigrants were met at the boats by manufacturers and their agents who hired them on the spot to work in the factories springing up everywhere. They were naturals for this industry, coming from small-scale industry in Europe. With few skills, and speaking little English, they found work earning one or two dollars a week. Industrial profits were high, but working conditions were horrific.

Wages in the needle trade were lower than other work, because most of it could be done at home. Tailors and cloakmakers earned more than unskilled workers, but work was seasonal. In 1921, the average male garment worker (in Toronto) earned $1,050 a year; the average female only $670—the wage needed by a family to survive was $1,655. There was a growing demand for cheap, well-made clothing, which manufacturers filled by more work at the same wage. Hours were long (80 hours a week), there were frequent accidents, and layoffs happened at the whim of a boss. Labour unions were formed, some with success, others doomed to failure.

Children went to work at a young age, 13-14, when their impoverished parents, even the tailors and cloakmakers, could not provide for them—neither adequate food, warm clothing nor education. It was difficult for girls to find work, but boys became newsboys, selling papers for one cent each. Many future businessmen got their start as newsboys.

At the corner of Park and Mt. Royal was Fletchers Field, where many kids from the Montefiore Home went to play soccer and baseball, among them Earl Greenberg, Sam Rasminsky, Max Matt, and Myer Gordon. Two of the Jewish soccer teams were *The Stern* and *Hakoa.* To this day, many remember that lacrosse also was a major organized sport there; among the teams was one comprised of the local Indigenous Peoples.

The Eastern European immigrants also brought with them their culinary skills. Jewish delicatessens slowly gained in popularity. Between 1900 and 1910 alone, four shops opened. Two foods that especially caught on and define Montreal were smoked meat and bagels—many kinds, many cooks. Hyman Seligman's *Montreal Bagel Bakery* opened around 1900, the first in the City. Some shops remain as popular today as in their early years. By 1920, eight more were established, including *Bens,* the oldest in existence today. In those early days, on Burnside, large smoked meat sandwiches went for 10 cents. They were served by Ben himself wearing a clean white apron.

By 1932, there were more than 30 delis, such as *Chenoy's, Etinson's, Rogatko's, Schwartz's* and *Shagass.*

Montefiore Home Alumnus Myer Gordon remembers that the boys from the Home (on Jeanne Mance) used to go to *Chenoy's* on The Main, near Mt. Royal, where smoked meat sandwiches sold for two for 15 cents in the late thirties; from there they went to the *Belmont Theatre* where they consumed their sandwiches and enjoyed an afternoon's entertainment.

> "Outside the Belmont was an elderly man (to us)—he may have been 40 or 50—who sold bagels from a push-cart. The bagels were about four inches around and very hard—like jawbreakers! He kept them warm over a gas jet flame. They sold for 1 cent each—in our price range, so they were very popular!"

Other favourite hangouts for the kids were *Shaps* (next to the Davis Y) for milk shakes—malted milks were 15 cents—and *Beauty's,* also around the corner from the Montefiore at the corner of Mt. Royal and St. Urbain. *Beauty's* was a family restaurant even in those days. Owned by the Sculnick family since 1942, it is still a popular landmark and now considered a 'premier luncheonette,' and selected in an April 2002 Macleans Magazine as one great spot for single diners—another sign of recent times.

Across the street was the 'Sports Arena,' where the *Montreal Maroons* professional hockey team practiced and wrestlers attracted crowds. The Davis Y had its own contingent of Jewish wrestlers and boxers. Some dated the girls from the Montefiore, and dates included dining at the above-mentioned restaurants. The 'Arena' was demolished in the late 40s, replaced by stores and an office building complete with bowling alley frequented over the years by many of the Alumni. This building too was demolished and is now being rebuilt as a new, modern complex.

The Canadian economy expanded and boomed between 1900 and 1914, and the garment industry expanded enormously...the sewing machine had been invented and there was work for everyone. Some of the most successful firms in the country were Jewish-owned, and they became one of the largest employers in the city, the first time they dominated a major industry. "As long as the consumer insists on having an all-wool ready-made, fit-you-as-a-glove, suit of clothes for $9.99, someone will have to turn it out," stated a 1911 article in the *Canadian Century.*

Most had started out as stores selling clothing and dry goods. Due to erratic deliveries, the entrepreneurs had switched to manufacturing. The firms of the "Lancaster Bunch", owned by the families of Lazarus and Lyon Cohen, Harris Kellert, Noah and David Friedman, and Harris Vineberg, dominated the garment industry in late 19th century Montreal. By the early 1900s, Solomon Levinson's *S. Levenson and Son* was Canada's largest men's clothing company.

The 1931 census noted that one in eight Jewish workers worked in the garment industry. In 1932, there were 462 women's wear manufacturers in Canada, most of them in Montreal and Toronto, and most of them owned by Jews.

Three stores belonged to the family of J. B. Miller, one of the founders of the Montefiore Home. The largest was on St. James Street, next to *Fraser's Auction Co.* It was a huge store, called *The People's Sample Store,* and when there was a sale, it was so crowded that customers lined up around the block to get in. Mrs. Miller was in charge of the business end of the store, while J. B. did the buying. As he was very friendly with all the companies from whom he bought, he bought heavily—too heavily. And as the Depression years came, the business failed.

Many other bigger multi-million dollar businesses came to Montreal, but so did the Great Depression.

J. B. Miller was also an avid reader. He knew everything that was happening in the world—he read every political book of his day. The floor of his bedroom was strewn with newspapers from every part of the world. Jews were also very evident at the time in the newspaper trade. *The Jewish Times* was founded in 1897 by two sons of the 'uptowners' Lyon Cohen & Sam Jacobs (later an MP in the Laurier and King governments)—the first Jewish-interest paper in Canada—printed in English, promoting Canadianization and the ways of the British Empire. It was founded mainly to counter the anti-semitism generated by the Dreyfus trial in France. It spoke for the philanthropists whose job it was to help the needy and advise the *shtetl* newcomers on how to 'comport themselves'—restrained and Anglo-Saxon in behaviour and attitudes.

Book stores appealing to the masses were opened, educating them about the world around them and reminding them of the world they left behind. When a store selling the socialist *Jewish Daily Forward* opened on Main Street in 1902, it became the first Jewish cultural centre in Montreal. Owned by Harry Hershman, who was involved with the Montreal Home, it evolved into the central gathering place of immigrant Jewish intellectuals. Main Street between Craig and Ontario, an attractive and interesting area, soon became a walking street, for gazing into shop windows, studying the latest in clothing.

Although the majority of immigrants had no time (nor interest) in reading books, every immigrant read the newspaper. The *Keneder Adler* (The Jewish Daily Eagle), a Yiddish language paper, was first published in 1907 by Hirsch Wolofsky. It attracted the East European immigrants as well as many of the brightest minds of the day. It steadily opposed assimilation and promoted a deliberate strengthening of Yiddish language and culture in this new land—excitedly intellectual and overly emotional. It served as the immigrants' window to the land and its people. They became well-informed about the assets of Montreal as well as its seamy side, criminals, gangsters and gamblers. The *Keneder Adler* remained in existence for 80 years. Wolofsky also published the English-language *Canadian Jewish Chronicle,* established in 1912.

The Community Grows

It was the immigrant Jews who arrived in Montreal prior to 1914 who paved the way for a new Jewish community, one where life could be prosperous and fulfilling.

In 1914 in Canada, the Jewish community became a significant minority rather than a negligible one—well over 100,000—the largest immigrant community, constituting more than 6 per cent of the population. Montreal in the 1920s was the major Jewish centre in Canada; in 1921, 52,287 Jews were listed in the census, about half of all the Jews in the country. By 1931 the Jewish population rose by 26.6%, mostly from a high rate of births. The Montreal Anglo-Jewish community was replaced by the crowded, noisy, Yiddish world of the Eastern European newcomers. Leadership remained in the hands of the 'uptowners,' but their control over the community in general was lost.

Clashes between the various interest groups became quite apparent. Anarchists, Socialists and Zionists/Hebraists...all felt their ideology was the best, and the ensuing struggles over the issues caused problems among all sectors. There were also class divisions among the workers, non-workers and manufacturers—all were separate organizational entities.

World War I greatly changed life in Canada. New industries geared to the war effort were born—among them, the manufacturing of uniforms, and munitions factories. There was more work and more money. All signs of unemployment disappeared. Jewish community and cultural activity increased, the papers appeared twice daily to keep up with the news. The most important cultural institution of the time was the Jewish Public Library. And in 1915, Montreal Jews organized relief committees to assist war victims: $60,000 was raised.

New factories, houses and roads were built. New neighbourhoods flourished. The Papineau district was one of these, built by Jews. The small houses greatly resembled the cottages in their home-towns of Russia and Romania. They built barns as well, hoping that the tenants would drink milk from their own cows and eat eggs from their own chickens. A real estate boom drove up the prices—Jews were attracted to this new business which proved most lucrative.

The end of World War I signaled a return to mass Jewish migration—European war refugees again making their way to Canada. But many of these new immigrants were different from the earlier newcomers. These were met by well-to-do relatives, already settled in. They found lighter work. The sweatshops had all but disappeared. The fur industry began to flourish. Dress stores were plentiful. The Jewish community was much more organized. The Jewish Immigrant Aid Society was in place to assist.

Neighbourhood House on Laval Avenue opened in the mid-twenties. It was a project of the National Council of Jewish Women, established to keep the young off the streets and to assist in their integration into the community.

Among the refugees were many orphans. The Montreal Hebrew Orphans' Home was overcrowded, and it was deemed necessary to open a second facility to care for the expected influx. The Montefiore Hebrew Orphans' Home, founded by a group of concerned citizens, opened in 1918 at 4650 Jeanne Mance Street. The Board of Directors for both Homes was comprised of volunteers anxious to help—'uptowners and downtowners'—volunteers with Federation and the Baron de Hirsch Institute at the Montreal Home; while a separate group was responsible for the Montefiore Home.

Jewish War Orphans of Canada

In the summer of 1920 there were more than 137,000 young Jewish orphans in the Ukraine, without homes nor means of obtaining regular sustenance. It was felt imperative by the Jews of the American continent to bring them over.

U.S. immigration laws did not permit such an undertaking; therefore Jewish relief agencies in the Montreal area took up this cause. Lyon Cohen, then president of the Canadian Jewish Congress, formed a Dominion-wide organization—asking the Canadian Government to grant asylum to 1,000 of these orphans—to be adopted by Canadian Jewish families. Only two hundred would be admitted, with full arrangements made in advance.

Mrs. Lillian (A.J.) Freiman of Ottawa was formally named Dominion President of the Ukrainian Orphans Committee, later changed to the Jewish War Orphans of Canada (she was also the founder of *Hadassah*-WIZO of Canada). Montreal committee members included Lyon Cohen, Rabbi H. Cohen, Leon Meltzer, S. D. Cohen, Louis Zucker, Lionel Coviensky, Harry Barsky, Mrs. Asher Pierce, A. Levin, Harry Hershman, H. Wolofsky, Miss Ida Seigler, S. Guttman, D.S. Friedman, Mrs. C. J. Gross, and S. W. Jacobs, K.C., M.P. Appeals for support were immediate and enthusiastic, showing the true charitableness of Canadian Jewry.

Across the country, other individuals and societies agreed to contribute $120 annually for the maintenance of orphans. Applications were taken from families willing to adopt the children once arrived in Canada—in Montreal, 56 families applied. Groups of women started to knit small garments for the children. *Hadassah, B'nai Brith,* local councils of Jewish Women, Hebrew and synagogue ladies' auxiliaries all cooperated in the work to be done. Non-Jews assisted as well.

On February 5, 1921, committee representatives sailed for Europe. They were appalled by the appearance of the children, aged four or five, eyes sunken, cheeks nothing but skin and bones, bodies almost skeletal. Of the over 1,000 children to be examined for eligibility, only 46 originally met the standard required. And they were older than had been stipulated, 4-12 years of age. Harry Hershman had reported very few children were left under the age of 6. He wrote home:

> "Children born in the Ukraine from 3-6 years old could not survive, especially if they had become orphans at the ages of 1 or 2. Those who survived are the fortunate ones whose parents were spared, and only superhuman sacrifices on the part of the parents saved them."

Delays dropped the quota from 200 to 150. The first group of Polish-Ukrainian Jewish war-orphans left on June 14th on the *Scandinavian,* which arrived at Quebec City the night of August 20th. The children were met by leaders of the Committee—welcoming speeches were in English and Yiddish. The next evening they left by train, for various destinations across Canada—21 to Montreal. Those who had been left behind in Europe came at later dates, from September through January 1922.

Of the 146 brought to Canada, 34 were reunited with relatives, others were adopted, some cared for in foster homes, and four put into the Montreal Hebrew Orphans' Home. The latter had one extra

> "thrilling experience when the Home's country branch at Shawbridge, where they were spending their first summer, was burned to the ground on August 10, 1922. Fortunately they were rescued."

Eight others were not as fortunate.

Reports gathered over the years showed that the children flourished. They became good scholars, musicians and professionals. And good citizens—enabled to live a true Jewish life. One of these lucky orphans was Faiga Fisher. Her story is both interesting and remarkable. Here it is, in her own words, written January 19, 2002.

> My birthplace was in the Ukraine (in 1912). My parents were killed in front of me in our blacksmith shop. Neighbours kept me until the war lessened, and sent me to an orphanage as arranged by local Jews. That's when Harry Hershman came with the two other leading Canadians—one, Mrs. Asher Pierce, the other I think was a member of the Bronfman family.
>
> I had a home with Mr. Hershman who adopted me, as a young child, directly from the European orphanage. Sorry to say that I was not an inmate of either Montreal orphanage, although I did my best to help the children.
>
> I have some memories of the Westmount (Montreal) orphanage, under the late Mr. and Mrs. Henry Bye and their sister-in-law Mrs. Shenker. I was an inmate of this Home only during my training as a social worker in 1934 or '35. I helped the children with their homework and helped them get sugar for their porridge in the morning, as Mrs. Shenker was not the kindest of the staff.
>
> I met my late husband Arnold Fisher who was a volunteer physical education teacher at the orphanage—his mother was a Board member of the Home. We married and had a wonderful life until he died on an airplane of a sudden heart attack. I was accompanying him on a business trip to New York at that time. I was left with three children and a business to carry on.
>
> I did the best I could to educate my children, and then stepped

out of squabbling with the paid manager who wanted the business for himself. My eldest son is a graduate of Harvard and M.I.T: I lost my second son at age 10 from leukemia. My remaining daughter and grandchildren are the lights of my present existence.

I am three weeks away from my 90th birthday; but have had two falls and been hospitalized twice. I was in rehab for awhile and now use a walker and an attendant to get around.

I have attended *Mishpocha* meetings* in Montreal and the only one I remember is Anne Reisler.

We always need improvements in child welfare, and Jews have been no 'slouches' in this regard. I have been a leader in my community until I became incapacitated. I won't mention all the positions I have held!"

* (ed.'s note: I assume she means reunions)

Faiga's daughter, Ginny Yaffe, related a story her mother told her—that she found conditions in the Home "terrible...right out of Oliver Twist." There didn't seem to be enough food. What there was, was neither seasoned nor sampled for taste, and the porridge was cold.

These seem to be the only adverse comments about the Home itself, but, as was pointed out by Mrs. Yaffe, that may be because we only meet at reunions with, or hear from, those who had good memories of their experiences—the others want nothing to do with remembering.

Meanwhile, Faiga Fisher continues to live on Cote des Neiges Road, and is a member of Temple Emanuel.

Faiga and the more than 140 orphans were fortunate. On July 26, 1921, an Order-in-Council was passed requiring all immigrants to Canada to have a valid passport from their country of origin, a measure which seriously affected the ability of future desperate and homeless Jewish refugees to enter the country.

The community worked its way north on and off Mount Royal. By the 40s, St. Urbain was almost 100% Jewish—a self-contained world of six streets: Clark, St. Urbain, Waverley, Esplanade, Jeanne Mance, and Park Avenue. By that time, too, Jewish settlement had spread north to Outremont, and west to Westmount and Snowdon.

Though turbulent, the St. Urbain ghetto was a comforting, diverse place of familiar sights and sounds. There were cafes and restaurants—coffee at *Horn's Cafe* was five cents; there were shops featuring traditional Jewish goods and mailing centres to send items 'home' to Europe; there were prayer halls and snooker halls, synagogues and afternoon Hebrew schools, *mikvahs,* public baths and medical clinics.

Many Jewish poets and writers had their start in Montreal; most came from the flood of Eastern European immigrant families at the turn of the century. However, the first significant piece of Canadian Jewish poetry appeared in 1863 with the publication of *Voices from the Hearth*, by lawyer Isidore G. Ascher. His collection of poetry, though written in a classical Victorian style, had its roots in traditional liturgy. As he returned to Britain, the early 'modern' notables were Montrealers A.M. Klein, followed by Irving Layton (who served as a tutor at the Montreal Hebrew Orphans' Home and as a Sunshine Camp counsellor), Mordecai Richler and Saul Bellow. The first book of Jewish poetry in Montreal was by J. I. Segal. Then there was musician Alexander Brott, and artists Moe Reinblatt and Stanley Lewis.

The development of Jewish Canadian poetry began in earnest during the 1920s in Montreal. Glen Rotchin wrote in the *Canadian Jewish News,* September 2001, that Jewish writers were in the unique position to realize the creative possibilities of living outside both the French majority and the English establishment, and so could maintain a strong sense of their own language and cultural uniqueness while at the same time exploring the opportunities presented by their adopted society.

Klein was the poet who helped shape self-awareness in Canadian Jews. The one who desired to reconcile Jewish heritage and language with the multicultural milieu in which he lived. Layton, on the other hand, wrote with a sense of moral indignation and rebelliousness, adding a fresh, brash vocabulary to Canadian verse.

Poet Irving Layton wrote of the Jewish district:

> "It was a turbulent neighbourhood, full of Jews, French Canadians, Slavs, Italians. Along the Main it was all Jewish stores."

The Main was positioned right between the Francophones and the Anglophones. In a 1970s interview, Layton said:

> "(The Main) was a great place to grow up. For a poet nothing could have been better. Nothing. Raw; vulgar; dynamic and dramatic; their smells and sounds and fights. It was altogether a rich and wonderful life. Sometimes I'm sorry for my children who lived in the suburbs and never had anything like this."

"From 1900-1950, according to Mordecai Richler in *The Street,* immigrant life on the downtown streets stood in the same relationship to the elegance of uptown:

> "Of the six streets, St. Urbain was the best—they accepted parcels from charity matrons on Passover; went uninvited to bar-mitzvahs and weddings to carry off cakes, bottles and chicken legs—they were not yet Canadian. Greeners, that's what they were..."

Richler wrote in *The Street*:

> "Downtown immigrants worked under appalling conditions in sweat shops, rented halls over pool rooms and grocery stores to meet and form burial societies and create *shuls*...began to struggle up a ladder of streets, from one where you had to leave your garbage outside your front door to another where you actually had a rear lane as well as a back yard where corn and tomatoes were usually grown..."

Yet, this generation of immigrants were the founders, in the main, of synagogues, theatres, societies, schools, unions and benevolent organizations. They laid the foundation of Jewish life in Canada in the 20th century and came to dominate Canadian Jewish society.

The synagogues were not only a place to pray, they were also social halls, cultural centres and schools. They united the religious and social life of the neighbourhood. They became the immigrants' safety net, a place to find understanding of their roots and their future.

The fraternal and mutual benefit societies were equally important to the immigrant community, based on the Jewish tradition of communal self-help. There was no government help; the resources of the established Jewish community were limited; they had only each other.

When the German Jews arrived in Montreal, they relied on the Spanish and Portuguese; when the Russian and East Europeans arrived, they, in turn, relied on the German Jews for advice, assistance and friendship.

About this time, the new immigrants were starting to make their mark, some in politics—Peter Bercovitch and Sam Jacobs; in figure skating—brothers Louis and Moses Rubinstein; in music—Pauline Lightstone (known as Madame Donalda), one of the world's leading opera singers and teachers, was the founder of the Opera Guild; earlier, in school—Marcus Sperber graduated first in his class in law at McGill University in 1900.

The School System and anti-Semitism.

Jews faced discrimination in schooling...forced to attend the Protestant Schools, limited in becoming teachers, limited in attending McGill University. Quotas were apparent. Non-religious middle- and working-class Jews sent their girls to the radical Jewish schools (now the *Peretz School),* while the boys attended the *Talmud Torah.*

As first generation Canadians, the young children spoke Yiddish at home. The first break with their parents' culture came at registration for school. To Anglicize their names helped them fit into the Protestant School methodology. And so, Chaya became Catherine, Chaim became Hyman, Laibl became Lloyd, and Yitschak became Issie.

Anti-Semitic remarks by a teacher at Aberdeen School in 1912 triggered a strike by 500 children. In negotiations with school officials, Rabbi Herman Abramowitz of the *Shaar Hashomayim,* and Hirsch Wolofsky of the *Keneder Adler,* put forth their issues; they were resolved, and lessons resumed.

In the 1920s, the new issue was Jewish schooling. The British North America Act of 1867 had endorsed Quebec as a Christian society. There were too few Jews to be noticed; they did not come under the provisions of the Quebec School Act; did not have a legal right to education. By 1903, Jews were permitted to go to Protestant schools, a system which worked well until the 1920s. There were now 12,000 Jewish students in the Protestant system (out of a total of 32,000). Some schools, such as Baron Byng (named after the Governor General of the early 20s) were almost entirely Jewish, but not one teacher was Jewish. It was famous for a high level of achievement in Academics—Latin, Music and Art—and prepared its students for university.

By 1923, the Protestant community felt that its values were under siege.

> "The children in their schools were not acculturated to King, country and the Protestant ethos. Their folklore was *Sholem Aleichem* and their history was oppression and poverty. They were 'foreign.'"

Again, the 'uptowners' and 'downtowners' had different aspirations. The former preferred the *status quo*—against further segregation, against remaining foreigners; the latter wanted separate Jewish schools wherein they could affirm Jewish cultural rights within a pluralistic society—without assimilating.

In 1930, a separate Jewish School Commission was approved. Premier Taschereau was attacked as a "Jew lover." Liberalism was now equated with "Jew-loving" and a new French language sheet, *Le Goglu,* was dedicated to smearing Jews.

Again, the 'uptowners' won the day. In late April, the Taschereau Cabinet appointed seven Jewish School Commissioners, six of them Westmounters. In May, Joseph Cohen, a Quebec MLA, suggested that the real aim of the commissioners was to reach an agreement with the Protestant School Board. On Dec. 12, 1930, an agreement was signed. Jewish children would stay in the Protestant system without being segregated; they would be excused for Jewish holidays; however, the Protestants would retain full control and Jews would not be represented on the school board or commission. Once again the 'downtowners' felt betrayed, condemned the Westmount Commissioners and called for their resignation. The agreement held.

The rising nationalism of the Quebec 'francois' had created a mood ripe for anti-Semitism, surfacing about 1913 with the publication in Montreal of a small, expensively produced book of anti-Semitic cartoons called *Montreal Juif: Dessins Gais.*

By 1930, Journalist Adrien Arcand was one of the publishers of three papers, including *Le Goglu.* Erna Paris wrote that...

> "perhaps the Jewish 'Anglos' were easier targets for the resentment of French Quebecers than were the powerful Anglo-Saxon barons themselves, particularly when wave after wave of immigration brought penniless Jewish peddlers who threw packs on their backs and travelled into the countryside, competing directly with French-Canadian merchants."

In 1934, the infamous Montreal interns' strike was one of hundreds of anti-Semitic incidents that occurred between the two World Wars. Samuel Rabinovich was a young medical student who came first in his class at the University of Montreal. As he started his internship at Notre Dame Hospital, all 14 of his fellow interns walked out, refusing to work with a Jew—concerned that their Catholic patients would find it "repugnant" to be touched by a Jewish physician. He resigned. It took until 1945 before restrictions were lifted.

There were also very few Jews in teaching and administration between 1933 and 1940—only a handful out of the thousands of refugee scholars, teachers, scientists, artists, musicians and writers driven from German universities. Jewish applicants at McGill were also discriminated against. Standards of admission for them were much higher. This quota was also dropped following World War II.

Jews, all foreigners, were a threat to the French-Canadian way of life. Modernism and materialism as practiced by Jews seemed almost demonic. Jews not only promoted egalitarianism and secularism, but they were also militantly anti-fascist. So, in Quebec of the 30s, it was easy to blame one's misery on the 'Anglo' in general, and the Jews in particular. Widespread, organized fascism died out in Quebec in 1939—only because Canada entered a war against a fascist country.

The Montreal of the thirties was known as the crime capital of North America, taken over by American gangsters thrown out of their own country for their criminal activities. Mayor Camilien Houde, city and police officials welcomed them—for a fee. Numerous killings triggered an investigation, and crime-busting Mayor Jean Drapeau brought an end to the mayhem.

Many Jews got into gambling. One of them—hoodlum, smuggler and yearning for big-time in crime—Charlie Feigenbaum was gunned down in August 1934 in the street on Esplanade, next door to where Myer Gordon's Vatch family had lived.

Even the orphanage boys were not exempt from these yearnings. The Montreal Hebrew Orphans' Home was home to brothers Cecil and Teddy Yanovitch and sister Vivienne. Teddy's chosen profession was reputed to be a collector for a major mob—the "insurance business." He was killed in a gun battle with police, reportedly in the 1980s. Cecil passed away in the fall of 2001; Vivienne resides in Florida.

Meanwhile, ordinary Canadians thought Jews were communists, although the real peril of the day was fascism. In fact, the total number of Jews in the Communist Party of Canada in 1937 was estimated at about 450. One of them was Fred Rose (Rosenberg), the only 'commie' M.P. to sit in Ottawa. He represented the Montreal riding of Cartier, which included St. Urbain Street, and was held by Liberal Sam Jacobs until his death in 1938. Rose was convicted as a spy for passing Canadian atomic information to Russia. *Time Magazine* described St. Urbain as "the Hell's Kitchen of Montreal—election scandals, strikes, the housing question, the climate in which communism flourished..." The people in the riding were humiliated. The "Jewish Radical Left" had a short life-span—50 years, born during the 1906 revolution and suffering its death blow in 1956 when it was known that Jewish writers and leaders had been murdered by Stalin.

Following the onset of the Depression in '29, the bottom dropped out of the Canadian economy by 1933. Twenty-nine per cent of the work force was unemployed; one out of 10 people on direct relief. Students dropped out of school to go to work. "No more immigration," shouted the Canadian Labour Movement. A third Order-in-Council was passed in 1931 and the doors to Canada slammed shut.

Although over 48,000 Jews had migrated to Canada during the 1920s, Jewish immigration was considered different from the rest. Jews were unable to enter Canada with other immigrants from the same countries of birth, i.e., Poland, Lithuania or Romania. They were identified not as nationals but Hebrew, and needed a special permit.

Sam (S.W.) Jacobs was first elected to Parliament in 1917 as a Liberal, and began his battle for the admittance of Jewish refugees to Canada. Though his family was well established in uptown Westmount—assimilated and anglophile—his constituents were the downtown Yiddish-speaking immigrants of Montreal (indeed, he served on the Board of the Montreal Hebrew Orphans' Home). Though close friends with both Premiers, Jacobs was most disappointed that the governments of Sir Wilfrid Laurier and William Lyon Mackenzie King were not open to immigration.

War Refugees

Between the rise of Hitler in 1933 and the outbreak of war in 1939, an estimated 4,000 European Jews were admitted to Canada—out of the close to one million who fled their homes and sought refuge elsewhere.

The saga of Canada and the Jewish refugees climaxed in a frenzy of activity on the part of the Canadian Jewish Congress and the Canadian National Committee on Refugees. Mass meetings were held across Canada in November 1938, deploring government policy, petitioning the Department of Immigration. Too late. Even after *Kristallnacht,* a somewhat sympathetic Mackenzie King did not let his private sentiments influence his judgement.

A million European Jews had left or escaped their countries of birth and were wandering in no-man's land. Canada's attitude—Europe's problems should remain Europe's problems. Mackenzie King's attitude was that the "virulent infection ravaging Europe might turn out to be contagious. Safety lay in keeping the distasteful messes of lesser nations at a distance." All humanitarian considerations were shunted aside, culminating in the now infamous case of the *St. Louis* in 1939. The ship, loaded with 900 Jewish refugees, sailed up and down the coast of North America, and was refused the right to land anywhere. It was later learned that these refugees were, in the main, a group of skilled, educated and moneyed people.

In Europe, Canada was seen as a remote, mysterious, pink Commonwealth blob on a school map. In Auschwitz, " 'Canada' was the name given to the area where victims' belongings were squirrelled away. In inmates' slang, 'Canada' meant an abundance of everything, off-limits and closely guarded."

And in Montreal, by 1942, the two Jewish orphanages were no more. Closed because they became too expensive to operate; closed because there were now other facilities to care for these children—foster homes, group homes, and in some cases, the parents who, because of better times created by the war, could now take their children home. However, at the war's end, due to the alarming strength of the CCF and the communists, King's government reversed its stand, and Canada became the first non-European country to approve emergency measures for the admittance of refugees from the camps.

FOUR HUNDRED BROTHERS AND SISTERS

THE ORIGINS OF SOME JEWISH ORGANIZATIONS
A Brief Historical Perspective

The Jewish community of Canada had its origins in Montreal.
—Erna Paris

Federation CJA, now an umbrella agency for social and community services in the Montreal Jewish community, began in 1863 when a small group of single men decided to take the burden of relief work off the elders of the community. At that point, they formed the Young Men's Hebrew Benevolent Society (YMHBS).

In 1891, eminent German financier and philanthropist Baron Mauricio de Hirsch, living in Belgium, was persuaded by the YMHBS to subsidize the settlement of Jewish refugees in the New World. He founded the Jewish Colonization Association (JCA) to sponsor Russian Jews in agricultural colonies in North and South America and funded large-scale settlements in Canada as well. When the late years of the 19th century brought a large number of destitute Eastern European refugees to Montreal, the YMHBS appealed, again—in writing—to the Baron. He sent an initial $20,000 (an immense sum in those days).

Soon after, part of the money was used to purchase a large store at 7 Elizabeth Street. Renovated and opened in June as the Baron de Hirsch Institute, it provided material relief, including jobs, loans, a free school for orphans, and a home for both orphans and immigrants.

When the Baroness died in Paris in 1900, she left a bequest of 600,00 francs ($89,000). In recognition and appreciation of their generosity, the Benevolent Society officially changed its name to the Baron de Hirsch Institute (BHI) Hebrew Benevolent Society...women were still not recognized in the naming of buildings or organizations.

The same year the cornerstone was laid for a new building on Bleury Street, which became the first central address for the community. The new building was officially dedicated on May 28, 1902 by the Governor General of Canada, Earl Minto. Federal and local dignitaries, politicians, and the cream of Montreal society were there—everyone but representatives of the group the building was to serve, the recently arrived Jewish immigrants.

The Institute had classrooms that could accommodate over 450 students; there was a large auditorium with stage and dressing rooms, library, administration offices and a large playground. Under the leadership of Lyon Cohen and Sam Jacobs, the Institute became the model for aid and philanthropy for the next generation—the main and largest organization responsible for the community and remained so until 1916 when Federation was born.

> "Every Sunday morning, an Uptowner in bowler hat and tailored suit would stand on the steps of the Institute and hand out dollar bills to anyone who asked. Men almost never came. They were too proud to ask for charity. But the women had children to feed. And a dollar went a long way."

These wealthy Jews were confident about their high status in Montreal society, yet also believed in duty.

The problems of immigration remained the major focus. While thousands made little or casual use of the Institute's facilities, a significant number sought assistance and guidance. The Institute, actively supported by 700 members, continued to supply them with food, clothing, shelter, medicines and transportation expenses.

Indeed, it was Montreal Jewry which built and provided the operating budget for the Institute, a clinic, two orphanages (*raison d'être* for this book), a sanatarium, an old-age home, an athletic and cultural club, a reform school, and many other organizations which dealt with the needs and problems of the immigrant community.

One of these was the Young Men's Hebrew Association, formed in 1909, meeting in a small room at the Baron de Hirsch Institute on Saguinet Street. The rent was $7.50 a month; the membership fee was 25 cents a week. By 1912, a membership drive brought in 1,260 people, making the Montreal Y second in size only to that of the 92nd Street Y in New York City. It wasn't until 1929 that the Mortimer B. Davis Y was built on Mount Royal Avenue. It was named for Sir Mortimer B. Davis, the first Canadian-born Jew to be knighted—he was also founder and president of Imperial Tobacco Ltd. He left a large bequest to the Jewish General Hospital, opened in 1934.

The flood of newcomers in the early 1900s was of such proportion a special response was needed. A Canada Committee of the J.C.A. was accordingly created; three members named by Paris—Mortimer B. Davis, Lyon Cohen, Samuel W. Jacobs, K. C.—plus three named by the Institute—D. A. Ansell, B. Goldstein, Harris Vineberg. These men, already well-known to Montreal's Jewish community, assumed responsibility for the initial costs of immigrants arriving in Canada.

The economic depression of 1907-08 necessitated the founding of organizations to assist the poor. The *Malbish Arumim* Society provided clothing; the Hebrew Consumptive Aid Society helped families of tailors and cloakmakers when one of them fell ill with tuberculosis; the Ladies' Relief Society discretely assisted families who wished to conceal their poverty; the *Bessarabian* Hebrew Sick Benefit Society was there in times of sickness. Organizations, previously active, saw the need and became reactivated.

The *Keneder Adler* newspaper, founded in 1907, was instrumental in the development of organized Jewish life by providing a network among the various Jewish groups.

Until 1908, the main source of funds for the costly operations for immigrants still came from abroad. In those days, the Old World supported the New World—bonds of Jewish responsibility for one another that endures to this day.

The cost to maintain the newcomers was heavy and mounting. In 1907, more than $6,400 was spent on relief for coal, matzos, clothing and medical attention. By 1910, the amount had risen to $25,000. Immigration continued to rise rapidly—in 1913, relief costs assisted 18,031 newcomers. Then costs started to decline. Why? Partly because of the rapid adjustments of many newcomers and partly because of those new organizations which arose to give specialized help.

One of the most effective self-help groups was the *landsmanshaft,* comprised of immigrants from similar *shtetls,* cities and countries. These organizations arranged for everything from health services to burials. The community opened dispensaries and clinics to provide medical services. The Herzl Dispensary, the first Jewish medical institution in Montreal, was opened in 1912 by a group of Jewish doctors and housed initially in a small building at 832 St. Dominique Street. In 1914, larger quarters were found at 632 St. Urbain Street, where it served an average of 1,000 patients a month. It provided free medical care for the community poor. It has been part of the Jewish General Hospital since 1974. The Mount Sinai Sanatarium (for T.B.) was founded in 1912 in the clear mountain air of Ste. Agathe.

The common thread to Jewish life in Canada 1914-1930 was the growth of organizations—political, cultural, social and charitable. By 1915, there were 71 Montreal Jewish organizations—including 16 synagogues, 6 labour unions, 10 sick-benefit societies, 18 syndicates, 8 cultural and 5 political organizations, and 8 charitable societies.

Surprisingly, it was the women who played the biggest role in philanthropic work, specifically in aiding the immigrants. Barred from being politically and economically active, they funded most of the early benevolent societies in the Jewish community. Their varied fundraising activities covered the costs of committees responsible for distributing relief and working with the needy.

> "A hodge-podge of organizations had sprung up in an attempt to meet real and perceived needs."

In 1912, under the leadership of Lyon Cohen, wheels were set in motion to form a central coordinating and fundraising body separate from the Institute itself.

And thus was born the Federation of Jewish Philanthropies in 1916. Founding agencies of Federation included: the Baron de Hirsch Institute, Mount Sinai Sanatarium, Ladies Hebrew Benevolent Society, Herzl Dispensary and Hospital, The Montreal Hebrew Orphans' Home, the Montreal Hebrew Sheltering Home, Ladies Jewish Endeavour Sewing Society, Young Women's Hebrew Association, Beth Israel Day Nursery and Infants' Home, Hebrew Ladies Aid Society, and Friendly League of Jewish Women. The Federation was housed in the Herzl Dispensary building on St. Urbain Street.

By 1910, Quebec nationalism intensified; attitudes toward Jews began to change. Jews felt an urgent need for unity. However, by 1915, the uptown and downtown factions were embroiled in a new conflict—both groups worried about the fate of the Jews caught in the war zones of Europe. A combined fundraising effort in Montreal netted $24,000 in donations. The problem? How to use this money. Uptowners, the wealthy, wanted contributions to charities at home as well. Downtowners, the immigrants, wanted all of it helping those overseas. As distribution was in the hands of the uptowners, $17,000 went to Montreal charitable organizations.

The downtowners 'saw red,' and, dreaming of a united Jewish voice, attempted to organize the many organizations into one Canadian Jewish Alliance—a voice that would express their political point of view They were Labour Zionists, left-wing socialists and Jewish nationalists—and they wanted the creation of an independent Jewish state in Palestine.

The Canadian Zionist Federation refused to cooperate, considering itself the national Jewish voice and believed that it alone should represent Canadian Jewry at the eventual peace conference at the war's end. The Zionist Federation called a counter-conference. Among their followers were the wealthy uptown Jews. This conference caused unprecedented bitterness and division within the Canadian Jewish community. Held November 14, 1915 at the *Gayety Theatre*, attendees included big names of the Jewish establishment—among them, Montrealers Clarence de Sola, Lyon Cohen, Michael Hirsch, Maxwell Goldstein and Nathan Gordon...

Nothing came of the conference—only the relief committee continued to function. The same with the Alliance—all that survived its meeting was the maintenance of relief work. However, it provided the impetus to forge a union between the Zionist Federation and the labour groups of the Alliance. Led by H. M. Caiserman, Lyon Cohen, A. J. Freiman and H. Wolofsky, the first meeting of a Canadian Jewish Congress (CJC) was planned. Elections took place all over Canada on March 2-3, 1919. With 24,866 votes cast, it was noted that almost every adult Jew in Canada had voted.

Lyon Cohen chaired the meeting. The undisputed leader of uptown Jewry, he spoke of the fear haunting many of the delegates as well as Jews throughout the country. "Would a Canadian Jew be seen as disloyal to Canada because he had organized something called the Canadian Jewish Congress which was calling for a national homeland and a declaration of rights for Jews everywhere in the world?" He thought not, because of the sacrifices made in common with all sectors of the community in the Great War:

> "Those privileges we enjoy here in Canada and which enjoin us to be loyal to Canada is a loyalty which takes second place to no other people in this grand country of ours."

Yet, while many Jews had been persecuted for their differences and wanted only to dissolve into a Canadian melting-pot, the circumstances in war-torn Europe and the chance to help end centuries of oppression permitted this new Congress to express more than one cultural view.

After the *Treaty of Versailles* had been signed, Congress delegates thought their issues had been resolved...minority rights granted, relief provided for war victims, and Britain committed to the Balfour Declaration. So they rested on their laurels, and over the years, the idea of a Canadian Jewish Congress faded. Even the problem of restricted Jewish immigration was soon handled by the Jewish Immigrant Aid Society, founded in 1920. Throughout the 1920s, JIAS was the most active Jewish communal organization—in terms of dealing with all aspects of Jewish refugee immigration.

With the advent of a new Federation decade, came a new era of giving. There was a short interlude of prosperity during the 1920s. Until the catastrophic advent of 1929 and the Great Depression of the 1930s. By 1932, one-third of Montreal's residents was on relief. The social scene was characterized by a veritable blossoming of philanthropy. Despite the austerity of the Depression, or perhaps because of it, a host of new *landsmanshaften* looked after their own by organizing schools, hospitals, old folks' homes, burial and loan societies. Jewish trade unions worked to assist the workers.

This period was one of not only additional income for Federation but also the recruitment of many local Jewish leaders of exceptional ability who rallied to the causes at hand. The Mount Royal Y served as a meeting place for the poor and unemployed.

Some of the other fledgling social institutions of the time were the Hebrew Maternity Hospital, 1914; Camp *B'nai Brith,* 1920; first high school class opened by Jewish People's School, 1922—a day school followed in '28; Jewish Laurentian Fresh Air Day Camp, 1929; the Jewish General Hospital, 1934—all appealing periodically for money from the Jewish community.

In 1951, Federation changed its name to the Federation of Jewish Community Services as indication of its expanded role in planning and coordinating activities. Another name change in 1965 takes us to the Allied Jewish Community Services. And in 1963, The Baron de Hirsch Institute celebrated its Centennial.

The Golden Jubilee Banquet of Allied Jewish Community Services took place in June 1967. It celebrated 50 years of service, from 1917 to 1967. The historical booklet for the event included a newspaper's comment that "Federation's growth is in public spiritedness and a better understanding of the needs of those dependent on others," and made mention of the Hebrew Orphans' Homes among the many organizations which relied on its assistance over the years. Its growing influence brought about many positive changes in those societies and community organizations, and paved the way for the present leadership development programs.

THE MONTREAL HEBREW ORPHANS' HOME

Including notes by A.D. Hart, *The Jew in Canada*, 1926

> *...the Old People's Home, under the supervision of the Federation of Jewish Philanthropies, was located in a small wooden building in Evans Street. It shared its space, moreover, with an orphanage. Some time later a committee was organized which established a fund for the purchase of an orphanage in Westmount, while another committee, representing the East Side, acquired another on Jeanne Mance Street, the Montefiore Home. The children of the Westmount orphanage, it is to be noted, were not admitted to the Westmount schools; they had perforce to attend the schools of Montreal proper, taking their lunch at the Baron de Hirsch Institute. The Montefiore Orphanage, on the other hand, suffered from no such handicap; its children attended both the Protestant schools nearby; and the Talmud Torah. Both institutions provided summer vacations in the Laurentians for their wards...*
>
> —H. Wolofsky, *Journey of my Life*

The First of the Homes

In 1909, well-meaning Jewish members of the community started a home in two old houses at the corner of Evans and Cecil Streets to care for immigrants, old folks and children—the Montreal Hebrew Orphans' Home and its companion Old Folks Residence and Sheltering Home (for immigrants)—according to Richard Kramer, whose mother was a cook in the Montreal Home. It provided a temporary home and shelter for orphaned, deserted and motherless children, the indigent aged and transients.

Evans Street ran from St. Urbain on the West a short distance East to Clark Street. At the corner of Clark and Evans was the Christie Biscuit Factory, from where the children could sometimes get a treat of broken biscuits.

> "It was a difficult outlook for Jewish children, especially without family support, and it is gratifying to know we (the community) rose to the challenge..."

By 1914, the Home's population had grown to 35 children and six aged folks. The orphanage moved to its own premises at 500 Claremont Avenue, in the western part of Montreal, in 1921. The Sheltering Home was converted into an Old People's Home, later moving to Esplanade between Mt. Royal and Marie Anne. Myer Gordon remembers walking by this home on his way to visit friends. He can still see the old folks sitting on the porch rocking. And in those days, old probably was around 60! This facility was the forerunner of the present Maimonides Hospital and Home for the Aged.

The Home was fortunate in the calibre and character of the men who served on the Board. Early Presidents were: 1912-1913, M. B. Stein; 1913-16, A. M. Vineberg; 1917-18, S. Kellert; 1919-20, Albert Lesser; 1921-22, Ascher Pierce; 1923, Jacob A. Jacobs; 1924, Moses Rittenberg. The Board of Directors for 1925 was: Advisory Committee; the Past Presidents; President, M. Rittenberg. Vice-President; H.M. Levine. Hon. Treasurer, S. Hart. Hon. Secretary; P. Meyerovitch. Board Members: Messrs. M. Albert, A. J. Alexander, F. Bramson, C. Fisher, A. Kellnor, I. Kert, Norman Friedman, H. M. Ripstein, J. H. Wener, F. Leopold, and Dr. A. P. Ship. Superintendent: Mr. Irving Gerdy.

Montreal Hebrew Orphans' and Sheltering Home 1918

Officers
A.M. Vineberg: Honorary President
S. Kellert: President
A. Lesser: Vice-President
M. Rittenberg: Treasurer
H.H. Cohen: Honorary Secretary

Board of Directors
M. Marcus; Charles Samit; H. M. Levinoff; P. Glickman; Charles Fisher; A. Kellnor ; D. M. Chorlton; Harry Gordon; William Albert; J. Goldstein; A. J. Hart

The Admissions Policy

Minutes of a Board of Directors' Meeting, December 4, 1918, by Saul Kellert, Chair, reveal some details regarding the admission of some children (not 'true' orphans).

> "This was the case of three children by the name of Pallett, whose mother was residing in Lachine and whose father was at the Front. These children were being neglected by their mother in a very serious manner and the Patriotic Fund was about to place these children in a Protestant Home. With great difficulty Federation had been able to place these children in a Jewish Home but for one month only; and was at present requesting the Orphan Home to take them in permanently; or until the father was discharged from the Army and that the Patriotic Fund would pay $30.00 per month for the upkeep of the children until the father was discharged.
> As it is contrary to the Constitution of this Home to accept children who are not orphans, this matter aroused considerable discussion. It was finally decided to admit these children, it

> being understood, that this was done under stress of war-time. The Secretary was instructed to write Federation and inform them of this decision...Mr. Fisher reported that at present there were vacancies for six girls and one boy."

Children were also discharged from the Home for behavioural problems. Boys will be boys, as the following note illustrates. Taken from the Minutes of the same meeting, December 4, 1918, Saul Kellert noted that...

> "The question of what to do in the case of Max Cohen was brought before the meeting. This boy was extremely troublesome and unmanageable as he stole away from the Home at all times and remained away for days; in some instances returning at 2 and 3 A.M., affecting an entrance through the coal hole, cellar, and through windows.
> It was decided after some discussion, to ask Federation to have him returned to his mother in Ste. Agathe, and the Secretary was instructed to inform Federation of this decision. Others were also discharged for misconduct, i.e. Hyman Monieson and Morris Schnitzer."

Meanwhile, in the immigration department, 255 men, women and children were cared for, and it was soon realised that the Home's quarters were inadequate. The following year the immigration work was discontinued, but the congestion was not relieved, due to the fact that the growing population of children reached a high of 50.

It soon became necessary to have two orphanages to care for the increasing number of children who needed care. And so the second Jewish orphanage, Montefiore Hebrew Orphans' Home, was founded in 1918. More about that facility later.

Excerpts of The Report of the Hebrew Orphans' and Sheltering Home for the year ending December 31, 1919, submitted by Harris H. Cohen, Secretary

"—On the subject of a new home for this Institution...urgent necessity—another year's experience has only emphasized and increased some of the difficulties of keeping our wards in the right surroundings for physical health, and under the proper influences for mental and moral wellbeing. The danger of fire in the building is a constant and fearful possibility...there is a constantly increasing number of cases demanding entrance which is impossible to consider.

—your Committee report on the Orphans' Home some years ago: overcrowded, unsanitary, unsafe, unsuitably located, having no playgrounds or recreation facilities, have no accommodation for the staff or proper sleeping quarters for the children, and in fact should be given up without delay.

Our finances—well looked after by Federation. Everything necessary for the welfare of the Institution was available through their management. We are duly appreciative...the disbursement for the year has been $14,408.85 including $775.43 being the cost of carrying our property in Notre Dame de Grace. Considerable painting and repairing has been done both at Evans Street and our Shawbridge House. An official survey of our property at Shawbridge has been made to define its boundaries. We made an effort last summer to derive some revenue from our vacant land in Shawbridge, with little success...

There were on December 31st under our care 42 children and 6 aged people, the children ranging from 5 to 15 years of age. Four boys celebrated their Barmitzvah during the year. One of our girls was given a course in a business college in the city to enable her to be self-supporting as soon as she left the Institution. In this regard, we must mention the lack of an efficient and sympathetic organization to follow up, advise and help those boys and girls who graduate, or are discharged from the Institution. All the care and effort taken during their stay in the Home is often in great danger of being lost for want of timely advice and kindly interest.

Our children receive their daily schooling at the Berthelet School...where Mr. Fullerton, the principal, takes a great interest in their advancement. Three children are now attending the high school. Hebrew classes of all the children (under the direction of Mr. Hyman) are held in the Baron de Hirsch Institute (as is) our Sunday School, under the able principalship of Mr. Leon Levine—the progress made is extremely gratifying, and much thanks is due to our Educational Committee...the children spent two months as usual at their summer home at Shawbridge, coming back to the city greatly improved by their outing...

...able to report splendid health among our wards, notwithstanding the dangerous epidemics that have swept the City, and in spite of the poor and inadequate facilities at our disposal to cope with such epidemics—we have to thank the conscientious workers in charge of the Home and our Medical staff for their untiring energy.

The Board would also like to express its deep thanks to those members of the community who so kindly and generously donated comforts and good things for the children. Space does not permit us to mention the names of all those kind people, but we wish especially to mention the Young Peoples' Hachnosis Orchim Society, who donated substantially towards improvements in both buildings; to the Local Council of Jewish Women who, under the management of Mrs. I. Cohen, have frequently entertained the children; to the Young Men's Hebrew Association; to the Baron de Hirsch Institute; to Mr. Mills, manager of *Loew's Theatre;* to Mr. Pomeroy, manager of the *Holman Theatre*; to the Young Girls' Relief Club of Sydney who donated $100.00; to the *El Pi Chara Club*; to Mrs. D. Slabotsky; Mrs. B. Weinstein, and to Mr. H. E. Lazarus of New York.

The Board looks forward to the Community during the coming year to fill the great need of this Institution—a Home suitable to the needs and commensurate with the size and importance of this Jewish Community."

Itemized Statement of Expenditure for 1919

Salaries	$3,5178
Bread	504.75
Meat and Fish	825.07
Butter and Eggs	300.00
Milk	834.71
Fruits and Vegetables	310.89
Groceries	1,270.77
Shoe Repairing	147.59
Clothing and Dry Goods	1,692.47
Drugs and Medical Supplies	315.94
School Books	18.48
Furniture and Equipment	364.57
Telephone and Stationery	135.27
Laundry	635.71
Coal	591.11
Rent and Light	242.28
Building Repairs	1,029.04
Ice	45.50
Sundries	70.87
	13,346.80
Interest and Taxes	1,062.05
	$14,408.85

The MHOH Seeks Larger Quarters

From the Minutes of April 15, 1920:

> "The Secretary was instructed to write to Mr. Leon Schwartz asking him to come to Montreal at the earliest opportunity bringing with him photos, plans and specifications of Orphan Homes to cost up to $100,000 and to house 100 to 125 children...also a letter to Mr. E R. Levinson of Winnipeg asking him to be kind enough to let us have the plans for the Home which was erected there. It was decided to have a survey made of the property owned by this Institution at Notre Dame de Grace. Mr. A. M. Vineberg will attend to this."

Discussions arose about the ways and means of procuring a new home just for the children. According to the Minutes of June 17, 1920, one option was to purchase, from Mr. Moses Vineberg, land at the corner of Cote St. Luc Road and Clanranald Avenue, at the rate of thirty-five cents per square foot ... pay one half in cash on the date of the passing of the deed of sale, the balance to remain as a first mortgage, payable in five years from date of signing—interest set at six per cent per year, payable semi-annually.

The second option—a Building Committee, consisting of Chairman J. A. Jacobs, A. Pierce, A. M. Vineberg, S. Kellert, M. Rittenberg, Wm. Albert and M. Markus, was to appoint an architect, draw up plans and specifications, sign contracts, etc., and to proceed to erect a new Home for, and in the name of, M.H.O.H. The other land in N.D.G. was to be sold.

After months of deliberation, at a meeting on September 19, 1920, President Lesser called for the consideration of purchasing the building and property of the Hervey Institute which could no longer meet its expenses. As this building was (1) comparatively new, (2) in a good location, and (3) built to house up to 150 children, it was considered by some members of the Board to be a good purchase. The cost—$100,000. Several members had inspected it and found that, with some alterations, it would be suitable for their own institution.

It was decided to purchase this building and property at 500 Claremont Avenue. The unanimous decision was that this was preferable to building a new facility. The Building Committee acted on behalf of the Home to look into details of the purchase. A budget for the Montreal Home for 1921 was set at a special Board meeting on April 14th, 1921...costs in the current facility were estimated to be similar to the preceeding year...

Estimated expenditure to September 1	$6,750.00
and from September 1st to December 31st	$6,750.00
based on the housing of 60 children	
	$13,500.00

Minutes of a special May 7th meeting described a campaign to raise the balance of the funds required to pay for ($100,000) and equip the new building ($25,000):

> "Mr. Rittenberg reported that about $94,000 has been subscribed already; of which $35,175 has been collected...It was decided to immediately issue a call for the second payment of one-third of amounts already subscribed..."

The question of soliciting new subscribers was discussed. A list of names to canvas was made from Federation's Annual Report—the cards to be distributed requesting payment of one-half cash by June 1st, the balance by September 1st. Voluntary subscribers would be solicited through ads in the Jewish papers after the results of the canvas were in, if the situation still warranted it.

According to author A. D. Hart, Moses Rittenberg, as President of the Montreal Home, spent much of his time visiting similar institutions to get some ideas for improving his facility.

The following was the budget as estimated for one year in the new facility, based on housing 60 children:

Superintendent	$1,500	
Assistants	$1,000	
Cook	$900	
House Help	$400	
Janitor and Wife	$900	
Teachers	$1,500	$6,200
Heating	$1,000	
Light and Power	$400	
Laundry	$1,000	
Food	$6,000	
Clothing	$3,000	
Drugs and Medicine	$200	
Postage, Stationery & Telegraph	$200	
Sundries	$1,000	
Insurance and Water Tax	$500	
School Books	$ 200	$13,500
		$19,700

The new Home on Claremont opens

Minutes of the Montreal Home Board of Directors Meeting of October 16, 1921, noted that more than 3000 invitations were sent to members of Federation for the official opening reception on Sunday, October 23rd. The following special names were added: Mayor of Montreal, Aldermen Rubenstein and Jacobs, Mayor and Council of Westmount, all Rabbis, Rev. Dr. Dickie, Frank Weldon, Mr. Simmond, Dr. Henderson, Head Master of Berthelet Street School, Prime Minister Mr. Meighen, P. Bercovitch, M.P.P., S. W. Jacobs, M.P., Senator Webster, and Mr. Taschereau. Committee members in charge of making arrangements for the reception were Messrs. Lesser, Kellnor, Levine, Albert, Rittenberg and Hart.

Record numbers of the Jewish community joined in the reception, most pleased with the new development. The proudest boast of the Montreal Jewry at that time was its new Hebrew Orphans' Home. President Ascher Pierce assured that the Institution's budget would be kept as low as possible, "consistent, of course, with the best interests of the children cared for."

At about the same time, the Home was approached by the Jewish War Orphans' Association. They were attempting to bring to Canada Ukrainian children orphaned by the War. They asked if these children could be housed in there for several weeks 'until they were disposed of (adopted).' The Home requested that this be submitted in writing, stating the number of children, the service required for their care, the approximate date of their arrival, and the length of their stay.

One Federation function was to coordinate the work of its various agencies. Accordingly, the activities of its central office, the Baron de Hirsch Institute and the Hebrew Orphans' Home were consolidated in order to simplify the admission of the children into the facility. A committee was to investigate and act on all questions of admission and discharge of the wards.

In the same Minutes, it was moved by Mr. A. Kellnor, seconded by Mr. D. Chorlton, that the applications on hand (for admission to the Home) be acted upon:

Dora and Barny Shapiro
Jenny, Sam and Sarah Novak
Mollie, Max, Jake and Morris Spector
Annie Rosenbaum
Minnie, Kate and Lionel Levy

Their acceptance was approved unanimously. Concerning the applications for the Pernikoff children, Charles Fisher reported that "their parents were in good circumstances and could look after them..."

The childen were moved into the new building in October 1921...there was ample room for 100 children. The 50 orphans now in the Home...

> "...were receiving the best of material care, and the advantage of a safe, sanitary, and attractive institution with a most modern and home-like atmosphere."

There were 12 dormitories—the Home was co-ed: girls roomed four to a room, boys the same. There were classrooms, lockers, gymnasium, music room, plus an isolation floor. This was a complete unit in itself, containing two infirmaries, a fully-equipped dental room, and other necessary facilities. The floor was fully equipped as a hospital in the fall of 1924.

Life in the Home was marked by privacy, individual treatment and informality, and with appropriate discipline—discipline, not as a group, but based on the need to develop self-reliance. Public appearances played down their status as 'orphans.' There was no public display to exhibit the children for the purpose of appealing for sympathy or funding, which greatly aided their morale.

From the fall of 1921 to fall 1922, 82 children were cared for in the Home. Nineteen were satisfactorily discharged, while eight were lost under sad circumstances—the catastrophic fire at the summer vacation home in Shawbridge (noted elsewhere). Entering the second year in the new facility, there were 55 children: 26 girls, 29 boys, ranging in age from 5-16 years. Of the 55, one was a foundling, nine were full orphans, 40 were half-orphans, while five were considered neglected.

In caring for the 40 half-orphans, the Home also gave practical relief to about 25 surviving parents, who, in most cases, might otherwise be an additional expense to the Family Welfare Department.

In 1922, after one full year in the new site on Claremont Avenue, President Pierce reported to Federation that

> "the children have grown accustomed to their new surroundings and are creating a real home atmosphere which gives us much satisfaction. We feel that the Home, with the activities organized under the supervision of our new Superintendent, Mr. Irving Gerdy, is of great benefit to the children and seeks to follow the highest ideals in communal child care. The Jewish community of Montreal has reason to be proud of this Institution, and we hope to bring our wards to manhood and womanhood to be a credit to ourselves and to the community at large."

An interesting anecdote...on April 7, 1971, a Mr. Claude Lepine called the National Jewish Archives in Montreal to say he had found a cane from the Home inscribed in 1922 to an *A. Pierce*—as noted above, Ascher Pierce was President from 1921-22, a Board member from 1925 on.

Sunday School was considered an important element in the children's education. By 1922, space was lacking, and then teacher Mr. Markus received an offer from the Baron de Hirsch Institute Sunday School, agreeing to incorporate the Home school with that of the Institute. He also arranged the fee to be paid to Mr. Cohen for his teaching of the Bar Mitzvah boys—$50.00. Sunday School was under the supervision of Mr. Arthur Vineberg, assisted by a staff of five teachers. Mr. A Chodesh, the new Hebrew teacher, conducted classes five days a week, with both morning and evening services, "there being more than a full *minyon* of boys in the Home."

By 1923 there was an appreciable advance in the children's Hebrew training. Mr. Chodesh, headmaster of the *Shaar Hashomayim* Hebrew School, employed modern methods of teaching. Friday Services were conducted at the Home, one of the older boys as Chazan. There was regular morning and evening davening. The children attended Sabbath Services at the *Shaar Hashomayim.*

And Home Director Mr. Kellnor reported in the October 16th, 1922, Minutes, that Mr. F. Bramson of Bramsons Taxicab Ltd. had very generously offered to take some childen back and forth to the Berthelet Street School every day. "The Secretary was instructed to write a letter of thanks to Mr. Bramson expressing our appreciation at his kindness and generosity."

Others were also bussed to the school at Bleury and St. Catherine Streets, some 10 miles away from the Home.

Four of the children were attending public high schools, and three were pupils of the Canadian School of Electricity on a partial scholarship given by the school. Two of the girls were at the Barnes Art School, while two others had a free scholarship at Shefler's Dance Studio, marking the third year Mr. George Shefler donated these scholarships to the Home's girls.

By the end of 1923, there was a monthly average of 65 children being cared for by the Montreal Hebrew Orphans' Home...69 in December '23, plus 10 children from among the refugees from Bucharest who were eligible for admission. The new President, Mr. J.A. Jacobs, noted in his year-end report that "wherever it has been found unnecessary to separate a mother and her children it has not been done..." He went on to write that...

> "influences that result from a monotonous routine have been studiously avoided. All who come in contact with the children express their admiration for their open and frank natures, coupled with consideration and orderliness."

At year's end, 58 children attended Berthelet School, five were at Baron Byng High School, two in Business College and three working. At the June closing, 53 were promoted, four graduating and 32 honours were earned. President Jacobs noted that

> "Our school situation, as is well known, is abnormal in that our children have a long way to get to school. Notwithstanding this drawback and our heavy schedule of Home activities, our children have done well in their school work."

In his report to the Board at year's end, President Jacobs noted that the health of the children was satisfactory, averaging only six calls per month for a physician to treat minor illnesses. The medical supply room was fitted with a supply of drugs and instruments for emergency cases. A dental staff was in attendance every Sunday morning...the dental room was fully equipped with all necessary instruments and chemicals. Dental problems were taken care of during the week at the dentists' offices. Eye examinations were conducted at the clinic of the Herzl Dispensary, which also filled prescriptions for the Home.

Some children were underweight. Special dieting built up most of them, with gains ranging from four to twenty pounds.

> "...one little lady who had to wear crutches and braces at the beginning of the year owing to a disease of the hip. She has discarded both and walks about now like a normal child. We are obliged to the staff of the Children's Memorial Hospital for their excellent treatment of this little girl."

By 1927, President H.M. Levine reported on two other support groups operating in the Montreal Home. The Sewing Society, under the direction of Mrs. D.M. Chorlton, provided a valuable service by mending the childrens' clothing, "a great aid in economy." This society was founded in 1902 to counteract the effect of missionary sewing classes which were trying to attract Jewish girls.

Sylvia Savitsky Rasminsky lived at the Montreal Home from 1933-42. She has many good memories of

"a lovely old home with a skating rink and baseball diamond on the property. We even had a piano teacher come in, and there was an elocution teacher as well. Who had elocution in those days? We were encouraged to listen to opera on Saturday afternoons, and one of the young assistants conducted current event classes...We had all the benefits imaginable. It was like an elegant camp."

Sylvia remembers that her mother, a dressmaker, visited every Sunday and re-made the used clothing from wealthy donors into beautiful dresses for the girls. She also recalls fighting over shoes with Annie Mitnick. Thinking back on it now, she finds it amusing, considering that Annie's feet were much bigger than hers!

In 'her time,' Sylvia well remembers that they had to go to Berthelet School, by foot, by street-car (the Home's own special school bus was not evident in the earlier days). Sylvia has one regret. When she won a proficiency award at school in grade 7, she was not permitted to attend a collegiate school rather than commercial. "We were supposed to get out and work as soon as possible." (Indeed, once a child reached the age of 16, he/she had to leave the Home.) The orphanage board turned down her request because its members said she would get married anyway. And Sylvia did—she married another orphan, Sam Rasminsky, with whom she was friendly as a teen in the Home. Sam was in the Montefiore Home first, then transferred to the Montreal Home when the former closed in 1936.

While the 'kids' in both homes were always well-treated, one supervisor in the Montreal Home, Maurice Ogulnick, was known to have 'over-disciplined' (mildly beaten) some of them. Sylvia defended his memory by saying that he was helpful in many ways, and he was great with the girls...after a Shabbat meal, he would take a group of girls into the gym where, sitting on mats, they held discussions about world news and politics. She remembers he also took them to Lac Masson where he would put 5 cents into the juke-box and teach them to dance. But, perhaps he did come over a bit strong to some of the boys...some of the wards can attest to that!

Recreation Programs

The Recreation Programs of that time contributed to the apparent happiness of the children.

> "There is little doubt but that the gem of childhood joy is preserved for our boys and girls, which is a blessing of much value since separation from one's people, mother and father, is such a blight. There is gladness in the eyes of the visitors when they see the children moving about with childhood ease and complacency...much to do with the good health and physical development noticed.
>
> There is little time left from schooling and the necessary hours for the necessities of life, but we are doing our best to create a diversification of activities that will correspond as closely as possible to normal experience of normal youngsters."

Activities included religious observances, Jewish/Hebrew education, history and ethics, domestic training, music, needlework, folk dancing and organized games, the fostering of individual hobbies, Hebrew, clubwork and social life.

Twice a week, all the children were given physical training and played organized games under the direction of Miss Herriott of the School of Physical Training, McGill University. Because the children got calisthenics in school, the Home paid more attention to games in its gym and to athletic teams: in winter—basketball, in summer—baseball, cricket and volleyball. Home teams performed up to par when playing against other clubs.

Birthday nights brought much pleasure to all. Mr. I. Rosenbloom furnished carefully selected films which entertained the children on Saturday evenings, followed by dramatic entertainment, music and dancing. They were also permitted visits to *His Majesty's, Princess* and *Orpheum Theatres*. Most of the graduates attended the weekly social events. The younger children enjoyed their own social evening every Friday night, filled with plays, recitation, songs and nursery games.

The children produced their own dramatic work—several playlets attended by members of the Board who were "delighted with the performance." For *Chunukah*—a play with tableaus, *Picture Out of the Past* (1923), was performed. Musical instruction was under the direction of Mr. Gerald Fels. Through the generosity of past president Mr. Ascher Pierce, mandolins were supplied and a mandolin club was formed.

In 1923, 12 boys were members of the Boy Scout Troop of the *Shaar Hashomayim* Synagogue—fully equipped with scout uniforms. Scoutcraft was seen as a strong character-building influence. It was hoped that a number of the girls would become involved with Girl Guides in the coming years.

Through these social and recreational activities, "we became a closely knit family group. In this way, we develop emotional and loving contact."

The 12th Annual Report by the Board of 1928 to the Federation of Jewish Philanthropies contained the following thoughts by President Samuel Hart:

> "For many years past it has been accepted as a principle in dealing with our children that insofar as humanly possible our charges shall bear no marks distinguishing them from members of other Jewish families in the City of Montreal. They are to us individuals who require the same attention and the same appreciation of distinct personality as our own children, and we have endeavored in all things to make them forget that they are orphans and to make them feel that their stay in the Home is a training place for their future as citizens in our community."

The number of children in the Home during 1928 averaged 86; ten new wards were admitted; nine graduated. The Alumni Group started several years ago and continued to retain contact with each other and the Home.

Bar Mitzvah boys in 1928 were Harry Brumer, Henry Fox, Alex Kushner, Moe Klein, Sydney Rosenbaum, Harry Avrith and Lionel Levy. A generous amount of money was raised as a Bar Mitzvah present, and entertainments were held.

Choral singing was part of the musical instruction offered to all the children, and was under the leadership of Mrs. Rossen, the matron. Miss Mary Vineberg was in charge of the sewing group. As well, Mrs. M. Margolick, with 'wide vision and sympathetic understanding,' directed a year filled with activity and accomplishments of the Ladies Auxiliary. Among these, funds were raised and provided an artificial leg for one of the boys. This enabled him to go out and earn a living. The Auxiliary also cooperated in purchasing clothing and furnished treats over the holidays.

How many of you remember Mrs. Reider, the cook? A newspaper article in April 1993 brought her to the attention of its readers and related some of her past. Which seems quite strange as she had retired in 1963 (and passed away in 1996).

Her daughter, Ernestine Justitz, set some of the record straight when the Gordons paid her a recent visit. Rika (not Rose, as the article called her) lived in Russia with her husband and daughter until she and Ernestine fled to Romania, then Germany, coming to Canada in 1928 where they had family. Says Ernestine, "My father never left Russia and was later killed in WWII as a Russian soldier."

Rika went to work in the Montreal Home in 1931; Ernestine, then 15, was living with an aunt. In 1935, they both moved into the Home.

> "I lived as a boarder with my mother until we got our own apartment in 1938 and mother no longer worked in the Home—living in an orphanage was not the way to live."

Ernestine later became a nurse and married. And is now a great-grandmother, living in Toronto and coming to some of the MHOH reunions!

Rika didn't learn to cook as a young woman. In Russia where she was born, it was considered a social disgrace for the lady of the house to soil her hands in the kitchen.

> "When I first came to Canada, I worked as a supervisor in an orphanage (The Montreal Hebrew Orphans' Home). One day the cook came down ill when the ladies auxiliary of the orphanage were due for the annual tea. So I found a cook-book and baked cookies and a cake for them. They all wanted to know where I'd found the excellent new cook!"

Mrs. Reider continued her new interest in cooking by reading every cook-book she could find. She seemed keen on sticking to a budget. And later, when she left the orphanage post, she embarked on a new career in cooking for others, i.e., at various synagogues. Soon she had a staff of six. "Cooking for two is wasteful—it's much more economical to cook for 600!" Obviously, her early Home experience made her feel "much more at home cooking for large numbers."

One of her budget recipes (Ernestine insists this was not one of her recipes) was for

> "Stuffed Onions: remove skin from two large Bermuda onions, parboil five minutes in salted water. Drain, remove part of the centres. Pour in 1/2 tin consomme over the shells, bake in 350 degree oven for 15 minutes until tender, basting often. Fill centre with boiled mashed potatoes, seasoned with salt, pepper and butter. Return to oven to brown."

(Another note from Ernestine—"My mother would never have used the term 'buttered' in any of her recipes (as the article wrote). She was kosher and used only oil.")

Still—A Problem with the School System

Over the years, one main problem remained in the education of the children. The Protestant Board of School Commissioners was still not induced to open its doors to Home children in any school nearer the Home than the Berthelet School which they still attended (however, as noted earlier, children from the Montefiore Home had no problem attending the local public school). There were rumours that the nearer Westmount Schools would not accept Jews, but it was said it was because the youngsters were not from tax-paying families.

Berthelet School was across from the Sommer Building in downtown Montreal; Berthelet Street itself later became a continuation of Ontario Street. Satisfactory arrangements were made with the Montreal Hebrew Sheltering Home, still at 18 Evans Street, for the provision of a hot dinner for the children, a vast improvement over previous arrangements. As well, to help relieve this situation, three classes were conducted in the Home for the benefit of the younger children.

In 1917, the Montreal Hebrew Orphans' Home looked after 46 children. After World War I, the number of orphans increased. By 1926, the new building on Claremont housed 105 children. Following is a sample of admission records from the Home:

Name	Born	Admitted	Discharged
Celia Dubin	Dec.12,1912	July 6, 1919	June 8, 1929
Wm. Goldstein	Feb. 5, 1910	Oct. 23, 1924	Jan. 21, 1927
Annie Israels	Aug. 14,1912	Nov. 21, 1922	June 1, 1931
Annie Klein	Jan. 19,1912	Nov. 15, 1925	May 26, 1929
Samuel Klein	Dec. 2, 1916	Nov. 15, 1925	Sept. 27, 1933
Lionel Levy	Apr. 9, 1913	June 15, 1923	Jan. 12,1930
Joe Waxman	Feb. 17,1912	Feb. 15, 1915	June 24, 1928
Etta Stotland	Apr. 11, 1913	May 23, 1926	June 19, 1929
Charles Alper	Dec. 1912	Jan. 1924	June 9, 1929
Louis Raven	Mar. 26,1913	Sept. 15, 1925	June 15, 1929
Winnie Andes	May 18,1915	May 30, 1929	May 3, 1932
Moses Velter	Aug. 14,1915	Jan. 1925	Nov. 21, 1931
Sam Bruner*	July 1, 1913	Dec. 12, 1922	May 25, 1929
Bennie Bruner*	Dec. 6, 1910	Dec. 6, 1922	May 8, 1927
Hyman Bruner*	July 10, 1912	July 12,1922	May 25, 1929
Sylvia Roseman	Aug. 15,1918	Dec. 10, 1928	Dec. 1, 1934
Hyman Goldberg	Dec. 1, 1915	Oct. 2, 1924	Died July, 1930

*Note: the correct spelling was Brumer; as attested by another brother Louis, who also was put into the Home in 1922, attended all the reunions and passed away in September 2001.

Applications from Federation, dated June 17th and noted in Minutes of a meeting on that date, referred to requests for the admission of Sam Rosensweig, "a former inmate." It was decided to accept him to remain in the Institution over the summer at Shawbridge. Another request was to re-admit Juliet Moss, aged 7—her mother had to be taken to the Sanatarium. She was admitted. Applications were also received for three Vincberg children whose mother had died of the 'flu.' This was a very sad case and one in which the Board would like to give assistance. But as the father was able financially to see that the children were cared for, it was considered unwise to create a precedent and therefore this application was rejected. Accepted for admission into the Home was another applicant, Joseph Goldberg, age 6.

The Beloved Byes

Alumni Abe & Edie Bye's mother, a social worker from New York's Hester Street, was hired as Matron because she spoke Yiddish. She met and married her husband Henry, treasurer of a local organization in Montreal. When Mr. Bye lost his business, Mrs. Bye got a job back in New York as the Matron of the Pride of Judea's Orphan Home. Abe's schooling was in the Bronx and Brooklyn—also the area *Murder Inc.* began...where bad guys threatened to kill their chickens if the people who ran the poultry market didn't pay them a couple of bucks...where Lansky and Shapiro started before they became part of the Mafia. Abe feels he turned out okay in spite of this.

Luckily, the Byes were hired back by the Montreal Home in 1929 in the positions of Superintendent and Matron. They ran the facility until it closed in 1942, and were very well liked by the children. The annual report notes that

> "their work merits commendation. We feel that they have rendered every cooperation in our attempts to economize and to maintain a high standard of service throughout our Institution."

From his time in the Home, Abe remembers the Montreal Minstrel Shows, Mrs. Reider's strudel, and Mr. Perry's *hamentashen* (he put pennies in them). He also recalls his favourite meal—hot dogs and mashed potatoes, the dumbwaiter going to the large laundry room in the basement, and the coal oil shampoos to kill the bugs, and, of course, Sunshine Camp...

Many, many years later, Abe wrote the following (after a reunion), "So glad we can still be part of the 'family.'"

As a child, Richard Kramer lived in the Home with his mother, Judy Gordon's mother had a close friend Kitty Lang. In conversation with 'Aunt Kitty' in the early '90s, Judy touched on the topic of husband Myer's stay in the orphanage. "Oh," says Kitty, "I used to play with a little boy whose mother was the cook at the Claremont Home. His name was Richard." The Gordons tracked him down to his home in Florida. He was in the Montreal Home because his mother, prior to coming to the orphanage, worked as a matron at the Vesta Street Home. And, indeed, he did play outside with some of the local children. He joined the Grenadier Guards in 1919 when he was only 15, and attended Strathearn High School. Abe Bye's mother later gave Richard a job in the Home at the office, which he later ran.

Richard wrote:

> "The future Mrs. Henry Bye was matron, and my mother was employed as cook and housekeeper (in the 1920's). In addition to caring for my younger brother and myself, my mother was also like a mother to more than 70 children. Many years later, on the occasion of her 70th birthday, these now grown children gave her a testimonial dinner in remembrance and gratitude."

The Third Annual Report (1919) of the Federation of Jewish Philanthropies of Montreal

> "...places on record its appreciation of the valuable services of Mrs. Kramer, our housekeeper, who has been connected with the Home for many years, and who has greatly helped toward giving our Institution its homelike qualities."

Richard's widow, Florence, is 95 at time of writing. She lives in a seniors' residence in Sarasota, Florida, and is still most interested to read *The Mishpocha* and generously sends in an annual donation.

In the Minutes of April 15, 1920, Al Lesser, Chair, informed the meeting

> "that Mrs. Kramer had received a very attractive offer to take a position elsewhere and it was felt that it would be advisable to offer her an increase in salary to keep her with us. It was therefore, moved, seconded and unanimously carried that this Board recommends to Federation that they increase Mrs. Kramer's salary by the amount of $15.00 per month to date April 1st."

The great crash of '29 caused havoc at the Home. It was the 20th year since the opening of the original Institution in 1909 and it experienced economic conditions parallel to the rest of the country. It was deemed necessary to cut back in as many areas of running the facility as possible, without impairing its high standard of services rendered. During the year, 96 children were cared for, 20 were admitted, and 23 discharged.

The health of the children could not be compromised. Dr. S. J. Usher and his staff on the Medical Board devoted their constant attention to the welfare of the children. All were immunized, assisted by Miss R. Ratner. With Dr. H. Israel as Chair, and a competent staff, dental treatment was available throughout the year. A new feature was the training of some of the Home's girls to assist the dentists—hopefully leading to similar careers for them when they left the Home. Another plus—free optical examinations and treatment was offered by Dr. J. Rosenbaum.

The Ladies Auxiliary continued to supply the Home with many necessary household commodities—a big saving. They cooperated in the purchase of clothing, shoes, household supplies, and paid for treats for the children. The various ladies' committees were from the *Shaar Hashomayim*, *Temple Emanuel*, *Shaare Zion* and *Spanish & Portuguese* Sisterhoods, who also provided the womenpower to supervise the school lunches at the Baron de Hirsch Institute.

Mr. George Vaz of Federation received the following invitation from Helen Matgolick, Chairlady of the Auxiliary.

> "The Ladies Auxiliary to the Montreal Hebrew Orphans' Home is having an "At Home" on Sunday afternoon, February 23rd. 1930—You and your friends are cordially invited to be present."

Any excuse to raise funds to help maintain the institution!

The ladies of the *Shaar Hashomayim* Sewing Circle, under the direction of Mrs. A.S. Vineberg, made up necessary articles with their own materials and donated garments made up at their weekly sewings.

All holidays were celebrated in fitting fashion, thanks to Mr. & Mrs. Henry Bye and Mrs. Konowitz who injected a tone of unusual interest. Sabbath morning services were discontinued in the Home as the children seemed to prefer attending at the Synagogue. Mr. Bye still conducted the weekday services every morning, attended by all senior boys. Religious training was under the chairmanship of Rabbi Charles Bender and his committee: Dr. H. Abramowitz, Messrs. P. Levy, L. Salomon and L. Faber. Sixty-one pupils attended the four classes, Jewish in content, modern in spirit.

A Visit of Importance

> "His Excellency, the Earl of Bessborough, Governor General of Canada, accompanied by Col. Willis O'Connor, A.D.C., visited the Montreal Hebrew Orphans' Home, 500 Claremont Ave., Westmount, this morning, and was received by the President, Mr. S. Ross Vineberg, and the Board of Directors of the Institution. The 76 inmates at the Institution sang the National Anthem, and His Excellency proceeded to inspect the building. Mr. S. Ross Vineberg and Rev. Dr. M. Abramowitz conveyed to his Excellency on behalf of the Directors and Montreal Jewry, a hearty welcome to the Institution and

expressed sentiments of loyalty to His Majesty's Throne and Person.

From there the Governor General proceeded to the *Shaar Hashomayim* Synagogue, being shown around the building by the Rev. Dr. H. Abramowitz and prominent members of the congregation.

The Governor General next visited the Baron de Hirsch Institute at 2040 Bleury Street, and was received by Mr. Marcus M. Sperber, President, the Board of Directors of the Institute, and the Trustees of the Federation of Jewish Philanthropies. His Excellency made an inspection of the building, visiting the Family Welfare Department, the Legal Aid Department, the Department of Colonization, the Employment Bureau, and the Administrative offices of the Federation...

Among those present at the three functions were Messrs. Allan Bronfman, Samuel Bronfman, A. H. Jassby, Ernest G. F. Vaz, David Kirsch, J. Levinson Sr., Horace R. Cohen, Clarence Michaels, Louis Salomon, C. B. Fainer, Max Finestone, Capt. W. S. Montefiore, J. Albert, B. Kaplan, Simon Kirsch, Philip Abbey, A. Greenberg, P. Garfinkle, Chas. Fisher, Dr. H. Israel, Henry V. Bye."

Financial Problems; Some Solutions

The cost to the Baron de Hirsch Institute and other community organizations to run the orphanages was high. Those parents whose children were looked after in the Homes were asked to pay a monthly fee if their financial conditions allowed. A "Ways & Means Committee" mounted fundraising campaigns to reach out to the general Jewish community. It was all too obvious that adequate monies permitted the admission of more needy youngsters and the ability to pay for the increasing burden this entailed to maintain a satisfactory life for them, i.e. healthier food choices, new clothing and more activities.

Federation fundraising was a common occurrence. A campaign for $150,000 was initiated, $125,000 was subscribed, and the Federation has ever since played a vital role in Montreal's Jewish community and in World Jewry. By 1922, donations formed the backbone of the orphanage structure—aside from money, $10 here, $30 there...Mr. & Mrs. B. J. Hayes donated 100 clothing hangers; Mrs. B. C. Feiner 6 bed sheets; Mrs. J. Dinovitzer and Mrs. Laurie fruits and vegetables.

The following letter is only one example received from the generous benefactors approached by ad campaigns and personal letters.

Bronfman Interests
205 St. James Street
Montreal, Canada
March Eighth 1928.

E.G.F. Vaz Esq.
Comptroller,
Federation of Jewish Philanthropies,
Montreal, P.Q.

Dear Mr. Vaz,

On my return to the City this morning I found your letter of the 7th instant in connection with the Sheltering Home. The matter will receive my attention right away.
Yours very sincerely

Allan Bronfman

Enforced Contributions

In an effort to raise funds, Henry Bye 'went after' the families of some of their wards, feeling it was imperative that they assist financially in the care of their children. As most of these families were quite impoverished, it was difficult to contribute. Others had some funds but were reluctant to part with them. Some were just never contacted. Hence a letter-writing and telephone campaign kept in touch with them, trying to elicit every dollar possible.

The following items are taken from a letter dated November 21, 1930, to the Federation's Comptroller, Mr. E.G.F. Vaz, concerning delinquent accounts...

> "Mrs. Rockman: Mother of one child, George, who was taken in the Home at the end of 1925. The mother has a stationery store on 2600 Coursol Street and has brothers running a business as Rockman Bros. Cartage Contractors. No effort has been made to make any of them help to pay anything towards the boy's maintenance."

> Mr. Morris Miller: Has two children in the Home since May 1926. The application read as follows: Mr. Miller has promised to pay $40. per month for the children's care in the Home and has given a deposit of $100 as a guarantee of his good faith. Miss Blumenfield claims she has no record of his account nor of any payments being made."

At the same time, Mrs. A.J. Freiman of Ottawa, a friend to Mrs. Allan Bronfman, wrote a letter to Montreal Home President Samuel Hart, expressing an interest in two Jewish orphans who were, at that time, residing in a Protestant Institution. She stated that the uncle of these children was most anxious to have them placed in a Jewish institution, preferably in Montreal, where he would be able to pay them occasional visits. He was also prepared to pay for their maintenance:

> "Would you please advise whether you are prepared to admit them to your Institution in consideration of a monthly payment being made, and if so what the charges would be."

She was informed that further information was required, i.e. names, ages, birthplace, present location, length of time in Canada, etc., at which time the matter would be taken up at the next meeting.

One item from the Montreal Home Comptroller's memo was about a man who had a good cash business (a store) and was thus financially able to pay the $15 per month to look after his son. He was allowed to "fall in arrear" over a period of two years, and so didn't seem to understand the importance of paying his account. It was felt that to take legal action would make him understand the necessity of paying each month—"to let it drag on for two years is poor policy."

The Will of the late Joseph A. Jacobs bequeathed that, at the death of his brother Solomon Jacobs, $25,000.00 be paid to the Mount Sinai Sanatarium. One quarter of the remainder of his estate was to be given to the Mount Sinai Sanatarium and one-quarter to the Montreal Hebrew Orphans' Home, and one-twentieth to the Neighbourhood House. On the 20th of December 1930, based on the net residue, the Montreal Hebrew Orphans' Home would receive $5,284.00...

In a further attempt to conserve monies during these early years of the Depression, the Montreal Home Comptroller realized that it was cheaper to purchase vegetables and fruit for the Shawbridge summer camp in Montreal than to buy it in the country...

$2.25	bag potatoes	versus	1.50	City Price
2.25	box plums	versus	1.75	City Price
40c.	doz. lettuce	versus	15c.	City Price
70c.	doz. cucumbers	versus	50c.	City Price
40c.	doz. beets	versus	15c.	City Price
30c.	doz. onions	versus	15c.	City Price
50c.	doz. cabbages	versus	20c.	City Price

In a letter to Mr. Greenberg, Chair of the House Committee, dated July 21, 1930, he further stated that

> "Seeing that there is no charge for express or freight in view of the fact that supplies are delivered weekly by the Mount Sinai Sanatarium truck, I would appreciate if you would give instructions at once to discontinue the purchasing of these supplies in the village, and continue as heretofore, by putting requisitions in the usual manner through the Purchasing Department so that purchases may be made in the City...."

Similar problems arose again in September 1932, when Federation of Jewish Philanthropies Executive Director Mr. George Vaz wrote to Mr. Greenberg about purchases for the Home, made without the knowledge of Federation's Purchasing Department, that were much higher than they could procure the same commodities for.

> "We found that the coffee was being purchased at 40 cents per pound, sardines $8.00 per case, delicatessen meat at 50 cents per pound, herrings at $1.00 per dozen, salami at 35 cents per pound....I don't have to tell you that it is essential that we save every cent in these times and I should appreciate if you would make Mr. Bye understand that the purchasing for the Institution is to be done by the Purchasing Department of Federation."

Home Superintendent Henry Bye replied to this slight within ten days. His comments, excerpted here were most insightful:

> "—ask me why purchases made instead of writing to Mr. Greenberg...purchases in question made while in Shawbridge—those made prior to that were allowed to go through so you have no cause to complain, 'our monthly food expense is very low'..."

As for the sardines, he had not bought any for a year—now purchased one half a case of 50 tins for when the children went on hikes—to give them sardine sandwiches for a change—Federation's purchasing agent suggested he buy the large barrel of herrings; Mr. Bye felt it was better and cheaper in the end to buy only a few dozen herrings at a time because "the latter had probably been in storage for a year and we don't want to be the goat for old stock."

And as for the coffee...that sent was too cheap a grade and it meant using more or returning it all the way from Shawbridge, "so we bought it ourselves."

The meat was purchased for the Field Day:

> "You may not know that we had quite a large gathering of visitors to whom we served lunch. The Committee in charge brought in a large number of prizes for the children; the suits, coats, dresses, pants and shoes alone saved Federation at least

$250.00. Now don't you think that these friends deserved a good meal from our Institution? Supposing it did cost a few dollars more than the cheaper food you could have procured for us, the fact that all those who were present complimented us for the refreshments served should have made you happy. The least you could have given us was credit for good judgement in giving the Home good publicity. Mr. Erlick was present and he can bear us out..."

All agreements are contingent upon strikes, accidents, delays of carriers and other delays unavoidable or beyond our control.

J. GILLETZ & CO.

BUILDERS

AND GENERAL CONTRACTORS

4392 CITY HALL AVENUE

PHONE BELAIR 1650-1

ALTERATIONS
STORE FRONTS
STORE AND OFFICE FIXTURES

PLASTEF
CEMEN'
BRICK W

Montreal, June 20, 1930

Mr. Vaz,
Federation of Jewish Phil.,
Bleury St.,
City.,

Dear Sir:

Enclosed herein find my evaluation of property, 500 Claremont Ave., Westmount, Orphans Home, for adjustment of fire insurance purposes.

I have mailed you my valuation in the month of March, but unfortunately you did no receive same.

Trusting that this will obtain the information required as on the last board meeting, r ter was taken up about having too much insurance, as the mortgage has been reduced and it is ı necessary to carry such amount.

Yours very truly,

J. GILLETZ AND COMPANY

Measurements of building of the Hebrew Orphans Home,
500 Claremont Avenue, Westmount.

Measurements taken Mar. 17, 1930

Size of building	120 x 41 x 50	246,000	c.f.
Hospital on roof	31 x 38 x 11	12,958	c.f.
		258,958	c.f.
	Value per cu.ft.	0.25	
	Total valuation	$ 64,739.50	

In another bid to save Federation's money, every aspect of the Home's expenses was studied, including the insurance—see the above letter of response from J. Gilletz & Company, Builders, to Mr. Vaz, assuring him that his rates would go down as the mortgage had been reduced.

Maintaining the children personally, and the costs of the building, proved to be an uphill battle as the years went by. As well, there were costs incurred by the Family Welfare Department for those children maintained in private homes. Federation assisted the Boards in negotiations with the Provincial Government in an effort to obtain a per capita allowance for each child. By 1929, there was still no definite action taken by the Government. There was evidence, however, that this issue was under consideration.

Through the diligent year-long efforts of such men as Mr. Peter Bercovitch, K.C., MLA, and Mr. Joseph Cohen, K.C., a conference with the Honorable Prime Minister Mr. Taschereau was arranged for August 19, 1930, at the latter's Provincial Government Office on Notre Dame Street. Mr. A.Z. Cohen was also asked to serve as a member of this deputation.

(Printed in Canada) FORM T.D. 2N

CANADIAN PACIFIC RAILWAY COMPANY'S TELEGRAPH

NIGHT LETTER

CABLE CONNECTIONS TO ALL PARTS OF THE WORLD

TIME FILED
CHECK

J. McMillan, General Manager of Telegraphs, Montreal.

Send the following Night Letter, subject to the terms printed on the back hereof which are hereby agreed to.

MONDAY, OCTOBER 13TH, 1930

THE HONORABLE L. A. TASCHEREAU,
PRIME MINISTER, PROVINCE OF QUEBEC,
QUEBEC CITY, QUE.

OUR EXECUTIVE COMMITTEE MEETS ON WEDNESDAY NIGHT TO GO FURTHER INTO THE SERIOUS SITUATION CONFRONTING OUR FEDERATED CHARITIES DUE TO THE PRESENT ECONOMIC CONDITIONS AND TO MAKE PLANS FOR OUR CAMPAIGN STOP THIS YEAR'S DEFICIT WILL AMOUNT TO OVER EIGHTY THOUSAND DOLLARS STOP WE RESPECTFULLY ASK AND WOULD APPRECIATE IF YOU WOULD INDICATE TO US YOUR GOVERNMENT'S DECISION WITH RESPECT TO THE JOINT PETITION FROM THE PROTESTANT FINANCIAL FEDERATION AND OURSELVES FOR A PER CAPITA ALLOWANCE OF 24 CENTS PER DAY TO CHILDREN CARED FOR IN PRIVATE HOMES AS IS ALLOWED FOR CHILDREN COMMITTED TO INSTITUTIONS OR A FLAT GRANT OF AT LEAST TWENTY FIVE THOUSAND DOLLARS STOP OUR CHARITIES NEED YOUR GOVERNMENT'S SYMPATHETIC ASSISTANCE NOW AS THEY NEVER DID BEFORE AND WE ARE COUNTING UPON YOUR WHOLEHEARTED COOPERATION

FEDERATION OF JEWISH PHILANTHROPIES
ALLAN BRONFMAN - Chairman Executive Committee
Marcus M. Sperber - President Baron de Hirsch Institute

Memo from the Home's Comptroller October 15, 1930

"I have been informed that the Prime Minister has unofficially hinted to Mr. Dawes, Chairman of the Executive Committee of Financial Federation, that he was recommending a grant of $15,000 per annum to their Organization. Despite the somewhat precarious position in which we found ourselves due to the issue of the School question, we have been successful in placing ourselves and the Financial Federation in a position where the Government, to my mind, is obliged to commit itself, and I am expecting in the course of a week to advice that we have been granted at least $15, 000.

In conversation with Mr. Sidney Levitt he informed me that there were a few children under the age of 5 whom we were boarding out, and that an effort was being made to have them admitted to the Orphans' Home. I addressed a memorandum on this subject to Miss Friedman, Supervisor of the Family Welfare Department, and I find that there are eight such children, costing us about $21.50 per month each for board."

October 30th, 1930
Mr. Samuel Hart,
President Montreal Hebrew Orphans' Home
400 Atlantic Avenue, Montreal.

Dear Mr. Hart:

I am pleased to advise you that I have been successful in having the Government agree to pay us 38 cents per day for children under 5 years of age cared for by us.

In view of the fact that seven of these children who were formerly boarded in private homes were recently admitted to the Home, this income, which will amount to around $1,000, will now go to the Home. This grant is made under the Creche Act, and even though we are not really entitled to it, the Government have conceded the claim that we made in this consideration.

Very truly yours,
Comptroller

As soon as confirmation of the Government grant was received, an application was made, amounting to an income of $1051.20 per annum. This request was not to be confused with the grant of 24 cents per day (for children boarded out, because this law applies to children 5-14 years of age); children under 5 years came under a different act known as the *Creche Act.*

The Montreal Hebrew Orphans' Home owned vacant land for which Federation had been paying taxes over a long period of years. The possibility of selling these lands at a fair price would recover the amount paid in taxes which could then be used to cover the boarding costs of its wards.

By February 1931, Family Welfare inaugurated a new feature whereby Federation could save a good sum of money while at the same time help a number of people from having to go on welfare. Mr. Bye reported to Federation on some of the people they were helping, who, at the same time, were helping the Home...

One example of this was a shoemaker out of a job and getting 'relief.' He was taken in hand by the Montreal Home and to date had repaired 22 pairs of childrens' shoes at a cost to the Home of $13.05. Taking into consideration the allowance he was receiving from Federation, the cost to the Home was still less than giving the work to a store.

Another man was receiving a weekly allowance of $7.00. Upon discovering he was a tailor, Home staff arranged to give him work repairing, pressing and cleaning the childrens' clothes. For this work, he also was given two meals and two car-tickets a day for six days.

> "The man feels he is earning the money he gets and...feels that as long as he has to work, he may as well be on the lookout for a real job."

Then there was the case of two painters, both with families, both receiving weekly allowances. The Home purchased supplies at the lowest possible prices through Mr. Abe Asch of Asch Signs, while Mr. J. Gilletz explained the kind of work required, and "so far they are making a good job of it." The cost to the Home? Lunch and car-tickets for a five-day work week.

> "We don't get, nor do we expect, a full day's work, but what we do get is value for the money Federation spends on them and we keep them from becoming habitual *schnorers*...from becoming a public charge."

"At a meeting of the Board of Directors of the Montreal Hebrew Orphans' Home held April 29, 1931, the following officers were elected for the coming year:

President:	Mr. S. Ross Vineberg
1st Vice-President:	Mr. Philip Abbey
2nd Vice-President:	Rabbi C. Bender
Treasurer:	Mr. Michael Margolick
Secretary:	Dr. David Tannenbaum

Messrs. A. Greenberg and J. Gilletz were appointed Representative Trustees to the Board of Trustees of Federation."

One Month's Supply of Food

In July 1931, Miss Sarah F. Wolff, B.H.S., Member, American Dietetic Association, compiled the following list of supplies for the month of January, as requested by Mr. E.G.F. Vaz, Executive Director of the Federation of Jewish Philanthropies. This food was for the maintenance of 85 children, ranging from 5 to 15 years old, and 15 adults:

Milk	390 gals.
Oranges	4 cases
Cabbage	2 doz.
Tomatoes	1 case
Potatoes	22 bags
Sugar	300 lbs.
Bread	725 loaves
Salmon	1 case
Sardines	2 cases
Lettuce	132 heads
Cocoa	25 lbs.
Coffee	10 lbs.
Tea	5 lbs.
Butter	170 lbs.
Eggs	132 doz.
Flour	196 lbs.
Cheese	30 lbs.
Crisco	50 lbs
Bananas	5 bunches
Peas	100 lbs.
Fish	375 lbs.
Sausage	36 lbs.
C. of Wheat	98 lbs.
Rolled Oats	90 lbs.
Pineapples	1 case
Beans	50 lbs.
Macaroni	25 lbs.
Onions	1 bag
Beets	2 bags
Apples	4 bshls
P. Rice	1 case
Corn Flakes	1 case
Carrots	4 crates
Chicken	120 lbs.
Meat	375 lbs.
Jam	30 lbs.
Barley	16 lbs.
Cream	15 qts.
Sour Cream	24 qts.
S. Biscuits	15 lbs.
Icing Sugar	10 lbs.
Coconut	5 lbs.
Matza Meal	24 lbs.
Celery	1 head
Honey	5 lbs.
Delicatessen	7 lbs.
Sauercraut	5 lbs.
Lemons	1 doz.
Jello	25 lbs.
Prunes	2 cases
Peanut Butter	10 lbs.
Flavourings	
Herrings	

"Having analyzed the requisitions, I would offer the following suggestions from a dietetic standpoint. The analysis shows that there are certain items that do not correspond to a normal diet list. Those foods that vary most in quantity from the list given me are as follows:

Food	Normal Quantity	Given Quantity
Milk	500 gals.	390 gals.
Oranges	6 cases	4 cases
Cabbage	48 heads	24 heads
Tomatoes	3 cases	1 case
Potatoes	15 bags	22 bags

A cut could well be made in the items 1 case Salmon and 2 cases Sardines. They are probably used as supper dishes and might be replaced by vegetables, since the diet is sufficiently high in protein without them.

Lettuce is very good but if the above suggestions in regard to increase in cabbage and tomatoes is adhered to, the 132 heads of lettuce could be slightly cut, especially if the cabbage is sometimes served uncooked.

In the winter months, 25 lbs. cocoa, 10 lbs. coffee and 5 lbs. tea are sufficient to give Cocoa to the children and to furnish tea and coffee for the 15 adults.

...It is hard to specify how much of the following items should be used. It would depend on the cost, the use made of them and other factors, such as occasion and preparation:

Cream	Icing Sugar	Sauercraut	Lemons
Sour Cream	Coconut	Delicatessen	Celery
Soda Biscuits	Matza Meal	Honey	Herrings
Flavourings			

This diet furnishes an average of about 2400 calories per head per day. Taking the average age of the children as 10 years and the number of girls and boys as equal, this figure furnishes the required energy. If the average age is higher than 10, or if the number of boys is greater than the number of girls, then the food requirement will be greater and the amount supplied would in consequence be insufficient.

The list makes no mention of seasonings, baking powder or soda, raisins or currants and I presume a normal quantity of these items is used, but is bought in wholesale quantities at certain periods.

In making an analysis of this nature it is impossible to state whether each individual is getting his proper diet. This could only be arrived at from personal observation. Also the quantities allowed for do not make any allowance for excessive waste."

The 1931 Annual Report for the Montreal Hebrew Orphans' Home revealed that 93 children had been cared for; 20 were newly arrived, some from foster homes; 23 were discharged, two were adopted by "very fine families."

The school situation remained the same...nothing had yet been accomplished in the way of obtaining better schooling accommodations. Twelve children attended high school, one by scholarship; 44 attended Berthelet School, one boy receiving a scholarship and a medal. The Home's library had been catalogued and was "in good condition," thanks to volunteers from the Jewish Junior Welfare League.

During the past year, Benjamin Goldberg, Joseph Goodman, Morris Simonoff and Hyman Singerman were Bar Mitzvahed at the *Shaar Hashomayim* Synagogue. They had received this religious instruction from the Rev. Dr. Herman Abramowitz and Mr. Lerner, Hebrew teacher at the Synagogue.

Hebrew instruction in the Home, after much experimentation, was now being conducted along the same lines as other educational institutions. There were 54 children divided into five classes; the curriculum embodied every phase of Hebrew instruction-religion, Hebrew, nationalism and traditionalism. The Byes, as Superintendent and Matron, supervised the daily services. Sabbath and Holiday services continued to be held at the *Shaar Hashomayim* and the *Shaar Zion* Synagogues. Even during summer vacations at Shawbridge, Mrs. A. Konowitz was successful in combining religious work with recreation.

The Ladies' Auxiliary (Mrs. M. Margolick, President), Home Sewing Society (Mrs. D.M. Chorlton) and the Hebrew Ladies Sewing Society (Mrs. A. Vineberg) provided many needed supplies to the Home, and treats for the children, arranged receptions, held a "Jam

Shower" and helped purchase, sew and mend articles..."15 shirt-waists, 44 dresses, 33 night dresses, 125 towels, 12 bloomers, 30 smocks, 55 pyjamas, 10 mufflers, 58 sheets, 26 miscellaneous items..." The vast numbers of 'co-workers' involved, not only from the above-mentioned Societies, but also local synagogues, were greatly appreciated for their time and caring, as well as their cost-savings!

Even the Journeymen Barbers Union earned thanks from Home President, Mr. S. Ross Vineberg, for services rendered during the year.

The health of the children, under the vigilance of Dr. M.W. Bloomberg and his Medical Board, remained excellent all year. To ensure their freedom from colds, a new heating plant and extra radiation was installed to better, and more economically, regulate the heating system of the building—all supervised by House Committee Chair Mr. A. Greenberg, Mr. Philip Garfinkle and Mr. J. Gilletz.

After Care for the Alumni

One problem studied by both the Executive Committee and the Board of the Home was that of offering only temporary shelter for some of the children. It was hoped to find a solution in the very near future. Another problem was the care of those children who have reached the age that made it necessary to discharge them into the outside world—usually at age 16. To this end, an After-Care Committee was organized under the chairmanship of Mrs. M. Rittenberg.

By the end of 1923, it was said that there was no official age at which a child must leave the Home—it was considered a duty to care for each child until he/she became self-supporting. The care given over the years seemed to be wasted when a child was sent out before being ready to cope with the outside world and life's problems.

The amount of education received varied depending on the aptitude of each child. Upon graduating from public school, it was the Board which decided whether the child, boy or girl, would go on to high school, business school or work. Those who were sent to work were given selected positions where there was a future, i.e. in plants where the employer has taken an interest in the progress of the child. Some of these firms were the *Berliner Gramophone Company Ltd.,* the

Bramson Auto Service Ltd., as well as Messrs. Felix and Sam Leopold. And according to Beatrice Hock, a volunteer in the Montreal Home, her father, Bunny Sabbath, a jeweller, was among the first to give employment to the older boys leaving the Home.

Only after it was found that the child was doing well in his/her position were arrangements made for discharge. Those who did leave continued to take a great interest in the Home, and came back for weekends and for social functions. Their visits were credited with building up an *esprit de corps* and a high moral tone among the rest of the children.

The Boards over the years felt it important to maintain continued contact with and supervision of the wards after they left the Home. One of their aims was the erection of a home where graduates could live at a nominal cost in a neighbourhood where contacts could be secured for them at the YMHA. They feared that being left to shift for themselves would negate the years-long efforts of the Home's care.

Some 'newly-liberated' youngsters attended neighbourhood schools and received an excellent Jewish education. Others couldn't afford to pay the small fee to attend high school and so dropped out at age 13 and went to work. Myer Gordon (in the Montefiore Home) was only one of these. He worked in all aspects of the needle trade, starting at the bottom, ending up as a travelling ladies' wear salesman, and still later on, jack-of-all-trades.

Mrs. M. Rittenberg's After Care Committee reported that, despite the financial depression, satisfactory positions had been found for those children who have left school, enabling them to obtain a start in life before they 'graduated' from the Home. It was apparent that there was a lack of proper homes where graduates could be boarded out at a low cost. A solution to this problem was being sought.

In a related vein, a letter sent to Mr. Vaz of Federation by President Philip Abbey, in January 1934, offered the names of Home children to be placed on unemployment relief:

> "I would appreciate it very much if you will do what you can for these children: Mary Boxenbaum, aged 18. Deserted by her parents, she was brought into the Home by the Salvation Army in 1921. Relatives were too poor to help her. She worked for the Ex Lax Co. for one week but was sent away as 'not fast enough for their work.' At present she is helping around the Home."

"Reva Velter, aged 15 1/2—admitted January 1925. She has a mother, two sisters and one brother living together. She worked five weeks at the *Ex Lax Co.* which 'promised to give her work as soon as they start up again.'"

"Mary Kantor, aged 16 1/2—admitted August 1929—related to Julius Block who made himself responsible for part of Mary and her sisters' maintenance. Mary took a business course (at a cost of $8.00) per month, starting November 1933."

"William Opalinsky, aged 14 1/2—admitted 1931. He was sent out of school as he was wasting his time. Given work in the Home's kitchen, he was occupied and kept out of trouble."

There always seemed to be children requiring placement in the orphanage. However, in a letter to George Vaz, dated August 24, 1932, Henry Bye maintained that there was no social work being done in any of the organizations. The Family Welfare Department would investigate the cases, send the children to the Home and the case was closed. He went on to say,

"We do not keep track of the conditions of the family after the children are in the Home; surely there must be some cases where the financial conditions of the parents had improved during the time the children are in the Home, and so there would probably be a possibility of making them pay for the maintenance or returning these children to their parents."

Sometimes even children with very serious family situations were refused admission into the Home. President S. Ross Vineberg pointed out that, if the Executive Committee would provide a grant of $375 *per capita* per year, so the facility would not exceed its budget, these children could be admitted. Lack of money became a double-edged sword...the miserable conditions at the family home caused by being poor, and the lack of public funds so vital to organizations in the social service field. Malca Friedman, Supervisor, Family Welfare Department, spoke of some examples of the children left in intolerable living conditions...

> "...five are living with their mother who is morally incapable of caring for them. The environment is so unwholesome that neighbours have repeatedly insisted that the community remove the children from the home. Nothing has been done for the past six months even though the situation had been brought to the attention of the Orphans' Home Committee. . . Another case is that of a three-year old living in a private home. Due to the woman's health, she can no longer look after the child. Rather than attempt to adjust him to another private family, we should like to have him admitted to the Home—without success."

Other childen were also hoping to be admitted. President S. Ross Vineberg was kept informed and urged to attend to the urgent cases:

Though it was urgent that the Marcovitch children be admitted as soon as possible, their case was slow to be considered. Mr. Bye said this matter would receive attention.

The Saslowsky boy was three years old. He was placed in the home of a French woman as a temporary measure. Since there were so few children at the Home of this age, and there had been a number of others in the past, the chances of him being admitted were good.

The case of the Lutsky children was not discussed with President Vineberg. These children had been sent to various Fresh Air Camps since the Home refused to admit them. Now, the father wishes to have them remain with him.

On the other hand, being admitted brings with it other problems, one of which is illustrated in the following letter of October 7, 1930, from Federation which continued to run the Montreal Hebrew Orphans' Home...

> "I am enclosing herewith statement of your account for the maintenance of your children at the Orphans' Home. It is most unfortunate that you have allowed your balance to accumulate to the extent of $135.00.
>
> We must impress you with the fact that we are in great need of funds and that our Institution is experiencing great difficulty in these times. By non-payment of your account or by

delaying in paying same, you are hindering us from giving the many children in our Home the various opportunities intended for them.

Our Institution cannot possibly operate and maintain your children and others unless payments are made promptly. We must ask you to give the matter your immediate attention and call in at Federation headquarters to make some payment on account and settlement of balance."

Questions

Is the above like being between a rock and a hard place? Are the parents taking advantage of the facilities/organizations? Or—are they still experiencing the hardships that forced them to put the children in the orphanage in the first place?

Is Federation taking a hard stance because they were running out of empathy in these days of the Great Depression? Because they knew they were being taken advantage of? Or were they being practical to ensure that they could carry our their mandate?

Always on the lookout for funds, Mr. Bye noted another source of income that had been neglected for years—the placing of the children on the Quebec Charity Act. So far there had not been a proper system of taking each admitted child and placing him/her on this list. This resulted in the loss of thousands of dollars which could have been collected over the years.

The comments fill one with mixed emotions. Are the organizations and caretakers of the children hardened by so many in need? Are they serving the children less because of their seemingly calloused attitudes—or was this simply the way things had to be managed to be workable, to be practical, to not be taken advantage of?

Henry Bye:

"The three Plotnick children were admitted in our Home in 1923. There is no proof to show they have ever been placed on the Charity Act, though at the time their father was a widower with a number of small children, working as a pants presser; never making a decent living. One boy was in the Home for two years; a girl for eight years; another boy is still in the Home. This means a loss to the Federation of $87.60 per child per annum...records found state that the father had a property at the time.

If so, why were the children kept in the Home for so many years? Besides, his position may have improved during the good years we had between 1923-29. We could possibly have made him pay something for their maintenance or returned some of the children to him.

Of course, there may have been the excuse, as in the Avrith case, that the man had re-married and is rearing a second family. You will realize that the whole thing is wrong, both in the interest of the children, the parent and the finances of the Federation."

Other cases involved the Simonoff and Kantor (Kantorowitz) families. At the time these children were admitted to the Home, they had not been in the country for five years, therefore not eligible to be placed on the Charity Act. Mr. Bye wondered why they were not placed on the list after the initial five years were up. He felt the system failed Federation by not properly listing the qualified children, thus losing the funding coming from their maintenance.

Mr. Bye further noted that the Montefiore Orphans' Home last year found a number of similar cases which had been neglected, and took the matter up with the proper authorities and received, in most cases, all the money it was entitled to.

Analysis of Income

January to December 1933	
Hebrew Orphans' Home	
Enforced Contributions	$1,238.92
Grants—Province of Quebec	$5,407.48
Donations	$5.00
	$ 6,651.40

Telephone Dexter 3466

Montreal Hebrew Orphans' Home
500 Claremont Avenue
Westmount, (Montreal) P. Q.

August 1st, 1934

Mr. Clarence Michaels,
Chairman of the Executive,
Federation of Jewish Philanthropies,
Montreal.

Re: Repairs to Claremont Ave. Building.

Dear Mr. Michaels:

The roof of the above building has been leaking for a little while now, and is certainly in need of immediate repair. This roof has not been repaired since the building was put up (as far as I know) and it is about time that some trouble is to be expected from it.

We are getting estimates on the cost of repairing same and the work will certainly only be given to the lowest reliable tender. So far it looks as though the repairs would cost approximately $300.

I can quite appreciate that we have exceeded our budget up to the present, and are doing our utmost to carry on within the limits obligatory to us. However, the extraordinary expenditure for repairs on the Home at Shawbridge brought on by the excessive cold this winter has made things a bit awkward for us.

The repairs to Claremont Avenue really should be looked upon as a capital expenditure, and feel quite safe that the roof will be in condition and will stand again a great number of years.

Will you please have that item passed at your next executive meeting so that we can get along with the work before the children return at the end of this month.

Assuring you of our complete co-operation with you and your very arduous task,

I remain,
Yours very truly,
Philip Abbey
President, Montreal Hebrew Orphans' Home
PA:ZW

1936—A Special Report from the President, Mr. Jacob Brodie

"This is the twenty-sixth year during which the Home has continued to serve the Jewish Community of Montreal in the field of child welfare work. As a result of the amalgamation arrangements with the Montefiore Hebrew Orphans' Home, we admitted 27 children from that Institution on June 30th, 1936; 23 of these children are still with us. After a series of meetings between representatives of our Home, the Federation of Jewish Philanthropies and the Montefiore...arrangements were entered into whereby all local Jewish children requiring institutional care are now looked after in our Home. Under the scheme of amalgamation, the Montefiore is now represented on our Board by six Directors, six of our Directors having resigned to make room on the Board for the representatives of our sister organization. The arrangement is proving a most satisfactory one. It is also a source of considerable saving to the Community both financially and in eliminating duplication of effort.

1936 was a particularly busy year in the Home. The sudden increase of 27 children in our population threw an added strain on our housing resources and considerable extra work on our staff. However, the situation was well managed and all difficulties were ironed out by the zeal and ability of our superintendent and his efficient staff of workers.

Population...during the past year, the Home has cared for 113 children. On January lst, 1936, there were 70 children in our charge. During the year, 43 were admitted and 20 discharged, leaving us with 93 children at the end of the year. However, after 1936, according to H. Wolofsky, '...the Montreal Home now houses less orphans than were formerly to be found in either of the combining institutions. Moreover, since Federation has adopted the policy of having those children placed in foster homes, the number is continually decreasing.'"

As a matter of fact, it was in 1938 that a child welfare department was created whose functions were to keep pace with social needs, including the prevention of juvenile delinquency, placement and supervision of children in foster homes, social study and arrangements for adoptions, etc. Federation kept pace in this manner.

When the Montefiore Home was closed in 1936, the remaining children were sent to the Montreal Home which was large enough to cope with this social problem. It was said the Homes were merged for the purpose of achieving a financial saving without impairing the philanthropic efficiency. The Jeanne Mance property was then renovated and equipped in an up-to-date manner for the use of the Herzl Dispensary and Hospital. In its first year of occupation of its new quarters, the Dispensary served 17,150 persons.

Even by the beginning of 1941, 54 children were still in the care of the Home. During that year, five were admitted and 12 discharged under the watchful eyes of Dr. David Tannenbaum and his Admission and Dismissals Committee. Their health remained good even though the general Montreal populace was stricken with a number of contagious diseases.

The House Committee, chaired by Mr. M. Cooperberg, made many improvements over the year. The new skating rink, and donations of skates and other sports equipment, enabled the children to enjoy the wintery outdoors.

The children participated in both outdoor and indoor sports. Some girls became members of Brownies and Girl Guides, meeting regularly at the *Shaar Hashomayim* with other groups. Entertainment Chair Mr. Arthur Shalet, with Mr. George Rotsky, arranged for visits to the *Forum* and several theatres, while a number of entertainments were held at the Home.

The Ladies' Auxiliary continued to render valuable assistance to the Home. Tutors were provided for "our wards" and fees were paid for some of the children who attended business college. The Annual Jam Shower was successful, and a Bridge and Keno was held; the money raised made it possible to continue the After Care work.

The Auxiliary held a reception in honour of the year's Bar Mitzvah boys: Joseph Miller, Reuben Reisler, Cecil Yanovitch, Moses Ticker, Nathan Cohen, Harvey Israel and Abraham Shmoiser. Monetary and other contributions were received and divided amongst them.

The After Care Department was most active during 1941, due to the rapid increase of those graduated, and the number of children being prepared for their vocational guidance tests. Miss Rachel Cohen, the social worker, used these results to find the right type of employment for each boy and girl before they left the Home. Suitable boarding homes were found when necessary, and access was arranged to various recreational centres. Contact was maintained by Miss Cohen for an indefinite period, depending on the needs of the individual."

A Montreal Hebrew Orphans' Home Summer Camp

Sunshine Camp

Montefiore Camp c.1935

Sunshine Camp

Sunshine Camp

Oscar Roth and Manny Cohen at Camp

Pearl and Sylvia Garfinkle, 1939

Mary Sokoloff and Vita Shein Seidler at Camp

Sunshine Camp

Overnight Hike at Camp

Row 1, back: Hy Jacobson, Abie Sokoloff
Row 2: Herbie Rasminsky, Ben Garber, Norman Bydoff
Row 3: Myer Gordon, Sam Rasminsky, Earl Greenberg
Row 4: Issie Shamovitch

Lac Masson Summer Camp location.
(The Dining Room was above the Rock)

Report of the President of the Montreal Hebrew Orphans' Home, 1942: Jacob Brodie

"Until June, 1942, the Montreal Hebrew Orphans' Home carried on the many activities for which it was established, caring for and providing satisfactory home surroundings, education, recreation and social and religious activities for orphan children.

In that month, in accordance with the decision arrived at to unify the services of the Montreal Hebrew Orphans' Home and the Child Welfare Department, the Building was vacated, and the children, at the conclusion of their summer holiday at Sunshine Camp on September 1st, were placed in satisfactory foster homes. Fifteen boys and five girls were returned to their own families which had previously been very carefully investigated. Two boys and one girl were placed with approved relatives after proper investigation and the Agency's satisfaction of their happiness and well-being.

Ten boys and six girls were, under the direction and supervision of the Child Welfare Department, provided with thoroughly good foster homes on a board and lodging basis. All have been accepted into these households as members of the families. Close and continued supervision by the Child Welfare Department is being maintained.

Two boys, aged 16 and 17, and one girl, aged 17, were considered ready and fit to take up suitable occupations. For these adolescents, satisfactory boarding homes were found by the Child Welfare Department, and all are now well on their way to becoming independent and self-reliant adult citizens.

...I should like to place on record my grateful thanks to all members of the Board of Governors and Chairmen of our various committees, for their valued efforts on behalf of our children, over the many years in which the Montreal Hebrew Orphans' Home has served the Community; and I look forward to a continuation of these fine efforts in the future. Also to the Ladies' Auxiliaries for their sustained interest in the children...

I wish also to extend again to the Superintendent and Matron, Mr. & Mrs. Henry Bye, the appreciation of the Board for their loyal and efficient services over many years, and to the Staff for the faithful discharge of their duties. To all friends and benefactors of the Home over its many years of services—I extend sincere thanks and, for their satisfaction, should like to say here that in its time, the Home served a laudable and worthy object and that many of its good offices and works will be carried on efficiently and practically by the Child Welfare Department."

The Montreal Hebrew Orphans' Home operated until 1942 (or '43, depending on whose records one reads), when it merged with the Jewish Child Welfare Bureau and became part of the agency's foster home care program.

As mentioned above, those remaining were returned to their parents or sent to group or foster care which was then available. One young Alumnus out in the world was Harry Kaminsky who joined the Merchant Marines and was killed in 1941 or '42 when his ship was sunk by a submarine in the St. Lawrence River. And then there was one Teddy Yanovitch, reputed to be a major local gangster, who was slain by police in a gun battle in the '50s.

Among the graduates and Alumni today are millionaires, auto- parts salesmen, secretaries, lawyers and judges, doctors and homemakers, auto parts salesmen, secretaries—spread across Canada and the U.S. Perhaps the Montreal Home's most famous 'alumnus' is poet Irving Layton, who taught some of the after-school classes and was a counsellor at Sunshine Camp. He attended one of the early reunions in Montreal.

And then, in 1985, a fascinating article appeared in the *Canadian Jewish News*, Montreal Edition. At that time, Joe King's "Frontline" was a weekly column on human concerns in Jewish Montreal:

"I'm calling from the Yukon," the man on the telephone stated, "and I need your help." The caller had dialed Montreal 737-2221, the number of the Jewish Information Referral Service, and explained that he had lived in the Montreal Hebrew Orphans' Home, at 500 Claremont, in the early '30s, and from there had gone on to a succession of foster homes.

Now for pension purposes, he desperately needed his birth certificate. And he wasn't even sure what name he had during his stay in the orphanage. During his life, he had four different names, for various reasons, as he moved from foster home to foster home.

JIRS began a search on his behalf—calling the Canadian Jewish Congress Archives to determine if they had a list of the children accommodated in the orphanage half a century ago—turning to the Protestant School Board of Montreal to seek records for his attendance at schools in this area, and bringing in Jewish Family Services which, as the Baron de Hirsch Institute, had and has been involved in the caring of orphans.

The JIRS has handled thousands of calls since its inception, but the Yukon caller was one of the most unusual assignments they had received.

The man had a sister, but he hadn't seen her for 30 years. He wasn't a true orphan; his parents, unable to provide for him in the Depression years, had given him up to the Orphanage.

The search for confirmation of his Montreal residence is continuing; Montreal City Hall had nothing to offer. JIRS continues to press for definitive information. And, if necessary, they will try to find the man's neighbours on St. Dominique Street 55 years ago. One of them, he told the JIRS volunteer who took the call, "was Mordechai Richler, the author."

The Montreal Hebrew Orphans' Home Sunshine Camp

This institution was fortunate in having a summer home in Shawbridge (now called Prevost), the foothills of the Laurentians, about 50 miles from Montreal. This large residence was the orphanage's summer home when the Berthelet Public School was closed for vacation. According to H. Wolofsky, he had a hand in starting this camp.

> "...It was at the time when Montreal was enjoying one of its periodic real estate booms. The Eagle was then located in The Eagle Building which also contained some real estate offices, including those of the Rabinovitch brothers and of Joseph Brenner. One afternoon, as all the building agents were whiling away the time at a card game, I broke in upon them with the suggestion that since business was now so very good, it might not be a bad idea if they acquired a building in the Laurentians where poor city children, otherwise unable to afford a country vacation, might stay for the summer. The notion strongly appealed to them; the card game was stopped; the matter was thoroughly discussed, and a fund of several thousand dollars was raised on the spot. Later, a building was acquired in Shawbridge. This committee did not function for more than two years, after which it was donated to the Federation of Jewish Philanthropies."

The new building, a brick cottage of two and one half storeys, was erected in 1924 on a tract of 24 acres owned by the Home in the village proper. The children slept on its wide open balconies and enjoyed surrounding facilities such as fishing, swimming, hiking, berrying, and playing fields. The Shawbridge Orphanage Summer Camp embodied the policy of the Home to normalize the experiences of the children under its care.

Richard Kramer remembered the 'swimming box' in the North River, the berry-picking on the mountain side, the oil lamps, and the only French his mother (the housekeeper) knew when the peddlar passed by—"*Avez vous des oeufs?*" He remembered that the assistant, Hatty Ashmeal, had a boyfriend (later her husband), Myer Kirsch, who was in an army camp in St. Jerome and who walked half the night to see her at the summer Home. And he remembered the dreadful fire...his mother and younger brother Milton, sleeping on the ground level porch, escaped safely.

That summer vacation of 1922 had a very unfortunate ending when the Camp was destroyed by fire at midnight, August 14-15th, with fatal results. The cause was unknown. Everyone was asleep and, aided by high winds, the fire completely destroyed the summer home. There was a tragic loss of 12 lives—eight of the Home's children, the Caretaker, Thomas Legault, his wife and two children.

The upper half of the building was never in use. The boys slept on the ground floor verandah, the girls on the first floor verandah, about 10 feet above the ground. The children who lost their lives were newcomers, and being unaccustomed to the open air, were placed indoors in a room next to the Caretaker's.

This unfortunate loss of children was a great shock to the Montreal community. The remains were brought to the City and interred in the *Shaar Hashomayim* cemetery. The funeral service was held at the Montreal Home, Rabbis Abramowitz and Merritt officiating. A period of mourning was observed at the Home.

An interesting fact—Alumnus Muriel Fishman discovered, by chance, (in 1999) a tombstone in Mount Royal Cemetery marked "Hebrew Orphans' Home." It commemorated the youngsters who perished in this fire.

The Federation soon after opened another facility. By 1924, the new home was completed. However, it remained unfurnished. Still, summers continued to offer an opportunity to spend over 10 weeks at the new, permanent country camp in Shawbridge.

Over the next few years, much time and money were spent in improving the facility. By 1927, the grounds were tilled and drained, a large porch was built, all sleeping porches were screened and a well was dug.

A wide variety of summer sports and recreation was available to all the children.

During the summer of 1928, the children made progress with their large truck garden, at that time one of the recognized Home activities. It was highly successful both from an educational and a monetary point of view and rated the best kept and best looking garden for many miles around. A large crop was produced, including 120 bags of potatoes and a large yield of carrots, turnips, tomatoes, radishes, onions, lettuce, Swiss chard, celery, Golden Bantam corn, peas, beans and pumpkins.

Mr. S. Ross Vineberg chaired the annual Field Day held in August. Visitors and Directors attended a wide variety of activities. Prizes were awarded for different field events, and greatly enjoyed by the children. The children's choir performed; refreshments were served. A very festive day for all concerned!

Another move, another camp, then known as "Sunshine Camp," opened in the '30s on Lac Masson, Ste. Marguerite—across the lake from the camp enjoyed by the 'kids' from the Montefiore Home... also called Sunshine Camp!

Each year, before the kids went to camp, the building was cleaned and repainted by Home staff and the high school boys. Materials were supplied by Mr. Abe Asch and his Sports Committee. (Coincidence—in his later life, Myer Gordon, an Alumnus of the Montefiore Home, married Judy Gold Asch—Judy's first husband Steve Asch's uncle, was Abe Asch—later of Scarsdale, New York!)

In 1931, new electric wires and fixtures were also installed, free of charge, by Mr. D. Mendell. Other supplies were donated by the following: Mr. Jack Rosenthal, Mr. A. Naimer, Mr. George Issenman and Mr. H. Silverman. Sports equipment was given by Mr. Philip Garfinkle which came in handy at the annual Field Day held each August. Again Mr. Asch and his Committee were on call—presenting prizes, not only to the winners of the sporting events, but to other children as well.

Everything was appreciated by all who came to visit and the children who lived amidst the improvements and were athletically inclined. There were a large number of graduates who were able to spend part of their vacations here. And one young lady, Betty Stern, who spent five years in the camp while her father was in the hospital.

Social and religious activities carried on throughout the summer, as they did in the city. Sabbath Services, under the capable hands of Mrs.

A. Konowitz, were held each week. And entertainments of Jewish interest were presented by the children, thanks to Mr. Martin Duchow who trained the children in group singing and acted as accompanist at all programs.

Tel. DEXTER 3466

Montreal Hebrew Orphans' Home
500 Claremont Avenue
Westmount (Montreal) P.Q,

Summer Camp
Lac Masson,
Ste. Marguerite, P.Q.

Twenty-fifth Anniversary Celebration and Field Day
Sunday, August 21st, 1938

Dear Friend:

The Home is celebrating its Twenty-fifth anniversary, which occurs this year in conjunction with the Field Day held annually at the Camp. You are cordially invited by the Board to be present at the Camp on Sunday, August 21st, to witness the anniversary ceremonies, as well as a full programme of track and swimming events.
This occasion will provide a very pleasant and most interesting outing. Refreshments will be served at noon. It is hoped that you will make every effort to join us Sunday.

On behalf of the Board, Yours truly,
BERNARD M. ALEXANDOR
Honorary Secretary.

DIRECTIONS:

By Car—Follow route No.11 out of Montreal to Ste. Adele then turn right on the road to Ste. Marguerite which leads directly to the Camp at Lac Masson, about 8 1/2 miles from Ste. Adele.

By Rail—Take C.P.R. train to Ste. Marguerite Station, whence taxi transportation to Camp is readily obtainable.

In his 1941 Annual Report, President Jacob Brodie wrote,

> "There can be no doubt as to the beneficial effects derived by our children from their stay at our camp in Ste. Marguerite. Fresh mountain air and wholesome recreation such as swimming, hiking, outdoor games and nature study give definite returns in good health, and undoubtedly help prevent possible illness throughout the year. In addition to the children from the Home, we also took care of 29 children sent by the Child and Family Welfare Department.
> We were again fortunate in having Mr. Jack Gross as head of Camp activities, Miss I. Kaufman as head girls' counsellor, assisted by Misses Sybil Freedman, M. Brown, C. Garfinkle, M. Berger, W. Jacobs...and Mr. M.A. Ogulnick as head boys' counsellor, assisted by Messrs. B. Battle, G. Gleason, H. Finestone and D. Landsman. The health of our children was in the capable hands of Drs. H. Mendelson, M. Siminovitch, and our resident nurse. To them as well as to Mrs. Kramer who has always graciously given of her time and efforts on behalf of our children during the camp season, I wish to express my sincerest thanks."

P.S. Jack Gross became a physician and lived for a time in Israel.

Sir Moses Montefiore 1784-1885—Excerpts from his Story

Throughout his life Sir Moses Montefiore represented Jewry itself. He became a roving ambassador for world Jewry,

> "so that vast area of the world virtually unknown to European society at the time of his birth, looked upon him with awe and respect."

The family name was derived from the small town of Montefiore, near Ascoli in Italy, the birthplace of his family in the 16th century. Sir Moses' grandfather, Moses Haim Vita Montefiore, was a merchant who settled in England in 1758. He laid the foundations for the family fortunes, and the resulting distinction.

Sir Moses was brought up in London. He was tall, stately...a British Sephardic Jew. In 1812, he married Judith Barent Cohen, connected by marriage to the Rothschilds. After founding the Alliance Insurance Company and other successful stock undertakings, he was not content to pursue riches through financial operations; he made Ramsgate his home and built a synagogue there which opened in 1833.

His first trip to the Middle East and Jerusalem was in 1827. He returned to Egypt to seek concessions from Mahomet Pasha on the treatment of Jews.

In 1837, Montefiore was made Sheriff of London and Middlesex, and was knighted by the young Queen Victoria upon her accession to the throne as an expression of her gratitude for his help with finance.

In 1846 he visited Russia and met with Emperor Nicholas to intercede on behalf of Jews in Poland and Lithuania. Over the years, Sir Moses and Lady Judith made many trips to Jerusalem, and in 1855 gave vast sums of money to "bring relief to the poor and distressed, and built hospitals, schools and agricultural colonies."

In 1863, following the death of his wife, Sir Moses made a fatiguing journey to Morocco where he obtained from the Sultan protection for Jews in the Mussulman State. His last journey to Palestine was in 1875 where he found the fruits of his charitable works resulted in marked improvements in social conditions.

When he died on July 28, 1885, the Lord Mayor of London spoke of Montefiore as

> "the most distinguished citizen of London...who devoted his life to the task of combating hatred, persecution and fanaticism, of severing the bonds of physical and moral slavery; and of aiding in the establishment of religious toleration all over the world."

Sir Moses Montefiore was the most well known Jewish philanthropist and Israel's benefactor. World communities turned to him for support—rarely denied. Synagogues, associations of friendly societies and hospitals took his name to pay him honour...

And so it was that the second Jewish orphanage in Montreal became known as the Montefiore Hebrew Orphans' Home.

The Montefiore Home

The Montefiore Hebrew Orphans' Home opened in 1918 to continue the care of underprivileged orphans. It was 'part and parcel' of the Jewish community's social services system, and came into being because the Montreal Home was unable to provide for the increasing numbers of needy children. Following World War I, these facilities had to respond to the continuing community demand and humanitarian necessity.

It was in what was considered a poorer section of town, at 4650 Jeanne Mance Street, and administered by a group of leading citizens representing this East Side (of Montreal)—all of whom had a keen interest in the Home's advancement and efficiency.

Among the most important of these was the man known as J. B. Miller—Julius Benjamin Miller. In a biography of Mr. Miller, written by his daughter Betty Miller Rosenthal, she writes that her parents were the co-founders of The Montefiore Home. To find out how this came about, keep on reading...part of J.B.'s story follows:

"My father was a very remarkable man and very brilliant...He was born in Pinsk, Russia, the son of a Rabbi of fine repute. His closest friend was Chaim Weitzman; they were both Talmudic scholars. The same Chaim Weitzman who was instrumental in having The *Balfour Declaration* signed.

My father fought in the Boer War and was wounded in the leg. He walked with a limp, but otherwise he fully recovered. In Canada, he was involved in buying for three stores, a family business (some details can be found under the 'new businesses' heading of that Montreal era).

J. B. was instrumental in bringing to Canada more than one hundred Ukrainian orphans whose parents had been slaughtered in WWI. Our family adopted one of these orphans, "Arnold," a boy of nine, and later adopted his sister, "Claire," as well. Claire was not too strong, due to being attacked and seeing her parents killed. My mother subsequently was instrumental in bringing seven of their immediate relatives to Montreal. All were educated and married in Montreal, and doing well.

This was only the beginning of my parents' charitable work. Father was the president of every Jewish organization in Montreal in his time. As well as his involvement with the Montefiore Home, my father also founded the first Jewish Hospital in Montreal—'The Hebrew Maternity Hospital.' He was also part of the 'Committee of Sixteen' who sponsored the 'Boys' Farm' for delinquent or wayward boys. If any Jewish boy would get into trouble, my father would never allow him to be sent there as records were kept, and it would have been a black mark in his future. Instead, he would personally contact the family of the boy and always helped to see the boy's problems solved. It never failed. Judge Choquette of the Supreme Court was one of his close friends, as were Sir Herbert Marler, the Honourable C.C. Ballantyne, Sir Mortimer Davis and many other prestigious men.

After my father's business went bankrupt, he fled to Israel where he was welcomed by his old close friend, Chaim Weitzman. Many of his friends there were happy to see him, and a banquet was given in his honour for all the wonderful accomplishments he had instituted for Montreal Jewry as well as Jewry in general. Later, he moved to British Columbia and opened another business there.

—there was a warm relationship between my father and Abe Vineberg, his son-in-law. When my father's eyesight failed and his hearing was impaired, he did not want to live. He wrote to Abe about his loneliness and depression, and Abe left his business immediately to be with him. When he died in 1934, Abe stayed on to salvage whatever he could and help wind things up. My mother had died of cancer three years earlier.

Never one to seek publicity, only those who were acquainted with my father personally, knew of his fine work and his brilliance, remembered him. My father, J. B. Miller; was a legend, nonetheless, in his time."

Montefiore Home annual budgets, incomes and expenditures were checked and audited by a Board consisting of a president, treasurer, comptroller and auditors. By 1924, original founding Board Members plus the newly interested, included the following:

Hon. President: Mr. S. W. Jacobs, K.C., M.P.
Hon. Vice-President: Mr. Bob Gradinger
President: Mr. M. Feldman
1st Vice-President: Mr. J.B. Miller
2nd Vice-President: Sol Z. Fels
Treasurer: Mr. B. Steinhouse
Fin. Secretary: Mr. Max Seigler
Record. Secretary: Mrs. D. Cohen
Corresp. Secretary: Mrs. H. Schafer

Honourable Directors

Mesdames: M. Blumenfeld, B. Gibson, W. Lustgarten, J.B. Miller, R. Ram, B. Steinhouse

Directors
Messrs: M. Abramovitz, M. Crelinstein, C.B. Fainer, A. Raginsky,

L. Raich, A. Rothchild, H. Schwartz, M. Simon, Schachter, Jos. Tabatchnick, Jos.Wigdor; Mesdames: N. Beecher, M. Crelinstein, M. Diamond, Ph. Gordon, Chas. Gordon, B. Halpern, M. Lefkowitz, B. Levy, E. Rosenthal, M. Rosenstein, M. Rosovitch, J. Weisburg;
Controllers: Mr. Paul Koenig, Mr. Abe Weiner
Hon. Solicitors: Mr. Louis Fitch, Mr. Nat S. Fineburg
Hon. Notaries: Mr. H. E. Hershorn, Mr. Isaac Kert

The Home was a modest three-storey red brick building, which accommodated some 65 needy orphan children throughout the year. The 'kids' slept in dormitories—boys on the second floor, girls on the third floor, which also housed the infirmary. An outside stairway on one side of the building led downstairs to the kitchen, pantry and dining room where the children ate at long tables. Food was plentiful, staff was caring..."Certainly no Oliver Twist experience." (This statement has been contradicted by Faiga Fisher, also quoting the Oliver Twist simile!) Offices for staff and supervisor were on the main floor. The Home also maintained a library and reading room. Books were provided by the Oneidas Club.

The auditorium doubled as a *shul,* with its own chapel—religious services were held regularly, both for the Home and neighbourhood residents. The children were given training in Hebrew and a back room was put aside for studying. The youngsters received a cultural, civic and vocational education, going to the nearby Bancroft School.

The only playground was the small fenced-in yard where the children played ball, pretended they were soldiers, or just 'ran around'. Used shoes were resoled to be warm and waterproof. When the yard was iced over to become a skating rink in the winter, some had skates, but, as Myer Gordon remembers, "I only had one!" Another boy had its mate....The children were divided into three groups...the first, up to nine years of age; the second, aged 10-13; the third, 14-16 years old. Says Vita Seidler, "While you would think the oldest kids would be in the first group, it was the youngest who were called the 'first group'-because they were the first to go to bed at night—6:30 p.m. in the winter; 7 p.m. in the summer!" The children were divided into three groups. The two older groups acted as 'big brothers/sisters' to the next youngest group, referring to them as their little brothers/sisters. So it was that the older children literally took under their wings the youngest, helping them when needed, whether going to school, etc. As the older groups 'graduated' out of the Home at age 16, the younger ones moved up, so eventually the younger children became 'big brothers/sisters' as well.

The third group—the oldest group—the first to leave the Home, sadly seems to be largely forgotten, according to Myer Gordon. As Myer was in the Home over the earlier years, he remembers many of them as he was growing up:

> "I was in the first group when I was six years old in 1927. At that time the children in the third group were the BIG boys and girls, probably around 15 and ready to go into the real world. Some of them attended the first four Montefiore reunions from 1957-60, but only a handful attended the combined reunions from 1989 on. Most of the first and second groups have been attending the latest get-togethers.
> Some of the names I remember are: Jack Spinner, his sister Anita, Abe Tolmasky, Arnold Golub, Harry Ostrofsky, Harry Zelfin, Charlie Bloom, Solly Kravitz, Moishe Resnick, Annie Greenberg, Willie Morganstein, Abe Sheiner, Jack Jacobson, Mendel & Godel Raffalovitch and Issie Rosenberg."

After they left, this group did visit the Home to be with the kids and help them both while there and when they left. Many opened businesses and were very successful in life. Gordon says:

> "Jack Spinner gave me a job in 1958 when I was off the road selling ladies' sportswear. And Willie Morganstein, who was manufacturing children's wear, gave me his line to sell on the road."

These were only some of the 'kids' who made the Home a home.

And in July and August, the children attended summer camp at various places as they became available...not luxurious, but out of the city—on Petit Lac Longue, Lac Brule, Ste. Agathe. One summer they pitched tents on the burned-out grounds of a hotel. One of the more formalized camps was on Lac Masson in Ste. Marguerite, in the Laurentians. While it was officially known as Sunshine Camp (as was the camp across the same lake used by the youngsters from the

Montreal Home), the campers there just referred to it as camp. Gordon remembers that sometimes "we took in extra kids at camp—poor ones. The neighbourhood kids envied us!"

For some, the Home experience was fun-filled, complete with summer camp and "assembly-line" bar mitzvahs (four or five at a time). For others, it was traumatic. Earl Greenberg remembers going to bed hungry many nights. Perhaps that is why he joined Hymie Jacobson to raid the kitchen after dark, scavenging apples and pastry to bring back to their cots.

But the Home is also where Earl acquired his first girlfriend, Sarah. He remembers they met during their dishwashing chores in Mrs. Mitnick's kitchen,

> "as we are every Saturday. Our hands are soaking in the greasy, dirty dishwater; savouring the touch of hands with every dish we wash, hoping we don't run out of dirty dishes...our hands lingering ever so long on one plate, your brown eyes (or were they blue—it's been over 60 years!) looking up at mine. We knew we were in love! Even today, when I look at my chapped hands, I think of you. Are yours still chapped, too? Hope to see you again at the next reunion."

Earl and Vita Shein also remember Mrs. Udica (but not sure how to spell her name!) She was widowed in her early 30s and worked in the Montefiore Home mending and refitting the used clothing for the children. She helped around the Home where needed, such as, after bathtime, she would use a black fine-tooth comb to search for lice in the children's hair. She also looked after a young child, possibly a nephew, Jerry, who was about 6 years old and lived in the orphanage. After she left the Home, she worked as a Hebrew Teacher for Workman's Circle.

At the 1989 reunion, Dave Cherry remarked about the impact the orphanage had on him. "At the Montefiore, we received clothing from the Malbish Arumin, an organization that helped the poor. Years later I became president of that society." Evelyn Shano remembered that "We all went to the same school, Bancroft, on St. Urbain Street, and we took part in the activities. But we always stuck up for one another." Ben Wiseman, now living in Florida, added, "We depended on one another."

Abe Tolmasky, Montreal, 1994...

"Whenever I leave the gang at our reunion, I go away with an empty feeling. It's hard to describe the thrill at seeing the faces light up as each one comes in and is flooded instantly with memories of days long, long ago. An outside observer could see immediately that all of us have fond memories of our time spent at the Montefiore Home.

I was there from November 1924 to late 1927 or early '28. We were not unduly punished or abused, or sexually molested. We had fun. We had a home, food and clothes, a yard and a basement to play in, and a skating rink in the winter. We were close to Bancroft School, Fletcher's Field and Mount Royal where we older ones tobogganed to our hearts' content. We had a nurse, Mrs. Milstein, to tend our aches, and Rabbi Shapiro who prepared us boys for Bar Mitzvah...there are so many memories.

One year we were in the Laurentians when school ended in November while our home was expanded. It was a long summer and fall for us, and we were running a bit wild. I remember coming back from a swim one day, dripping wet, and Arnold Golub told me to poke my thumb into an open electric socket. I remember the shock to this day!"

In another note one year later, Abe wrote that the names Archie Blankstein and Mr. Talpis, mentioned in a story by Arnold Golub, came to mind. (Mr. Talpis did some fundraising and accounting work for the Montefiore Home.)

"It goes back 65-70 years, but I remember them. Blankstein took us occasionally to the circus or to see a movie. Talpis used to walk to our *shul* on Saturday, though he lived in Westmount. He wouldn't drive or ride on the street car on the Shabbat."

When Max Matt, former resident of the Montreal Home, became Supervisor of the Montefiore Home, at age 19, that was the beginning of lifelong friendships. Because he was an orphan himself, he could understand the children's thoughts and actions. And once the children themselves understood Max's history in orphanages, they could understand him better. Max tried to make the children believe they could overcome anything if they tried. He still had to use 'tough' methods once in a while. Like the time he overheard swearing and threw a bar of soap at Abie Stoffmaker saying, "Take a bite."

Another time, Bennie Garber and Abie Stoffmaker were to be punished by Max, a strapping, common in those days. Max gave Benny six light lashes. But Abie came out smiling. Why? He had put telephone books in his pants (the books were thinner then!)

From eating soap to playing sports at summer camp, experiencing joint Bar Mitzvahs, being treated to two suits/dresses a year, to going to bed hungry some nights, most of the former residents remember the special bonds formed between the 'brothers and sisters.' That's what keeps them coming back to the annual reunions.

"Oh, you were in an orphanage? How were you treated?" Vita Shein Seidler, a 70-something orphan, has heard this question over and over again (but it wasn't until after the 11th annual orphanage reunion in July, 2001, that we all agreed it was time to tell the whole story—this story).

Vita moved to Toronto in 1991 to be closer to her sons and grandchildren. As soon as she settled in, she started calling some of the 'kids' from the MHOH. To Vita, in her mind's eye, they are all still kids, never mind that they are all in their late 70s and 80s now.

> "Like magic, a few of us got together and the fun started. Each had stories to tell, remembering some of the funny things that had happened in the Home. I laughed so much that tears came streaming down my face. At the end of the evening, I went to bed thinking what a nice time we all had, going back to our childhood days without worries or care."

Vita recently shared two stories that 'popped' into her head at a recent get-together. As a newly-arrived 4 year old from Russia in 1930, she was put into Bancroft School's kindergarten, then called "Scribble and Pencil." She spoke very little English. One day she had to go to the bathroom, but in her excitement forgot any words of

English she might have known and, putting up her hand, she pleaded, in Yiddish, "*Ich vil gayn pishen.*" Teacher Miss Hoffman, asking another little girl to translate, was told that Vita had to go to the bathroom. Miss Hoffman gave permission for the girl to accompany Vita downstairs to the basement washroom, but told her "to come right back; Vita can return on her own." Instead, Vita, so scared to be alone in the basement ran home—back to the orphanage.

Years later, as an adult and fully Canadianized, Vita thought she saw a familiar face from her childhood on a summer visit to Old Orchard Beach, Maine, a popular spot for Montreal vacationers at that time. Yes, it was Miss Hoffman! Vita began a conversation with her, finally getting around to relating her old story. Her former teacher roared with laughter, but couldn't believe that she didn't understand poor little Vita's pleas all those years ago.

Another painful memory of Vita's orphanage years also had a school setting (she recalled only nice or humorous memories of the Montefiore itself). One of her classmates in third grade was Tamara, whose father would send her outgrown, but clean—good condition—clothes to the Home. Vita was given a special dress of Tamara's, one with smocking, which she proudly wore to school the next day. Tamara looked at her, and yelled, "Oh, that's my dress that my daddy brought to the orphan's home!" Vita never wore it again.

> "As kids, the worst punishment was being sent to bed right after supper, especially in the summer when it was still light outside. Four of us, Mary Sokoloff, Ida Sklar (Lewis), Evelyn Shano (Furlong) and myself decided to play some games to amuse ourselves. What to do? One of the kids had the idea of playing Hide & Seek. But where to hide? We had lockers for our clothes, stacked one on top of the other. Ida and I picked the lower lockers. Evelyn, who weighed a good 110 lbs. at 8 years of age, was quite big. She picked the top locker! Mary had to find us. As the lockers were the only place to hide, she found Ida and me right away. She soon found Evelyn in the top locker but couldn't get her out. She started to scream and we didn't know what to do. Our only solution seemed to be to call our 'big sister.' It took a few of the staff to pull Evelyn out. While they were trying, we started laughing and couldn't stop! This episode earned us another two days of punishment!"

Vita remembers going to the movies at *The Canada* on St. Lawrence Blvd. with Mary and Ida. A ticket was 10 cents. But first they stopped at *Oscar's Biscuit Store* where a large bag of broken chocolate biscuits cost 5 cents. Hoping not to have to share with anyone else, they ate the whole thing...and were they sick! "Oh, were we sick!" Vita and Mary were comics at heart. They wrote Laurel and Hardy-type skits, which they performed for the kids during the week. They rehearsed at the Davis Y, then went to *Shaps* for a treat. Both wanted to go to California to be comedians, but when Vita met Eric, she stayed in Montreal. P.S. She and Eric have been married 57 years.

As a result of a few elocution lessons given in the Home, Ida and Vita came to love reciting poetry—learned by heart—complete with gestures. No other children were interested, so the classes were stopped. By the way, Ida 's father was known as the 'banana man.' He went from door to door with his horse and wagon!

Here are some other anecdotes about some of the others in the Montefiore Home...

Willie Label and Abe Senderoff were like 'clean twins.' They brushed their teeth four or five times each day, and every night, they shined their shoes! They stole the cream off the top of the milk bottles, and chewed their milk! Willie, at 83, still swims and plays tennis daily, especially as a Florida snow bird. Twice a widower, he presently has a lady-friend. Abe, never married, lives in New York.

Godel Raffalovitch, at around age 19 or 20, married a little girl who was a dishwasher in the Montefiore Home. The ceremony was held upstairs in the Home shortly before it closed in 1936.

Hy Jacobson also recalled some of his memories in the Montefiore Home. He entered at age 7 in 1927 and stayed for about 9 years. He learned early on that, for him to survive emotionally, he had to 'hang around' the cook. He had keys to the pantry and one day locked himself in there with all the strudel. Max Matt had one heck of a time getting him to come out!

Hy related an anecdote about a school in London, England, which discussed the type of punishment to give kids who stole. Each one was given a penny a month for being good; one penny was taken back each time they were bad. Hy felt young kids steal because they are deprived of love...the school gave money to compensate.

Hy preferred to be known as Hymie in the Home, but adopted the name Harold when he went to war. He kept that name for a few years, did his banking as Harold Hymie, and in the early '70s again became Hymie. "Funny enough, my brothers, sisters and relatives prefer Harold, so I let it be, with them." Hy became an architect, retired at a young age. He ran a bed-and-breakfast 'for friends' only! He never married but kept himself busy with volunteer work, i.e., Palliative Care Services of the Queen Elizabeth Hospital. He also promoted the occasional 'New Age' type philosopher who passed through Montreal.

One thing most former residents of both Homes remember is the solid preparation they received for the tough world of post-Depression, pre-war Montreal. Sam Rasminsky and the boys even learned how to type and do shorthand. "They called us 'the secretaries,'" Sam remembers, making sure to remind us that he was 'all man' and went on to play hockey with *The Baltimore Clippers* in the 1945 season! "Yet," adds Rasminsky, "if it weren't for the Montefiore Home, we would have been out on the streets."

One neighbour of the Home was Abe Grosser who lived across the street. Abe was a frequent visitor; in fact he seemed to spend more time at the Home than his own home. In 1994, Harry & Rebecca Lenetsky (both now deceased) met him and he expressed an interest in receiving *The Mishpocha* newsletter. He later met Vita Seidler and the Gordons on a visit to Toronto, after which he not only wrote the following, but attended the 1995 reunion:

> "I wish to express some thoughts and remembrances of the MHOH. Living across the street from the Home, I spent most of my time there, made many friends. When they held 'Tag Days,' I was always called to help out. I also remember that, when the boys and girls had their friends visit and it was time to go home, I was told I could stay.
>
> I remember back a long way to when Mr. Lerner, Mrs. Rachel and Max Matt were in charge, and Mr. Talpis looked after the office...Myer (Gordon), you sure didn't change since I last saw you over 50 years ago—except you have grey hair. But your face is the same! One of the boys I bowled with was Joe Miller. I was surprised to learn that he was one of the group..."

A friend, Menda Weinstein, related to the Gordons an anecdote about her grandfather, one of the Home's Directors, Rabbi M. Blumenfeld, a moyel as well–like the well-known Rabbi Colton.

Rebbitzen Gittel Blumenfeld was a homemaker who suffered two great losses. Her two daughters died within a few years of each other, one in 1919 when a deadly plague hit Montreal; the other died of tuberculosis around 1923. She was so heartbroken that she spent her days sitting by their graves, talking to them. After some months of doing this, she decided she had to find something worthwhile to do, and put her compassion to work with the Montefiore Home's Auxiliary.

EIGHTEENTH

ANNUAL REPORT

of the

Montefiore Hebrew Orphans Home

For the year ending Dec. 31st, 1935

MONTEFIORE HEBREW ORPHANS HOME

4650 Jeanne Mance St. - Montreal

Varied reports excerpted from the 1935 Annual Report
(Report of President George Issenman.)

> "...many ardent and zealous workers who respond when called upon...nothing was too hard for them...They neglected not only their businesses, but in many cases their families. For what? Just to see that our unfortunate children should not be in want of anything we could possibly supply them with...I am very happy to note that each Chairman has pointed out the importance of the cooperation and help they have been able to get from their Committee members..."

Honorary Officers 1935

Honorary Presidents
M. Abramowitz , A. Cooper, J.B. Miller (the late),
S.W. Jacobs, K.C., M.P., H. Wolofsky, M. Feldman, L.B. Daniels,
Alderman Max Seigler

B. Gradinger, A. Raginsky—Honorary Vice-Presidents
Mrs. D. Cohen—Honorary Secretary

Executive Officers
George Issenman, President
Jack Brodie, First Vice-President
I. Popliger, Second Vice-President
I. M. Rubinovitch, Third Vice-President
Morris Cooperberg, Treasurer
H. Handman, Comptroller
Moe Feldman, Chairman of the Board
Lyon W. Jacobs, K.C., Solicitor
Max Matt, Executive Director
Mrs. M. Crelinstein, Mrs. D. Cohen, Mrs. W. Lustgarten,
Mrs. H. Schafer, Mrs. I. Weisberg

Board of Directors
Mrs. R. Bernstein, Mrs. H. Segal, Mrs. B. Vosko, Mrs. B. Gibson, Mrs. M. Handman, Mrs. S. Lerner, Victor Cape, A. Naimer, Wolfe Bialik, J. Josefo, S. Klinger, M. Deskin, B. Goldenberg, Louis Briskin, D. Cohen, H. Smith, Mrs. M. Deskin, Mrs. M. Rosovitch, Mrs. M. Voskoff, J. Block, L. Kert, L. Liebman, A. Feiner, H. Cohen, B. Vosko.

Admission Committee Report, Chair, M. Abramowitz

Eleven meetings were held over the year, to consider certain applications, as well as to study the present 'inmates' with a view of placing them elsewhere if their age and circumstances would permit.

> "I have always felt that to keep a child in an institution too long was inadvisable, in as much as it only isolated the child from the outside world..."

On January 15, 1935, there were 47 children in the Home, 29 boys and 18 girls, ranging in age from 5-17. During the year, three more boys and three more girls were admitted, only one foreign-born—a drop attributed to the stringent immigration laws recently adopted by Canada. Seven boys and one girl were dismissed, leaving at the end of 1935, 45 in all—25 boys and 20 girls.

By the end of 1935, 198 children had been admitted and cared for since the founding of the Montefiore in 1918.

> "Today we point with pride to some of the graduates who have organized themselves into an Alumni, and are actively participating on behalf of the children at the Home...the only one of its kind in Canada, and one of the very few even in the United States that has been so successfully administering to the needs and welfare of our children...a great credit to our Home and we feel that this is an outstanding example which proves that the children are instilled with a deep love for the Home that has given them shelter during their years of childhood..."

House Committee, Mrs. M. Deskin, Chair

Mrs. Deskin notes that examination and supervision of the children's diet showed that they have been receiving the best and most wholesome of food. During 1935, the Home used: "1,480 pounds of butter (almost 3/4 of a ton at a cost of $444.00); 2,912 gallons of milk ($728.00); 7,300 loaves of bread ($365.00); 1,560 dozen eggs (18,720 eggs @ $550.00); 4,160 pounds of meat (over 2 tons @ $600.00); 780 pounds of fish ($100.00); and about 200 bags of potatoes."

The total sum for clothing and shoes was $428.88, but did not represent all the clothing deemed necessary. Through the personal interest of Mr. M. Cooperberg, the boys received suits and overcoats twice a year, while the girls were supplied with dresses through the courtesy and cooperation of Mr. L. Briskin—usually in time for the High Holidays. Their generosity represented a savings of approximately $1,000.00. Both these gentlemen also actively assisted with many personal problems faced by the youngsters.

The religious festivals were observed in true Jewish spirit. Numerous donations were received throughout the year...of foods, fruits and delicacies which delighted the children at festival times.

Education, S. Lerner, Chair

All the children attended public schools, except for one who was underage (at that time). Six were in high school—four boys and two girls, one of which would graduate in June. According to teachers at Bancroft School, the children's work and behaviour was considered highly satisfactory.

Hebrew and Jewish education was also open to all in the Home. Teachers Mr. Kaplan and Mr. Pozmansky were employed, at a cost of $600.00. Classes were held on the premises—Mr. Lerner arranged these programs when convenient to the Home—not have the children meet at different classes at various times in other Hebrew schools, i.e. the United Talmud Torahs. The curriculum included Prayers and their translations, Jewish history, Bible, grammar, debating. Services were held each morning. During this year, six boys celebrated their Bar Mitzvahs—Sam Rasminsky, George Rockman, Jack Senderoff, Aaron Kirshenbaum, Seymour Black and Louis Bloom.

Mr. Lerner organized and conducted religious services on Saturdays and the High Holidays, to instill a true spirit of Judaism. The general public was invited to special ceremonies commemorating festivals and holidays. In 1935, the total income of the High Holidays was $880.40, which exceeded that of the previous year by just over $100.00.

Maintenance, M. Deskin and H. Handman, Co-Chairmen

This Committee had only been operational for several months. To date, $360.74 was spent on building maintenance: $161.56 used for replacements in the plumbing system, $78.29 for furnace repairs.

Physician's Report, M. Naihouse, M.D.

The Medical Staff was under the supervision of Dr. M. Scherzer, while Dr. Louis J. Rosen and Dr. Wm. H. Wise have provided dental treatment to the children for many years.

> "...Since April 1935, we have not had any really serious illnesses. Mild influenza cases predominated...inflammations of the ear drums...a little anxiety about one adolescent girl, who, while working in a factory, became pale and weak, lost her appetite and strength, became nervous and unable to sleep. Upon examination I could not find any sign of disease...attributed her condition to the strain of work. And so it proved to be. A few weeks of compulsory rest, supervised feeding and medication restored her health completely.
> ...during the summer vacation in the country we had no trouble as had been expected—the usual intestinal upsets, etc. There was only one accident, one of the older boys jumped out of a tree and fractured both bones of his right forearm. To serve as a lesson for future management, I am compelled to tell you, though reluctantly, that the boy was taken to a French physician in Ste. Agathe, who could not find anything wrong with the arm. I happened to come out to the country the same day and saw the real trouble. I was able to set the arm in good position as was proven by x-ray taken at the Mount Sinai Sanatarium where I took him the next day.

All this I am telling you without undue pride, only wishing to stress the two following points: that no matter how difficult it is for the attending physician to make visits to the country, that method has to become an established tradition; physicians willing to be associated with the Institution must also agree to lose some of their time and income, and visit...frequently. Secondly I would urge the management, in the event of necessity, not to trust the children to the care of a country physician, but bring the child to the city.

...one child developed a heart defect...one adolescent girl developed a stone in the kidney...one younger child had a disease not often seen in this City—Glandular Fever. It is rather contagious, but never serious. On the whole, I am glad to report to you that in spite of the handicaps we find ourselves in, due to financial stress, not being able to supply the children with everything that could contribute to their well-being, the children have not suffered here any more than they would under the care of parents of moderate means and they have been a great deal better cared for and possibly many diseases averted because of the possibility of watching over them daily...."

Treasurer

Mr. M. Cooperberg reported that

"in the fiscal year ending December 1935, the Montefiore Hebrew Orphans' Home realized, from all its activities, the net sum of $23,123.76. The disbursements totaled $19,092.98, and we were, therefore, left with an operating surplus of $4,030.78.

After strenuous months of fundraising, these figures are indeed encouraging, as, through this operating surplus, the deficit of $9,160.18 (excluding the mortgage of $10,000.00) with which our Home was burdened at the end of 1934, was reduced to $6,129.40 and a mortgage of $9,000.00 at the end of this year.

> We are all very happy at this marked improvement and we owe our deep appreciation, not only to those who generously gave in answer to our appeals on behalf of the orphans, but also those ladies and gentlemen who are ever ready to offer their time and labour when called upon in connection with the various activities during the year..."

Comptroller

The services of a comptroller required a great deal of time. Mr. Max Handman visited regularly to go over every invoice, checked them thoroughly, and when cheques were issued for the payment of certain bills, it was his duty to scrutinize them and ensure no errors occurred. He checked the income and expenditures and found the monies well accounted for. He had installed several well-merited reforms in the bookkeeping and system of payments. One change was that a monthly audited report is procurable; another—that vouchers were to be attached to cheques before he would sign them—ensuring not only economy and good judgement, but also a substantial savings.

Tag-Day

Alderman Max Seigler was Chair of the 1935 Annual Tag-Day held in July which brought in "an amount well worth the effort." "Uncle Max" has also taken part in every activity held over the past year and is also Chair of the summer Sunshine Camp. His chief concern—finding various ways and means of safe-guarding the health and lives of the children.

Fund Raising

George Issenman, in his capacity as Board President, wrote the following about an important campaign in the 1935 Annual Report...

> "The annual fund-raising Campaign, which was held the week of September 15th-23rd, was under the capable leadership of your 1st Vice President, M.J. Brodie. He will no doubt explain to you the system of the inner organization, and will point to

> the trials and tribulations he was faced with, but I know that his modesty will not allow a true acknowledgement of these facts. In my experience I have learned to appreciate the amount of work and energy that must be concentrated upon a Campaign in a city the size of Montreal.
>
> For 7 or 8 weeks, your Chairman spent many hours of each day in the Home, directing the work. Some criticism has been passed regarding the expenditure involved in the collection of nearly $7,000.00. I wish to state publicly that if our Campaign Chairman would have had sufficient workers to canvass the cards which were placed at their disposal, twice or three times the amount raised could have been secured without extra expenditure.
>
> For the efforts of Mr. J. Brodie, I can pay no greater tribute than to state that our Campaign organization needed his leadership and I sincerely trust that Mr. Brodie will be as actively associated with our future Campaign as he was in the past year."

Staff, an Alumni Group and benefactors staged several mini fundraising events to help out, including dances and sporting events. Even at showers, weddings, bridge, and bar mitzvahs, collections were solicited, and donations made. A core of 'outside men' assisted them when the Home's financial difficulties got out of hand.

Lists of donors and subscribers appeared in the Annual Reports, and were comprised of such names as Monroe Abbey, H. Abramovitz, Mrs. E. Abugov, *Acme Clothing,* R. H. Adelstein, Mrs. M. Albert, *Alboin Textiles Co.,* Amalgamated Union, Mrs. Z. Amsel, Mrs. Fanny Aronoff, *Art Knitting Mills, Associated Screen News,* Mrs. L. Azriel, *B. B. Wholesale Bananas Reg'd.,* Dr. David Ballon, *Banque Provinciale du Canada,* Mrs. Dora Barash. (As you can see, the list is only an early sampling by alphabet!)

As part of the 1935 Annual Report, hundreds of names were listed, all proud to support the Montefiore Home. There were two categories-subscribers who paid an annual fee of $3-$5, and donors who paid what they wished. Some donors included...

Bronfman Interests and B. Aaron	$300	plus $500 as subscribers
M/M M. Cooperberg	25	
Dominion Bridge	50	
H. Feldman, St. Henri Syndicate	95	
M/M J. Gallay	22	
Jack Golden, Imperial Life Assurance	15	
George Issenman, Electrolier Mfg. Co.	42.50	
M/M S. Klinger	28	
Liberty Smelting Works	52	
Sir Charles W. Lindsay	15	$25 subscriber
J. W. McConnell	25	
Peerless Clothing	10	$25 subscriber
Pesner Bros.	10	
Price Waterhouse		$25 subscriber
Russian Polish Hebrew Sick Society	23	
Elijah Silverstone		$100 subscriber
Marcus Sperber	5	
J. Sternthal	12	
Sun Life Assurance Co.	25	

Also in April 1924, Max Matt wrote to a Mr. & Mrs. Slotin thanking them for the party they gave to the orphans in celebration of their son's Bar Mitzvah. They were kind enough to remember the children and share with them a day to remember, just as they and their son will always remember his important 13th birthday.

Copies of a 1935 Campaign letter and "GIVE" brochure follow. It was designed by learned men of the time, but yet might seem strange to us in the new millennium. The campaign phrases were put forth very simply, very straight-forward and very old-fashioned. Hopefully, they worked!

• Generosity is Always Rewarded
- - GIVE ! !
$20.000 CAMPAIGN
MONTEFIORE HEBREW ORPHANS HOME
GIVE WITH A HAPPY HEART
ESTABLISHED 1919
HELP A CHILD
4650 JEANNE MANCE
OBJECTIVE: $20,000.00
SEPTEMBER 15 to 23, 1935
CONTRIBUTIONS THANKFULLY RECEIVED AT THE "HOME" » »
4650 JEANNE MANCE STREET - - MONTREAL
Guardians of Coming Citizens
— And The Ten Reasons - -

GEO. ISSENMAN, *President* MOE FELDMAN, *Chairman of the Board* MORRIS COOPERBERG, *Honorary Treasur*

$20,000.00 CAMPAIGN

"Answer the Cry of the Helpless Orphans - *Help! Give!!*"

יתום אתה היית עוזר

"The poor committeth himself unto thee; thou art the helper of the fatherless." —Ps. 10. 14.

SEPTEMBER 15 to 23, 1935

FOUNDED 1919 מאנטעפיארע בית יתומים 1919 געגרינדעט

MONTEFIORE HEBREW ORPHANS' HOME

• CAMPAIGN HEADQUARTERS: 4650 JEANNE MANCE STREET • HArbour 8278-8279 • MONTREAL •

CAMPAIGN ORGANIZATION

ALLAN BRONFMAN
Honorary Campaign Chairman

JACOB BRODIE
Campaign Chairman

JULIUS BLOCK
BEN GOLDENBERG, B.C.L.
Co-Chairmen

ADVISORY COMMITTEE

LYON COHEN
JACK KLEIN
A. RACINSKY
M. RUDOLPH
ELIJAH SILVERSTONE
M. TANNENBAUM

GEO. ISSENMAN
MOE FELDMAN
Chairmen, Special Names Committee

MORRIS COOPERBERG
Chairman, Employees' Contribution Committee

ALD. MAX SEIGLER
Control Chairman

H. R. COHEN
Chairman, Speakers' Committee

STANLEY HANDMAN
MAX FELDMAN
Co-Chairmen, Publicity Committee

OSCAR REINHART
Chairman, Revision Committee

A. JACOB LIVINSON
Campaign Director

Montreal, September 17th, 1935.

TO SYMPATHIZERS
WITH OUR ORPHANS.

My dear Friend:

You will doubtless remember our Appeal written to you, under date of September 9th, for a Subscription or Free-will Donation to our Cause.

We feel, in that connection, that you will welcome this reminder in which we again draw your attention to our plight.

Therefore, we once more desire to assure you that any Contribution to our Funds, that you, in your goodness, decide to make, will be doubly welcomed at this time, when budgetary resources of the Home are at such an extremely low ebb, that even our minimum services stand endangered as a consequence.

Certainly your Sympathies are with this Noble Work.

Express this Sympathy in a material way by making - - a Generous Contribution as a token of your interest in the Welfare of our Orphans, and for the Institution that, as a Mother, tenderly watches over them, day in and day out.

We remain,

Yours very cordially,
MONTEFIORE HEBREW ORPHANS' HOME

J. Brodie - Chairman 1935 Campaign.

JB:GB
Encl. 1

6 Years of Constant Service
Montefiore Hebrew Orphans' Home

שפטו דל ויתום, עני ורש הצדיקו

"Defend the poor and the fatherless: do justice to the afflicted and the needy." —Ps. 82. 3.

"Think and Thank - - *Give With a Happy Heart*"

Hundreds of Orphans Hel[p]
"Sunshine Camp", Lac Masson

Report of the President of the Montefiore Alumni-1935

Ladies and Gentlemen: I take great pleasure in presenting in the following lines a brief resume of the activities and accomplishments of the Montefiore Alumni during the five years of its existence.

To begin with, this group originally was formed by a number of the graduates of the Montefiore Home, with this object in mind—that in some way they would endeavor to show their appreciation for thc finc treatment that they had received while at the Home. Late in the year of 1931 these very same graduates staged a dance and although the net profit was not what was anticipated, it showed nevertheless that there was good material that could be worked with and improved upon with the proper help. And as time went on, they succeeded in interesting some outside men to join the group, men who really appreciated the cause for which this Alumni stood. These men, together with the graduates, formed what is today a solid and well founded group, whose sole purpose it is to assist the Home in its financial difficulties in regard to its educational department. This group is today seeing a number of older children through High School as well as supplying the younger children with school books and other supplies as deemed necessary by the Home.

The past summer the Alumni took great pleasure in sponsoring a sports outing at the summer home for the children and presented cups and prizes to the winners. They also supplied sporting goods, all in all making a saving for the Treasury of the Home.

This year the Alumni has witnessed its most successful year since its inception and hoping to also take under its care the Jewish and Hebrew education of the children. If it pleases God and our Fund allows them, there is a very happy thought that another branch of the Home's difficulties will be overcome.

On behalf of the Montefiore Alumni, I wish to express my deepest appreciation to the Officers, Board of Directors and the Staff of the Montefiore Hebrew Orphans' Home for their cooperation in our past ventures and express the hope that we may count on them in the future. Wishing them every success in their undertakings.

I am, respectfully yours,
J.L. Yates,
President, Montefiore Alumni.

PHONE HARBOUR 8278

Montefiore Hebrew Orphans' Home
4650 Jeanne Mance Street Montreal

May 18, 1936

Mr. George Issenman,
President, Montefiore Hebrew Orphans' Home .
4082 Marcil Avenue, Montreal.

Dear Mr. Issenman:

The amalgamation of our Home with the Montreal Hebrew Orphans' Home now being almost accomplished, I feel that my services will no longer be required and I hereby beg to submit my resignation.
As I shall need all of my time to make my future plans, I will appreciate being relieved of my duties at the end of the current month.
May I take this opportunity of assuring you that I have considered it a privilege and pleasure to work under your direction for the past years.
At the same time I should also like to extend my thanks for the cooperation you have always given me.
Wishing you every success in your own as well as your endeavors on behalf of the many helpless children, I beg to remain
Sincerely yours,

MONTEFIORE HEBREW ORPHANS' HOME
Max Matt
Executive Director

On the same date, Max also sent Mr. Issenman the following letter, wherin he expressed his concerns for the care and upbringing of the children. (The lengthy letter has been excerpted.)

Dear Mr. Issenman:

"...As I am about to disassociate myself from my work I feel it my duty to clarify some aspects of amalgamation... points of which have hitherto not been discussed fully. Being an employee it would have been unwise and impractical for me to produce arguments in disfavor and which would tend to antagonize amalgamation...brought about in the fact that the community will be saving thousands of dollars annually as well as in the fact that the Montefiore Home has not the proper accommodation...

To produce enough grounds for reasons to the contrary, one would have to be idealistically inclined almost to the extent of displaying tyrannical qualities. From my angle, silence and inactivity have been the most logical... With you, as one who has been so greatly responsible for the amalgamation, I must be candidly free in displaying sentiments. You will no doubt be actively associated with the Hebrew Orphans' Home in the future and knowing that you have always been interested in the welfare of the children, I take the liberty of placing with you the disadvantages of amalgamation as seen by my wide intimate experience.

That which an orphan has lost can never be replaced, try what we may, and an institution can only provide food and lodging and when, at its best, can give the child a year or two of high school education... the Home records show this statement is neither minimized nor exaggerated. Thusly handicapped, the institution can only do one thing...plan the child's life not pertaining to his welfare at the Home but rather to make him realize what is to be expected upon his discharge. After all, we must agree that the most important object is to prepare the child for the future.

Aside from the physical and moral care he received at the Home, there are only two ways of accomplishing the above—1. to continue contact with the outside world (activities and interests outside the Home)... 2. to encourage association with his/her relatives.

The Montreal Hebrew Orphans' Home is handicapped in supplying those needs inasmuch as it is isolated from that part of the city to which he is bound to return upon his discharge at the age of 16. It is admitted that, as well as heredity, environment plays the next most important part in a person's life.

Now follow the child who has been placed in care of the Home by his poor relatives who live, let us say, on Colonial and Duluth. The child is five years old and his fate is to remain at the Home the next 10 or 11 years—a sixth of a person's lifetime and at the most delicate part of his life. The child has been living under refinement (at the Claremont Home) and has learned to appreciate a higher standard of living...under the best of conditions: cars, chauffeurs, clothes and the nicer things in life. This has left an almost indelible impression and the child begins to believe that the same advantages are in store for him when he grows up.

But what a deplorable distraction! His relatives have long since discontinued contact, or if some still exists, it is not significant. The boy is now 16 and with his grip in his hand, he finds himself one day on the streetcar destined for Colonial and Duluth. He lives with his relatives, but as should be expected, does not get along with them. He does not like their manners and habits for which he has been taught differently. What a come-down for him after having spent such a big part of his life under favourable conditions. Friction soon develops between him and his people for he finds it almost impossible to readjust himself. The Home has done its share and the boy cannot expect any more help from it and if, in the rare case such help is forthcoming, what can the Home do to help the boy in his readjustment? Almost nothing.

The only contact which the Hebrew Orphans' Home can supply the children is when they travel downtown to school (aside of the weekly visits of the relatives which soon wear off). This condition has been bewailed by the community which has accused the City of Westmount for not allowing the children to attend their schools. People have often expressed themselves that it is (not good) allowing children to travel daily such a distance to and from school.

But, Mr. Issenman, this is not a handicap. It is a blessing and not a curse, for the only contact they have with downtown is when they go to school, and the little harm done by this inconvenience is insignificant to the harm that would be done if they actually did attend school in this vicinity (in Westmount, so removed from their real life environment).

I feel that you will realize more emphatically the responsibility the Hebrew Orphans' Home undertakes when a child is admitted. I feel also that the confidence I have placed in you will be given of your interest adequately. We must not feel for a moment that in amalgamation all difficulties have been overcome. We have been successful only in solving the financial problem and little solving the problem directly affecting the future of the child.

The thoughts herein described...have been motivated by a spirit of sincerity in my personal interest in the welfare of the orphans. Wishing you every success in your mission on behalf of these children, I beg to remain,

Respectfully yours,
Max Matt

Max Matt still has these original letters, and gets as annoyed now by the amalgamation as he was then.

And he continues to feel that those children in the Homes were better off in their later years than those going from one adoptive home to another.

And, by the by, George Issenman never answered his letter, nor responded to his suggestions.

When the Montefiore was closed in 1936, some remaining children were sent to the Montreal Home which was large enough to cope with this continuing social problem...it was said the Homes were merged for the purpose of achieving a financial saving without impairing the philanthropic efficiency. A second reason was that the building and the Montefiore name itself continued as a facility for various organizations, among them, the Herzl Clinic. Fundraising under the Montefiore 'banner' continued through 1943.

Other children were returned to their parents or sent to group or foster homes which were then available. From the experiences of some at that time, it seemed as though foster parents took in children (for the most part), not as much to care for them, but to use them as household help and babysitters. It's tough to tell it as it is/was, but orphanages were deemed by far the better choice by the children—if one had a choice!

Even though the Jeanne Mance property was no longer operated as an orphanage, the name was retained and the building continued to be used by, and for, several other organizations. It was immediately renovated and equipped in an up-to-date manner for the use of the Herzl Dispensary and Hospital. In its first year of occupation of its new quarters, the Dispensary served 17,150 persons.

However, money remained tight. By the end of 1939, the balance in the bank was $269.50, cash on hand, $16.48, making a total of $285.98. Not very much to maintain the operating costs of the building itself.

In a letter to Mr. E. F. Vaz of the Federation of Jewish Philanthropies, dated August 22, 1940, Montefiore Home President George Issenman wrote that the heating boilers are

> "in such condition that they cannot be used for the coming winter. We have an estimate from several plumbing houses and the lowest is $500.00 for the installation of a boiler of sufficient capacity to take care of the building during the winter months. This boiler has been used for three winters (a fact known by this writer) and is guaranteed by J. Becker & Co., who are the lowest tenders."

Mr. Issenman also called into question the maintenance of the building itself. Revenues to the Home were decreasing constantly, with barely enough to take care of the caretaker, coal, lighting, etc. He felt compelled to ask Mr. Vaz to assume not only the costs of the boiler repair, but also the interest on the mortgage as it comes due.

By the end of December 1940, conditions worsened. Mr. Issenman once more wrote to Mr. Vaz noting that the Board will have to consider discontinuing the present setup of the Montefiore Home. Statements of the past 12 months, showing receipts and disbursements, indicated that the receipts are decreasing to a point where there was not sufficient income to maintain this Institution without calling on Federation for a further contribution.

> "You are no doubt aware that Federation is already paying the interest on the mortgage and the civic taxes."

A meeting of the Board of Governors was slated for January 2nd at 4650 Jeanne Mance Street.

PHONE HARBOUR 8278

Montefiore Hebrew Orphans' Home
4650 Jeanne Mance Street, Montreal

January 7th 1941

Mr. E.F.G. Vaz,
Federation of Jewish Philanthropies,
2040 Bleury Street, Montreal, Que.

Dear Sir:

Re. Montefiore Hebrew Orphans' Home Jeanne Mance Street

I am herewith enclosing statement of Receipts and Disbursements for the past twelve months. I would like to draw your attention to the fact that the Revenue is gradually diminishing to a point where some changes may have to be made.

The dues and donations amount to $789.00 for the past twelve months, and will diminish considerably as there is no collector out, as we cannot get anybody to work due to the lack of interest by the public. There is also a reduction in the rent of $212.00. Altogether we estimate that there may be a shortage of between $500.00 to $600.00 during 1941.

A number of the old Directors of the Home held a meeting on January 2nd with reference to the above, and have decided to put the matter up to the Executive of Federation. All parties concerned are reluctant to recommend the closing of the Home, due to the fact that there is a Synagogue in the establishment, and services are being held there every Friday evening, Saturday and all Holidays.

It was suggested by Alderman Seigler that we rent the place to the Jewish Immigration Aid Society, who are willing to pay approximately $1,000.00 per year. That of course would also show a loss, as the amount required for maintenance would be somewhere around $1,500.00 to $1,800.00. May the writer suggest that you assume the coal bills, repairs, telephone, and by so doing the establishment could be continued almost indefinitely.

Yours very truly
Montefiore Hebrew Orphans' Home
per: George Issenman

P.S. At present the building is being used twice weekly by the Neighbourhood House, and also the W.S.S.O. for which we do not receive any renumeration.

More Recently...

Over the more recent years...occasional articles in *The Toronto Canadian Jewish News* have attracted some most interesting responses, and brought back more memories of those past years. One such article, printed about the orphanage in late 2000, led Miriam Schneiderman Young to write from Montreal. She was interested in reading about the story and Irving Pfeffer, and wanted to know if anyone remembered her father. He was Morris Schneiderman (from the $.05-$1 chain) and was President of the Montefiore Home for several years.

As a child herself, Miriam recalls some of the stories he related about the Home, and remembers how dedicated he was to the children. Faiga Fisher is now known to Miriam through her activities in the Jewish community. "The other person I remember my father talking about was Dr. Giselle Freedman, the Home doctor and a fine woman." Miriam noted that she was the youngest of four children and her father passed away in 1968 at the age of 77.

Another response was a phone call from Sally Vineberg. Her husband, the late Marcus Mortimer (Mort) Vineberg, was the grandson of Julius Benjamin (J.B.) Miller, a founder and board member of the Montefiore Home. Mort's father, Samuel, married a daughter of J.B., whose name is on the plaque on the Jeanne Mance Building. He moved to Rupert, B.C. in 1929, and died in 1934.

J.B. Miller was instrumental in keeping the Montefiore Home going over the years...his name was featured most often where issues and concerns were critical. He continually wrote letters to the *Keneder Adler* re the importance of this institution.

Sally put us in touch with Miriam Altman, the niece of Annie Shisgal, whose maiden name was Gross. She still lives in Montreal. Her brother was Arnold Golub, now deceased, who moved to New York years ago (a write-up of Arnold's life story appears in the biography section of this book).

News about some other Montefiore Alumni...Issie Shamovitch lives in Michigan, is in his eighties. A diabetic, he has lost both legs from the knees down. Myer Gordon keeps in touch with him, as well as with Moe Letnick (whose bio will bring you up to date). Myer and Earl Greenberg also used to visit Issie Rosenberg in his seniors' residence until he passed away in 2001.

In between reunions, some Alumni keep in touch with each other, especially when aware of sickness. Muriel Fishman and Lester Dick are in constant contact with Myer. They had remained close with Charlie Berman, phoning and visiting, until he took sick and died in the fall of 2001.

And it was an amazed group of 'girls' at the first reunion when they learned that their old gal-pal Tsippa Wiseman was now known as Tina Rosen. She had an older sister Celia who was not put in the Home. Supervisor Max Matt started calling Tsippa Celia by mistake and that name stuck. It translates to Tina, which is what she began calling herself after she left the Montefiore Home.

P.S. As for the 'Rosen', she later married Leonard Rosen.

The Montefiore Home's Sunshine Camp

Alderman Max Seigler was the Chair of this other Sunshine Camp. In his 1935 report to the Montefiore Home Board of Directors, Mr. Seigler wrote...

> "This camp offers our children the opportunity of spending their two months of summer vacation in fresh air and sunshine. The site upon which our Camp is built is one which cannot easily be surpassed in beauty, as the entire 12 acres of well-wooded land fronts on the lake...It has the advantages of seclusion and privacy; even though it is located within a few hundred yards of the Post Office."

Speaking of the lake however, there was one unexpected point of danger lurking. The pipes that pumped up water from the lake were slightly exposed in different places, not entirely covered by the grass leading to the kitchen/dining room area. One day, Myer Gordon was on his own, walking up to the dining room, when he accidentally stepped on one of these pipes. Trying to jump off, the other foot also hit the pipe. He sustained burns on both feet about 3" in diameter. Taken to the infirmary, Myer was in bed a couple of days, unable to walk.... 'blistered like boiled eggs.'

Gordon also remembers some good times at camp. And exciting times, like when the King of Siam visited Ste. Agathe in the 1930s! And when the boys used to make toys out of odds and ends they found 'around'...like umbrella parts, some of which became fishing rods to catch pickerel behind the camp buildings...others became bows and arrows on demand! And when some visiting Alumni strung their buddy Jack Spinner's shirt up the flagpole!

> "While the younger boys sleep in a dormitory and all of our girls are housed in 10 rooms above that, our older boys are able to rough it, more or less, in tents with permanent wooden floors. Our dining room is built on the waterfront, with a capacity of 125 children at one sitting and with the kitchen on the same floor, we are provided with all conveniences.

This building, as well as the dormitory, have been covered with new metal roofs during the year. Both buildings are electrically lighted, solidly built, and in good condition. I would recommend, however, that the incoming Board make the improvements suggested below.

Levelling-off the playing field; at the suggestion of the Canadian Amateur Swimming Association, a pier at a distance of about 150 feet from the present one should be erected. Under such an improvement our children will be able to swim from pier to pier—always under the supervision of our counsellors, thereby reducing to a minimum the chance of an accident; lining the inside walls and ceiling of the dining room with B. C. fir; installation of motor and tank on the upper grounds to facilitate the bringing of the drinking water from the well. This water, by the way, is annually treated by the Provincial Health Bureau, and their reports show this to be excellent.

In conclusion, I earnestly desire to thank all those people who have made this Camp possible. One can have no greater pleasure than to visit our Camp and to note the happiness and enjoyment that our children have during the summer. "

Boxes of Tissues were the Centrepieces of First Combined Reunion

Raye Bye, wife of Abe, whose parents were Superintendent and Matron during the 1930s wrote:

> "...As an outsider looking into the hearts of human beings, trying to put myself in the situation they have experienced, is rather difficult. But I have shed more than just a tear, in awe at the togetherness of the 'brothers and sisters'...the warmth, the love, the recapturing of memories...the profound emotions that run high, the smiles that hide the pain of the 'good-byes'—not knowing what 'next year' will bring, are enough to melt one's heart. If only we could encapsulate the countries that are in constant battle and let them peek into these reunions—it would melt their hearts and humanize their existence..."

And still, over 60 years later, residents of Montreal, Jews and non-Jews alike are completely unaware that the city housed two orphanages in its midst. Oh, certainly those living on the same street knew, but the rest remained totally ignorant, whether by choice or by circumstance. But, to the amazement of those involved, one way or another, it is almost unbelievable that such an important institution of those days remains unheralded.

Some Alumni of the Montefiore Home first met again in 1955, 13 years after the last orphanage, the Montreal Home, closed. This is how it came about...

In 1955 or so, while former supervisor Max Matt was visiting Montreal, some of his 'kids' planned a get-together with him at the Capri Hotel...Myer Gordon, Harry Lenetsky, Ida Sklar Lewis and Celia Wiseman. Someone said, "Let's have a real reunion!" Myer and Ruth Lenetsky (Harry's first wife) agreed to look into it.

It took two years to accumulate names from everywhere, all over Canada, the U.S. and even England, although the majority of the Alumni still lived in Montreal at that time. The reality came about in 1957 when the first reunion was held in Montreal. Three more followed in 1958, '59 and '60. They were held at the Mount Royal Hotel, Rogatgos and the Ritz Carlton.

The Montreal Home also had reunions, mostly when Leah Weiner came to town from Los Angeles. Then Sylvia and Sam Rasminsky would call some of their Alumni to meet. Over the years, these attendees included Frank, Harry, Johnny and Sam Baker, Jenny and Katie Gold, Eli Hartz, Shirley and Harvey Israel, Joe and Moishe Miller, Harry Miller, Yetta Miller, Annie Mitnick, Harry & Leo Schwartz and many others.

The financial report for the '59 reunion, held on May 16th at the Mount Royal Hotel, follows:

	Rec'd	Paid	
Monies for Banquet	$420.00		
Dues and Donations	$85.00		
Monies for Pictures	$43.00		
	$548.00		$548.00
Hotel for Banquet		$403.72	
Tips		$25.00	
Orchestra		$100.00	
Amusement Tax		$9.60	
Photographer		$57.50	
		$595.82	$595.82
		Loss	$47.82

Loss to be paid for from monies on hand.

Orchestra in attendance: Mr. Segall, RE 87594
Hotel Caterer: Mr. Albeti
Assistant: Mr. Hofer
Photographer: Mr. Jack Markow

In 1960 the planning committee, for what was to be the last Home reunion for another 29 years, held a meeting.

M.H.O.H. ALUMNI GROUP Feb. 1960

A meeting was held on January 20th at the home of Ida (Sklar) Lewis. In attendance were Vita (Shein) Seidler, Lynn Cohen, Ben Wiseman, Moe Adelstein and myself. Discussion was centered on the coming reunion and to possibly further the Sick & Welfare activities. Since the turnout for the meeting was not as good as anticipated, no decisions were made but it was decided that a meeting be held in the near future. Plans have been completed for the next meeting as follows:

MISS MONTREAL

THURSDAY, FEBRUARY 25, 1960, at 9:00 p.m.

Miss Montreal will charge a minimum of $0.75 per person which will cover food and drinks that you may wish to have. Discussion will be about the coming reunion which has been set for May 14th at the Mount Royal Hotel or some other place, which will be decided upon. Other topics will be taken up during the evening. Please note the above meeting date on your agenda as there will be no follow up other than this letter. Please make this February 25th a date...

With best wishes for the coming year,

Myer Gordon

PS. The reunion was held at the Mount Royal Hotel.

The Montefiore Hebrew Orphans' Home Alumni
request the pleasure of your company
at their Fourth Annual Dinner Dance
Saturday Evening, May 14, 1960
at six thirty o'clock
Mt. Royal Hotel
Peel Street
Monteal. Quebec

$7.50 per person *R.S.V.P.*

Some 27 years later, in Toronto where some Alumni from both Homes were living, a small group began to meet for lunch every now and then—when, again, someone said, "Let's have a reunion!" As there were people from both orphanages, it was decided to have a combined reunion.

Sophie Kazdan Feldman, Myer Gordon, Earl Greenberg, Herbie Rasminsky, Sam and Sylvia (Savitsky) Rasminsky and Harry Schwartz put their collective heads together and started the planning process. Much work had to be done...more names and addresses were needed. Sylvia took over the duties of obtaining the names for the mailing list from her Montreal Home; while Myer was in charge of the Montefiore Home addresses.

After many months of searching—countless letters and phone calls—the list grew to 150 Alumni. It was difficult to contact many of the former residents because they had changed their names...whether to simply anglicize them or to find a new identity for themselves...we do not know for sure! As well, we later learned that some of them were confined to the Douglas Hospital, Montreal. Two Alumni, Tillie Hoffman and Sam Florian, visited with the latter regularly.

To determine the dates and times for the reunion, Myer called Max Matt in Bloomfield, Connecticut, to find out what was most convenient for him. Myer considered Max the catalyst for holding reunions..."after all, who was more important than our supervisor, need I ask?"

Toronto, July 1989... so much time gone by...so much time to grow mellower, to reach some hard-won personal success, to realise that they missed their 'brothers and sisters.' "We were all like siblings," said Evelyn Shano Furlong who came from Los Angeles.

This first combined reunion drew 100 Alumni, including spouses. The Saturday dinner was held at Belinda's Restaurant, Sunday's catered luncheon at the Gordon residence. The first meeting, the camaraderie was overwhelming...some hadn't seen each other for 50-60 years!

The tissue centrepieces were well-used. There was much hugging and kissing, reminiscing, teary eyes...evident the entire weekend.

And like all reunions, it unleashed a flood of memories. Evelyn's classic reminiscence from that first weekend was that, "although we were all so close, we never had sex in the Home." To which Benny Garber responded, "You were only 11 years old, for God's sake!"

There were dinner jokes about after-dark raids on the pantry, Benny's porridge packages which found their way to the garbage, and the mad scramble for small change left laying on the floor after dances. And how Sam Rasminsky scrapped with "a big French guy" on the way to and from school every day.

Claire Tolmasky Margolian's reaction to this first reunion: "... successful, enjoyable—and for me, near-traumatic...I was truly moved and surprised by my reaction...It must have been a difficult job (to organize the reunion), or perhaps a labour of love."

Moe Letnick wrote

> "...I cannot express the feeling of seeing everyone after so many years. The emotional impact it had on me will last all my life. Even though I couldn't remember the names, the faces I knew. It still brings tears to my eyes just writing this and reminiscing the old times. . . "

And this, from Abe Tolmasky: "...Seeing so many I haven't seen in 50 years or longer was a thrill I'll never forget or get over. We were really brothers and sisters while we were at the Home-the good old MHOH... on that reunion weekend, you made us feel young again..."

His brother Saul added...The feeling that went through the crowd, of camaraderie-the feeling of love and friendships renewed, the feeling of warmth, of excitement and appreciation of seeing Max Matt and so many others, and the feeling of sadness for many who weren't there... "

"Reunions are happy and sad. All those old faces," said Toronto's Eddie Rosenberg. "It's been such a long time."

Sam Schwartz, living in Florida and brother to Harry, Leo and Libby, had to miss the '89 reunion as he was on a trip to South Africa. "...I feel that I missed one of the greatest events in a long time..."

This initial reunion was the start of our Archives. Many pictures were taken, the *Toronto Star* and *Canadian Jewish News* sent reporters and photographers. There was even a segment on CITY TV...including Evelyn's and Benny's remarks about (non) sex in the Homes!

The several hundred letters received over the years are kept in special books, as are copies of *The Mishpocha* and photographs. There are also about eight large bristol boards with photos and articles... most are taken to each reunion where they are eagerly looked over and discussed by attendees. As a photographer, Myer ensured that a pictorial record was made of each reunion. In later years, Lester Dick and Harvey Israel would send in their photos as well. This 'library' has provided much of the content of this book.

The original committee organized the first five reunions—except for the second, held in Montreal and coordinated by Leo and Laura Schwartz. After that, Sam and Sylvia Rasminsky and Harry and Ann Schwartz spent the winters in Florida. So Judy and Myer Gordon took over, with advice from Vita Seidler and Earl Greenberg. *The Mishpocha* said when and where, and the cheques came in!

Organizing the reunions has proven to be quite a challenge...trying to make them at good restaurants with private rooms. And trying to find a bit of entertainment to spark the interest of attendees. There have been musicians, caricaturists and magicians. Myer has been the MC and shares his witty stories, bringing laughter to all. Other Alumni tell their own jokes and personal stories of their Home experience. The late John Brownston especially loved telling his jokes! And hearing Irving Pfeffer's comments about his life in the Montreal Home, and about his later success in life, is always a treat. After all, how many Judges do we have in our Alumni?

Says Myer, "Spouses are the core of the reunions. They participate by attending, paying attention and making every effort to feel part of what is going on. Bless them all."

Their quarterly newsletter, *The Mishpocha* connects the orphans of the past to the older adults of today. Initiated by Myer and Judy, it contains articles, photos, anecdotes, family news, and change of addresses sent in by the Alumni...keeping everyone in touch over the years between the now-annual reunions, held mainly in Montreal (the odd Toronto function is thrown in every so often to appease the expatriates living there)!

Judy's *Mishpocha* was the key to keeping the Alumni together. Says a slightly biased Myer, "Her creativity brought in phone calls and many lettters were received over the ensuing years." When donations were needed (for the publication, subsidizing reunion meal costs, and providing confidential financial assistance to those Alumni in need), everyone came through as best they could. And when we stopped asking for donations, there are still some who provide them annually...one of these, Florence Kramer in Sarasota, Florida, who wants to keep a connection to her late husband Richard's early life in the Montreal home with his mother, cook and housekeeper.

When Hy Jacobson asked. "What is it that brings us all here to reunions?" many Alumni responded... "To see how we are aging." "To recapture our youth. We're family and when you stop to think about it, at a reunion we have at least 15 brothers and sisters (aren't we lucky?) with a need inside to see each other." "We are here in the heart, not intellectually." He wrote, in 1989, that he was "looking forward to (the first reunion) seeing our brothers and sisters—the right words to describe the bonding we experienced in the Home."

The Canadian Jewish News of September 1995 contained an article by reporter Miriam Chinsky about the sixth combined reunion. It again brought Montefiore and Montreal alumni to Toronto for a weekend, though the majority still live in Montreal. "They cluster around a table covered with old snapshots brought by their former supervisor Max Matt, trying to identify themselves and friends from the early days." Max, then 84, travelled from Connecticut with wife Wanda, and posed happily for more photos with 'his girls.'

Now in their twilight years, many ex-residents feel an added urgency to get together. From the initial mailing list, many have passed away over the past few years. The list is down to 110, with about 48 active attendees...and this number includes spouses.

Over the years, we have lost many 'brothers and sisters'... On behalf of the MHOH Alumni, Myer Gordon sends a charitable donation in their memory. "It is the least we can do."

At this writing, 2002 will mark the 13th reunion of the MHOH Alumni. And each year's event has been a little bit different. Myer Gordon took snaps of different groups for the albums...of Harry Lenetsky standing proudly with his granddaughters visiting from New York and Vancouver; of Sam Rasminsky who talks about when he was invited to try out for the Montreal Canadiens, and when he went to Baltimore but left the team to come home to marry Sylvia whom he had met when they were both in the Montreal Home; of Tina (Celia Wiseman) & Leonard Rosen who talked enthusiastically about their trip to Holland for the 50th anniversary of D-Day.

Over the years, family members came to learn about their parent(s) early life in an orphanage. Among them were the Rasminskys' four daughters who made a big hit because they were the first family to come. That same year Myer's son Alan attended and made a video of the reunion. Others included Ida Sklar's children and grandchildren,

Max Matt's two sons and one daughter-in-law; Manny Cohen's whole mishpocha; Ben Wiseman with some of his family...and Jack and Hymie Jacobson came one year with sister Sally.

There was even a reunion in Florida. In February 1995, Harry and Ann Schwartz, encouraged by Myer Gordon, organized a beautiful dinner and invited all local Alumni plus the 'snow birds.' Even Max Matt came! Those attending included Nat and Bess Alper, Ruth and Dave Furman, Arnold and Gert (Miretsky) Golub, Willie Label, Alice and Joe Miretsky, Sam and Sylvia Rasminsky, Aaron and Dorothy (Shmoiser) Solomon, Ida Sklar Lewis, Anita Spinner, Jack Zukerman & Rose, and of course, the Schwartzes!

In 1998, at the August reunion in Montreal, the Alumni presented a beautiful clock plaque to the Gordons—lovingly inscribed...

> *For your timeless devotion in organizing, creating and arranging our yearly reunions. With much love from The "Sisters" and "Brothers" of the Montefiore Hebrew Orphans' Home and The Montreal Hebrew Orphans' Home, August 1998*

Special thanks to Beatrice Hock for instigating this presentation.

People, Voices from the past excerpted from the quarterly *Mishpocha*

> "...you must know that, among the best things that have occurred in my lifetime, are the years spent in the MHOH, for which I am forever grateful."
>
> Riva Savitsky Schuman, Tulsa, Oklahoma, 1996

Max Matt, North Africa, 1943 (from a letter sent by Max to Abie Sheiner during WWII, and presented by Abie to Max at the 1992 Montreal reunion!)... "...your letter was most interesting and contained plenty of news about the old gang. Well, Abie, old boy, North Africa, what I have seen of it, is not what I expected. Plenty of Arabs, and since it is forbidden to write derogatorally about any Allies, I shall just say that their mode of life is far from anything an American can ever get used to....Mind you, I'm not referring to any natural beauties I have seen-I am merely trying to convey to you the very different mode of life that exists over here...Try to give my address to as many of the boys as possible as I sincerely hope that some day one of the boys will contact me. I can think of no bigger surprise nor treat than just such a happening."

Edie Bye, Montreal, 1989... "...I will not be attending the reunion but... appreciate being asked and receiving your bulletins. 500 Claremont was listed as my home address from Sept. 1930 to Sept. 1942 which means I have known some of the people (who will be attending the reunion) for a very long time, although I haven't seen most of them recently. I do wish you all a very Happy Reunion with some laughs for the "Good Old Days." (P.S. Edie has been attending ever since!)

Helen Greenberg Zawalsky, Ottawa, 1989 "...At our reunion 30 years ago, I was so emotional about it that I had a difficult time recalling and recognizing so many faces and names. I can't tell you how much I am looking forward to another wonderful evening with all our "kin", and yes, there will be teary but happy exchanges of our many memories. Poor Max Matt—he's really in for a million hugs and kisses. I shall never forget him..."

Dave Cherry, Montreal, 1989... "...although this happened 58 years ago, I still have a vision of all the boys and girls in my mind who were at the Home... I hope to be well enough to attend with my wife, to be with all of you as this would be something very special in my life."

Ben Wiseman, Florida, 1989...Ben came to the first reunion with his wife Freda and two daughters—Susan, Toronto, and Karen who brought her own two young children from Tulsa, Oklahoma. "I learned about the reunion from a *Canadian Jewish News* notice sent to me by a friend. In the Home we were as close as brothers and sisters. We depended on one another."

Evelyn Shano Furlong, California,1989... "We all went to the same school, Bancroft on St. Urbain St., and we took part in the activities, but we always stuck up for one another."

Willie Morganstein, Montreal, 1989... "Imagine, if you haven't seen your family for over 30 years. That's what it's like being together now."

Myer Gordon, Toronto, 1989... "All the reminiscing at the dinner last night and today; it's not about what happened 30 years ago (at the last reunion)...We all went back (in time) to the orphanage!"

Dr. Jack Gross, working at the Hebrew University of Jerusalem, 1990... "I'm glad Sylvia tracked me down. I have fond memories of Sunshine Camp and am delighted to hear of the success and activities of our alumni...I would appreciate your continuing to send me news."

Sylvia Rasminsky, Toronto, 1991... "about two years ago we located one of our 'sisters' from the Montreal Home, who was living in a foster home for the elderly. She was quite ill, both physically and mentally, and very unhappy, as she was fed in the basement, alone, away from the other residents due to her condition. Thanks to the efforts of many who still remember her she is now in an apartment by herself... assisted by numerous alumni from the orphanage, who phone her, take her shopping, out for lunch, help her write letters...Her greatest pleasure is hearing from her 'brothers and sisters'... "

Myer Gordon, Toronto, 1992..."One of the happiest weekends in my life...to see brothers and sisters whom I haven't seen in 50-60 years! Jack & Abe Senderoff, Sarah (Connie Gore) Bercusson, Moe Letnick, Abe Sheiner, Caroline & Tillie Hoffman, Ben Garber, Jack Zukerman, Harry Lenetsky, Sophie Feldman Kazdan and so many more...and I've gained friends from the Montreal Home."

Vita Shein Seidler, Toronto, 1992... "I really looked forward this year to celebrate the 50th anniversary of the two Homes...the highlight for me was meeting Sarah Bercusson Gore (Connie) after not seeing or hearing of her for the last 40 or so years! Knowing perhaps that this might be the last big get-together (I hope not) made me want to enjoy it all the more. Seeing the Senderoff Brothers for the first time in years reminded Abe about the time he used to love milk, and chewed it, as he was told it would give him big muscles! We had a good laugh over that...he didn't think anyone would remember that!..."

Shirley Israel Feldman, Montreal, 1992... "When I tell people how we residents of the MHOH are getting together after 50 years, they are amazed and delighted beyond belief. How wonderful, they say, and I agree!... I am sorry to hear about Phyllis Sokoloff's (Felicia Sotell) demise. I believe she attended the last reunion and to my regret I never had a chance to converse with her. I had not seen her since the orphanage disbanded. She had a brother Jimmy (Jack) who used to attend our summer camp at Ste. Margarite/Lac Masson..."

Nettie Avrith Shragie, Montreal, 1993... "Thank you for doing such a marvelous job. I know it takes time and effort. I was brought up in the Home on Claremont. Most of the names I do not recognize—maybe it was after my time. I know the Brumers—I washed dishes with Harry every other week. I remember Hilda Matt who took dancing lessons, and her brother Max, the Randolphs, the Israels, and the Velters..."

Beatrice Sabbath Hock, Ottawa, 1993... "...another reunion...a great success!...It seems to me that everyone was 'glowing' with the pleasure of being together..."

Helen Zawalsky, Ottawa, 1993... "...back to earth again after a wonderful nostalgic weekend. As always it was a joy to see our brothers and sisters—swapping stories, bringing back countless memories...The hotel was absolutely beautiful—it reminded me of our dormitories...what a coincidence!"

Manny Cohen, Montreal, 1994... "It's only two days since our reunion and I'm already getting lonesome. Bless you both (the Gordons) for putting in the time and effort to keep us all together."

Saul Tolmasky, Montreal, 1994 "...may God grant you both the health and strength to carry on. You have made a lot of (old) people feel happy and young again."

Tina (Celia Wiseman) Rosen, Montreal, 1995... "Glad to be included on the list for the next reunion... happy to be with all of you... Your *Mishpocha* news is such a pick-me-up, we read it over and over..."

Beatrice Sabbath Hock, Ottawa, 1996... "The reunion was truly the 'best yet'! I gathered so many lovely memories to add to the past ones. You should feel very happy to know that your great efforts and enthusiasm paid off....you accomplished the impossible—pleasing everyone who attended!" Bea was not in the Homes but volunteered at the Montreal Home as a teenager, assisting the youngsters with their homework. Her father, the well-known Bunny Sabbath, gave many of the 'graduates' (over 16 years of age) their first jobs.

Reva Savitsky Schuman, Tulsa, Oklahoma, 1996... "Though I regret my lack of participation, you must know that among the best things that have occurred in my lifetime are the years spent in the MHOH, for which I am forever grateful."

Florence Kramer, Sarasota, Florida, 1997... "...Through your Alumni group (and *The Mishpocha)*, Betty Sandell has started quite a correspondence with me and has sent me photos of Joe and their daughters... I read a copy of Joe's biography... fascinating. I think that man is a genius, what he has done and accomplished in his lifetime..."

Lester Dick, Kirkland, Quebec, 1998... First came to the 1991 reunion, then started again in earnest in 1998. Now he wouldn't let even one year pass him by! In between reunions, he phones Alumni who are not well and generally likes to keep in touch with his 'family.'

Raye Bye, Montreal, 1999..."The *Mishpocha* Reunion is a time for rejoicing—a connection with the past—with 'brothers and sisters' who come together to share secrets of past and present as well as plans for the 'tomorrows'...The essence of this joy is coming together and feeling as one... we all look forward to the reunions as there are so many stories to be told and so much to be proud of..."

Edes Sarner, Toronto, 1999...joined us at this year's reunion for the first time. She volunteered as a teenager at the Montreal Home, giving piano lessons and starting a jazz band! Now 85, she enjoyed meeting some of her former pupils, one of them a tambourine player!

Manny Cohen, Montreal, 1999..."We could not let time go by without writing you to wish you Happy New Year and to bless you for all the days and hours you spend on behalf of us kids, keeping us...in touch. Mary & I had such an empty and sad feeling that we could not attend this last reunion. It was the first time...It did my heart good to see all the photos in *The Mishpocha*—they keep our memories alive."

Rebecca Lenetsky, Montreal, 2000..."...when we left the hotel after this weekend's reunion, I felt a pang of sadness for those I had met over the years who are no longer with us, including my husband Harry who was in the Home. Although I was not in either orphanage—lucky enough to have had both parents—I felt a strong sense of kinship with those who were. From Harry I had heard so many vivid stories, such as about when he, as one of the oldest, regretted having to leave when his mother remarried. He had such great esteem for Max Matt.

After Harry had left, and the Montefiore closed, he had established himself and was married, when he got a long-distance call. The voice at the other end said, 'Do you know who this is?' and Harry answered, 'Max Matt!' Harry was delighted that, after so many years, Max thought enough of him to find him! Shortly afterwards, the reunions started, and I am ever so grateful that Harry had a chance to meet with all his old buddies again. He enjoyed each reunion immensely."

Harvey Israel, Montreal, 2000... "Our last reunion was superb. I felt a closeness to all you guys like never before. Let us keep these reunions going for a long time..."

Judith Stolov Kazdan, Toronto, 2000...a marathon runner for years, competing world-wide-still at it in her 80s. She "thought it was great to have these get-togethers after all these years!"

Ruth Smilovitch Furman, Florida, 2001..."...can't attend reunion, but extend our best wishes to everybody...very much enjoyed the poem in the June issue of *The Mishpocha*...plan to submit it to our condo newspaper. Thank you too for the donation in memory of my brother Solly. His children were also most appreciative..."

Beatrice Hock, Ottawa, 2001... "...Myer, you're the head of the 'family'...the one who keeps the group together..."

Irving Pfeffer, San Francisco, 2001... "I have a special place in my heart for Charlie Berman (recently deceased) who was a room-mate of mine at the orphanage. The list of deceased keeps growing but we are still in there kicking."

To answer Vita Shein Seidler's earlier question, "How were you treated (in the orphanage)?" it seems that the majority of those keeping in touch through letters, phone calls and reunions have many fond memories of their stay in their respective Homes. Only a few complained of maltreatment by a supervisor; some were homesick for their families, which is natural; others had problems with the food.

But when one really thinks about the situation in those times, it was often the only, and so the best, choice. They were fed and clothed, had instant playmates and activities, and summer camp. There weren't too many who could brag about that in the 'outside world'!

The Alumni learned to cope with differences, they educated themselves into careers and professions, married and were wonderful parents to their own children. Relishing that opportunity as only they could.

Bar Mitzvah boys Moishe Cohen,
Willie Morganstein and Dave Cherry

L-R: Abe Tolmasky, Charlie Bloom, Harry Zelfin
and Arnold Golub, 1939

Myer Gordon and Sammy Rasminsky 1941

Issie Rosenberg and Willie Label, 1942

L-R (front): Sammy Rasminsky, Ben Garber
L-R (behind) Herb Rasminsky, Eli Lenetsky.
At the ball field. Sam played for The Generals.

L-R: Joe, Morris and Ray Miller; Sylvia Zimmerman

Moe Letnick sketched by Counsellor Jerry Waldston in 1942

Ben Garber and Ben Gordon, London 1943

Sketch of Supervisor Maurice Ogulnick 1943

BIOGRAPHIES OF SOME MHOH ALUMNI

Moe Adelstein

"My father put me and my younger sister Minnie in the Montefiore Home in 1930 after mother had passed away: I was 8 years old. I remember playing hockey on a small rink and watering it many a time!

I also remember the Alumni of 1930 visiting the Home and taking some of the children to *Her Majesty's Theatre*. The Alumni and MHOH staff were all so kind and caring.

My father remarried one and one-half years later and took us out of the Home to live with him and our new stepmother.

For the next six years, I spent all my time at the orphanage, and attended Bancroft School with the children in the Home. I also spent some summers at the camp in the Laurentians. I remember having my Bar Mitzvah at the Home as well, but don't remember who the other boys were.

After leaving the Home, I worked in a men's sportswear factory.

I married Jeannine in 1944. We have two children—a married son with one child, and an unmarried daughter. My sister Minnie married Hy Leibovitch and moved to Edmonton. Her grandson was married in Toronto October 2001.

Ever since Myer Gordon, his wife and the committee started the combined reunions in 1989, we have attended all of them. I am grateful for the reunions, because even a once a year get-together is a *mitzvah* for me."

Nat Alper's Life Story

"If I could live my life over again, I would want to grow up with a mother and her love. That's what I always missed most." Nat was just six months old when the Cossacks murdered his mother; she was only 30 years old.

Nat was born in Boiarka, a small village in the Ukraine, 25 miles south of Kiev. He was the youngest of six boys born to Sima Sklarsky and Jacob Alper...they were simple hard-working people. Young as he was, his only memories of his earliest years come from his older brothers Max & Issie.

Life in the Ukraine was hostile and restricted for Jews. The 1917 Russian Revolution created even more social and political chaos. The White Russians were seen as allies by the American, British and Germans who all came to Russia hoping to save the country from communism. In 1918 Trotsky and the Bolsheviks won the final battle for Kiev and took full control of the Ukraine.

Life in the Alper family's village was fairly quiet for several months...the calm before the storm.

They were followed by years filled with calamity...the pogroms that killed his mother, the treacherous, traumatic trek across Europe and the long trip by ship to Canada, arriving in Halifax December 31, 1923. The passengers' entry visas were stamped January 1, 1924, so the ship waited just outside Canadian waters, then moved leisurely into harbour at the appointed time.

Representatives from JIAS helped them disembark, finally putting them on a train heading west. There were about 250 in all, none speaking English. As the train approached Quebec City, officials walked up and down the aisles, pointing to someone, saying, "You're going to Vancouver" to another, "You're going to Winnipeg." "You're going to Toronto." Eventually, they came to Nat's father. "You, Mr. Alper, will get off in Montreal."

In Montreal their first home was the Jewish Immigration building on Notre Dame Street, where they stayed for about one week. Then came a visit from the immigration authorities of the Baron de Hirsch Institute. They insisted that Mr. Alper couldn't possibly work and properly care for six children at the same time. With that, they took four of the six brothers away and placed them in the Montreal Hebrew Orphanage. The two eldest could remain with him as they were over 14 and could work.

Nat was five then. So, his earliest memories began in Montreal where his first happy home on Canadian soil was a Jewish orphanage. To him, the orphanage was beautiful and the children were cared for with kindness. "I met kind and caring people there who treated me with affection. My father did his best for me, but never could give me that same kind of love."

Nat's story is not a glamorous one, but he feels the first years of his life were the ones that shaped him the most. "If my childhood had been more comfortable and complete, I might not have made financial stability a number one concern. I might not have wanted as much. But when you are born with nothing and live for years with even less, security becomes an obsession. I was always driven to succeed."

At five, Nat was the youngest in the orphanage, and "that was just fine by me, because I got lots of love and extra attention." The girls who worked there fussed over him in the most wonderful ways. They'd hug him in the morning, bathe and dress him. His brothers Myer, Charlie and Max were also well-cared for, and loved their new home, but not as much as Nat. He remembers that period as one of the happiest times of his life. Everything was planned out for him...at three o'clock there was a meeting; at four o'clock there were lessons, and at five o'clock there was always something else to do. Nat felt very secure.

There were about 100 youngsters living in the Montreal Home back then. They were clothed, fed and sent to school. On Saturdays they went to the *Shaar Hashomayim* Synagogue. If the circus came to town, someone would always take them out to see it. And during the summer, they'd spend terrific weeks at a camp near Shawbridge, in the Laurentians north of Montreal. All the rich Jews used to come up there to play with them on weekends. Sometimes they'd even give them a little money. Nat remembers having to run up a hill as part of some game, and if he made it to the top, the prize was a dime. "As far as I could tell," say Nat, "living at the orphanage was like staying in a big hotel. Everything about it was excellent."

The building itself always seemed huge to Nat, though it was probably only three or four stories high. The rooms inside were enormous, and Nat recalls the dining room had a very high ceiling. Nevertheless, despite the seeming grandeur, the youngsters lived together in fairly close quarters. They slept in dormitories, six to eight in a room. At mealtimes, everyone sat together at long rectangular tables in the dining room...at least 18 children at every table. Prayers were recited, and then the orphanage staff would appear with wonderful kosher meals—filling breakfasts of orange juice, cereal and toast; tasty suppers of meat or fish with rice or potatoes and salad.

The children went to Berthelet School on Ontario Street. "They used to bus us quite a distance, because no one wanted Jews at the schools in Westmount." At noon, they would have a lunch of soup and a sandwich at the Baron de Hirsch Institute on Bleury. "The sandwich was fine, but the soup always seemed to be burned!"

Meanwhile, Nat's brothers and his father were living in the Jewish quarter of Montreal. His stepmother Bubell (from Bucharest) had finally joined them, and Nat's half brother Dave was born in 1925.

After about four and a half years in the orphanage, Nat and his brothers were sent home to his father and Bubell. "Home" took some getting used to. After the years of being babied at the orphanage and accustomed to a good life, the sudden changes were dramatic for Nat and his brothers. The accommodations weren't much better; food was not as plentiful...Nat had to get used to dining mostly on potatoes and herring.

Nat was never comfortable with his step-mother. He felt she never treated him fairly, never pampered him. Half-brother Dave always got the cream at the top of the milk bottle, was the first to be served and seemed to get the best of everything! Nat recognized that he had been spoiled at the orphanage, but Dave's preferential treatment made him angry. Today he regrets that his anger hurt his relationship with Dave, because Dave was a wonderful kid brother, and "it wasn't his fault."

The Alper family had little money for toys, so Nat got his enjoyment from playing with his friends, spending summers at the *B'nai Brith* Camp in the Laurentians and occasionally getting into trouble. "We felt a lot of anti-Semitism in those days. If we'd venture into a French neighbourhood, there was always a chance we might be beaten up, just because we were Jewish."

Nat quit school at age 12 and never continued on to high school. He felt he just wasn't cut out for academia...he was too interested in making money. He realises now that it would have been wiser to continue his education. "I never really felt right about not having a degree." But he had no choice about attending Hebrew lessons and remembers that 20 people came to his Bar Mitzvah, but he doesn't remember a single present. His father brought home a bottle of liquor, some herring and onions, and "that was that. "

Now, thinking back, Nat doesn't recall a happy childhood. Though his years at the orphanage were fine, once he returned home, he was usually troubled. His father was too wrapped up trying to support his family and put food on the table. Nat's feelings changed only when he started earning a wage and no longer had to ask his father for anything. He always had that drive, more than ambition—an obsession. So he worked, while his friends played.

Odd jobs and boxing at the YMHA filled his time until his first full time job in the shipping room of a small clothing factory...he thinks it was the *Merit Blouse Company.* He trained as a dress cutter, joined the union and went to work for a larger company, *Sapera Brothers,* in the same Sommer Building which, coincidently, housed Berthelet School which he had attended while in the Home.

His salary to start was $60. a week, then raised to $125. and he started living like a mensch. He bought clothes, went bowling, out to dinners and movies. His favourite restaurants were *Shaps, Pumpernicks* and *The Snowdon...*roast beef meals for 75 cents!

Nat hoped one day to open his own business, and each week he saved a few dollars towards that goal. But then came World War II, which again changed his life. He enlisted in the RCAF in 1942, aged 23, and served until '45, but never overseas. He found those years the most enriching...for not only was he serving his country, but the service opened his eyes to the world. In Montreal he'd been living in a cultural ghetto—all Jewish. The only ethnic interaction was mostly unfriendly. Air Force life offered the opportunity to travel, play sports, extend his education, and meet many fine people, Jews and non-Jews. This experience dramatically improved his outlook on life. He was well-fed and sending his father $10 a week to help with the rent.

At war's end, Nat moved back home. But his new life experiences had changed him and he couldn't cope with the restrictions and the bickering between his father and Bubell. One of the many occasions when Bubell moved out and Nat's father had to go to court, became the basis of the internationally acclaimed film, *Lies My Father Told Me.* As told by a cousin Seymour Alper:

> "Gedalie was a junk dealer and they lived in two rooms at 4900 Clark...Gedalie had a horse named Pitou, 'parked' behind the house. Now Bubell had moved out and hired a lawyer who sued Gedalie for alimony. His lawyer explained to the judge that Gedalie had no money; that he needed his horse to make a living and with the money he made, he had to feed it. If he didn't feed the horse, he could make no living and if he made no living, he could not pay alimony. The next day, headlines in *The Montreal Herald* read, MAN FEEDS HORSE BEFORE WIFE!"

Yet his father never complained. He was happy to have food on the table for Shabbat...the rest of the week didn't seem to matter. While Nat respected his father's strength and spirit, he wanted more than a good Friday night meal. It was his father's sorry situation that fuelled his ambitions. He didn't want to end up like him, so he was driven to prove himself and somehow repay his father for his life of sacrifice.

Nat returned to work at *Sapera Brothers* from 1945-48, when he and two friends started their own dress manufacturing business, *Jul-Mac Fashions.* Due to their inexperience, it did not flourish and he went back to *Sapera Brothers*—but not delighted to be there.

Nat was still a poor cutter when he first met Bessie Goldberg during a skiing weekend in Ste. Agathe. She looked so pretty standing at the top of the hill that he knew right away that he wanted to marry her. He told her so on that first day. She laughed and thought he was crazy! She wouldn't give him her phone number, so months went by before Nat was out on a blind date with a friend. His friend's date was Bessie. Nat arranged to switch dates (which was done in those days) and the evening worked out splendidly.

Nat's intentions were good, but he wasn't religious or wealthy enough to suit Bessie's parents, who, relatively speaking, were very well off. But she was the girl for him, and Nat wouldn't give up. He borrowed money to buy an engagement ring, popped the question and Bessie said yes. They were married in March 1949, Nat aged 29,

Bessie (well, that's still her secret!). Following a wonderful New York honeymoon, the newlyweds settled back in Montreal on Park Avenue, near St. Joseph Blvd. The rent was a whopping $60. a month.

Monthly bills were hefty and money was tight. Nat was still a cutter, Bessie a bookkeeper. But soon Nat was promoted to production manager and things started looking up. They loved going to clubs—a favourite, the *El Morocco*—and even bought their first car, a glorious blue Chevrolet at a cost of $1,800.

Part of Nat's job was negotiating with the unions...intense pressure as it was a case of economic survival. When Nat left *Sapera Brothers* in 1953, he was a bundle of nerves. To get away from the scene of the stress, Bessie and Nat made a getaway to California where Bessie had some relatives. Relaxing in the warm heat, Nat felt refreshed. Then, chatting about a cousin's travel business and agencies in general, Bessie had an idea. Newspapers in California and other States had large ads for employment agencies. Back in Montreal, a look through the phone book showed not an employment agency in sight. They opened one in 1953 at 1405 Peel Street. It was hugely successful right from the start.

They had struck at the right moment. *Ace Personnel* was the first official employment agency in Canada (not counting a similar business run by a woman out of her home in Vancouver). Before long, it employed a full time staff of 12. Nat recalls, "During one particularly hectic period, there was such activity around our office, the police showed up to investigate. They'd seen so many young women waiting in our lobby; they suspected we were an escort agency and these were our call girls. We quickly explained that we specialized in permanent and temporary placement of the legal kind only!"

In his capacity as an entrepreneur, Nat also became active in the community, joining the Lions Club and then *B'nai Brith* Maple Leaf Lodge in 1978, becoming president at one point.

Business boomed through the 60s and 70s. Nat and Bessie lived a good life. Moved to a nicer apartment on Linton, hired a maid and when son Michael was born, a live-in nurse. Daughter Shelley was born soon after they purchased their first home in the newly developed area of Cote St. Luc. The children flourished, the house was renovated and life was good. Eight years later it got even better when they moved to a much larger home in Hampstead. Then, suddenly

"I was just another guy with big bills and high taxes...plus expensive furniture and increasing stress. I was never good at handling stress."

Nat plunged even harder into *Ace Personnel* like a man possessed. In 1965, the anxiety and long hours caught up to Nat and he suffered a serious stroke. Lucky to be alive, it took him several years to regain his equilibrium and mental strength.

Bessie ran the business while Nat was incapacitated...it was her baby anyway, and when Nat returned, he concentrated on finding suitable applicants for people at the top, presidents, CEOs. It was a great deal calmer. Then, in 1989, feeling the need for a rest and a change, they sold *Ace Personnel*. Sad to say, the new owner ran it into the ground, for which they felt quite badly. It took time to adjust, to fill the vacuum left by not working. Golf took up the slack and they now enjoy their retirement immensely.

Nat's regret? He spent too much time working and not enough with his children as they were growing up. Son Michael became a doctor, the first university-educated member of the family. Daughter Shelley is a physiotherapist. Their accomplishments brought Nat a peace of mind and faith in the future for a father who grew up with nothing.

But he looks at his dear wife and knows there is much to celebrate—his family and the life they shared together. All caring and considerate. They now enjoy their three grandchildren. All those years of work and worry have been worth it. "I have been blessed."

And to add to his celebration of life, Nat's children threw him a big 75th birthday party...the first birthday party he ever had.

John Brownston's Story

John Brownston, late of Sacramento, California...A magazine article about his major 'planned gift' to McGeorge School of Law, noted that John 'ran away from a Montreal orphanage at the age of 16,' did odd jobs, then joined the Canadian Army. Facing many traumatic experiences and minor injuries in Italy, he decided that if he lived through 'this lousy war', he wasn't going back to Canada but to sunny California. After being in the jewelry business for a decade, he enrolled in law at McGeorge, opened his own law practice and became wealthy. So, years after being a runaway, John couldn't help but add that "...I confess that I am pleased to be among the number of orphan's home inmates who have achieved a modicum of success." He makes it sound so easy!

John was born in Winnipeg, the fifth of six children of Molly and Samuel Brownston. The 1929 crash resulted in his father losing his furrier business and their home being foreclosed. They moved to Montreal into a succession of rented tenement flats. "My father kept moving around, seeking work wherever it could be found, and later when my mother was so ill she couldn't take care of my younger brother Martin and me, a social worker picked us up and delivered us to the orphans' home on Claremont—in 1931. I was 10. My older siblings were not placed there because they were already either in school or working."

"It was a strange experience at first. I wasn't happy there, but attempted to adjust as best I could under the circumstances. When I was 12, my mother passed away from cancer." John attended Berthelet School with most of the other kids his age from the orphanage. He graduated from 7th grade first in his class, received a scholarship permitting him to enter Baron Byng High School at no charge (in those days tuition was charged to attend high school, plus the cost of books). While still in Baron Byng, John did indeed run away at about 16 years old. He managed to get a series of part-time jobs; the first delivering packages on his bicycle in the evenings for a neighbourhood drug store (*Cooperman's* at St. Lawrence/Prince Arthur Streets) for the grand sum of $2.50 per week, including every second Sunday from 9 a.m. to 11 p.m...to private homes and one or two brothels in the neighbourhood. Brothels were considered good customers at that time, ordering somewhat more expensive sweet-smelling lotions and creams, etc., and being good tippers!

Summertime, John left this job for one in the Laurentians—for $5. a week, plus room and board. After the summer, he worked evenings and weekends to earn money for food, rent, etc...as dishwasher, bus boy, waiter—eking out a living during the depression years.

When Canada entered World War II in 1939, John quit high school before graduating to enlist in the Anti-Tank Battery. Three weeks later, he crossed the Atlantic. After basic training, completing a radio/signaling course and assigned to drive the Commanding Officer in an armoured car with a machine gun and radio (sort of a roving tactical H.Q.), he located in Croydon, Surrey. There he was encouraged to enroll in a local Polytechnical Institute (at no charge—a Canadian Government pay-off), where he worked towards his B.Sc. degree. Military duties and frequent maneuvers interrupted classes, and John eventually sailed away to invade Sicily in July '43. This campaign through, he was involved with the invasion of Italy, under Field Marshall Montgomery.

John was sent home in 1945, having completed almost three years towards his science studies. He had hopes of studying law at McGill University but hadn't completed sufficient undergraduate studies. Not wanting to hang around for another Canadian winter, he arrived in California in April 1946. As a condition for being permitted to leave Canada (an exit permit was required at that time) he had to give up most of his Veteran's benefits. He still hoped to return to college, but found work as a fine jewelry salesman, shifted throughout the State, taking part-time courses in various state Colleges, adding bits and pieces to his education. While in Sacramento, "deciding to start my own business, I left my job, found a location and, at the same time, qualified as a beginning student at McGeorge School (part of the University of the Pacific), graduating in 1961. My fine jewelry business prospered and allowed me time to study law...I sold the business upon passing the Bar Exam and found a position in the field of law in a Stock Brokerage as a trainee."

Somewhat disillusioned, John left after 8 months, securing a position with the *Better Business Bureau,* exposed to every conceivable rip-off, swindle, racket, consumer fraud, etc. This was followed by a stint in the newly-created Department of Consumer Affairs, but the low salary prompted John to hang out his own shingle and enter private practice. There he lasted 36 years! His ventures into partnerships, real estate, business management were so successful,

John, "at the risk of appearing immodest, noted that his net worth was in the 'millionaire class.' In my wildest dreams, during the hungry years of the Great Depression, I never envisioned my abilities to achieve what I have. I don't know if it was luck or brains, possibly a little of both..."

P.S. John used to come to the reunions (in the later years with Trish). He loved presenting a stand-up comedy routine as part of the evening's entertainment...when he could get Myer off the stage!

Manny, Nathan and Yetta Cohen—Nat's story

Father Harry Cohen was born in Lodz, Poland, at that time a textile centre called the Manchester of Poland. The family owned a jute mill. Because of the economic and political turmoil caused by World War I, he immigrated to Canada in 1919, where he met and married Montrealer Ida Shapiro. He soon realized his Canadian dream of being independent when he became a scrap metal dealer, later switching to the more profitable coal business.

Manny was born in 1924 on Victoria Day, or what he, now fully bilingual and full of humour, called *Jour Dollard des Ormeaux* as the French named it. His sister Yetta was born in 1926; brothers Nathan in 1928, and Abe in 1934.

The Depression created many business opportunities for Harry, and he became known as a *shvitzer* or hustler. Among his varied occupations, Harry sold items at the *Jean Talon Market,* frequented by Italian immigrants. It was here Manny, aged 10, met his future wife, Mary Nanni, whom he married in 1947. Manny, aged 11, was helping his father distribute chickens; he had lost an eye when an anti-Semitic bully attacked him with a stick.

Manny joined the Y in 1931, aged 7. "The Y was a bastion, the Y was my home-away-from-home." What began as a place to hang out turned into a life-long commitment, including a 17-year stint as a part-time boxing coach. Manny also boxed for the Y, winning the Golden Gloves in 1942. The purple and pink silk robe he wore was recently donated to the Y. He was assistant coach in 1943 when they won the *Jack Dempsey Trophy* with the most championships.

Mother Ida died in 1938 following a lengthy illness, leaving Harry to raise four young childen. Unable to cope, he put the three oldest children into the Montreal Hebrew Orphans' Home, and sent the baby to live with his sister, Sarah Berenbaum. Manny was also taken in by his aunt when he was 16—when most children were 'graduated' out of the Home.

While in the Home, Manny first became involved in boxing at the Davis Y, and when he left his MHOH facility at 16, he headed back to the Y to continue the sport he loved.

In 1939, Harry returned to Poland to sell the family-owned jute business. His Montreal family never heard from him again. In 1946, they learned he had perished in Auschwitz, the only Canadian to die in the Holocaust. Manny moved out of his aunt's house in '47 after the family cut ties because he had married a non-Jew. They reconciled three decades later.

Being part of the Y also helped Manny in his business life. His friends in the *schmata* trade preferred to deal with him than strangers, and encouraged him to start his own business. He worked for over 50 years as a manufacturer of industrial pressing equipment.

Today, Manny lives with Mary, his wife of 54 years, in Chomedy. They have three children, David, Ann and Bernice, and six grandchildren. At one of the MHOH reunions, the whole Cohen clan attended to learn more about their father's background as a young man.

Moishe Cohen (Morris Cowan)

Moishe Cohen was in the Montefiore Home in the same group as Jack Jacobson, and bar mitzvahed with Abe Sheiner, Willie Morganstein and Dave Cherry. For Morris, this event was a memorable one. He recalled the kindness of the staff.

He later became an inventor of items used in the medical field and did well in real estate. Most important to Morris was his work as a playwright. His wife Ruth informed us from their New York home that he died in the summer of 1987, only a few months after writing the following *Ode to Life*. It attests to the appreciation he felt for the many people who enriched his life, and most significantly, to his capacity for deep love. "Perhaps his experience at the orphanage contributed to this...I know his time at the orphanage was one of fun and camaraderie...a positive experience..."

Morris Cowan wrote a celebration of his life in May 1987 as he lay dying in his hospital bed. To the reader, it is both depressing and uplifting at the same time. It points out the necessity of enjoying every moment of your life every moment you draw breath, of making the most of your life...for "who knows what tomorrow will bring." Perhaps this ability for a positive attitude was his survival mechanism, derived from his years in the orphanage. Partial excerpts follow...

> "When lying helpless in bed, one's energy ebbs slowly into nothingness, unable to contribute even a single thought to life's ramifications. Its every passion, every sound and movement triggered by passion. The plucking of a musical instrument. The full-throated song. All mundane activities are now so full of need and purpose. Ha, to partake of these! When, Oh God?
>
> One can be fully grateful for all life's blessings when one is fully deprived.
>
> Only then do all of life's nuances stand out in full colour and necessity...Oh, to be part of it again. To participate, to contribute with all of one's ability. What a joy! Will it ever be mine again? If yes, I promise never again to squander one ounce of it...to contribute all I can where I am needed.
>
> Of all the plays I've written, this is by far the greatest. It fathoms the rock bottom of life. No drama can equal it. Its finesse cannot be equalled. This is life in the raw...touches the raw nerves of life. What can be more basic?...Suffering is part of the grand scheme of life. In its misery it embellishes life's true purpose, which is more and more life.
>
> Life's imperfection is also the school of basic learning...We can complain, but to no avail. There are no listeners, only law-givers. Death is a small price to pay for relief.
>
> This is my ode, to the joy of life, to the means and people, friends, relatives who made it possible...my praise of life's wisdom, even its cruelty, for who knows a better way. The idea is to be whole again. Life was and can be beautiful again if given a second chance. But life is not that kind...This ode is

> to the eternity of life and its immutable laws, harsh as they are; for without them, life would cease...Dignity is all. We came and leave with it whatever its measure...
> Does life offer a second chance? Probably not...a second chance might be selfish...What have I done to deserve a second chance? Still, we hope against hope to be the chosen one. So, accept the inevitable, final, bitter pill. Suck it to the last grain and say it was good, certainly the best available. Lay your pen down, man. This has got to end. You get A+ for effort but F- for intuition and insight. Count your blessings and depart in dignity...
> Life is change and without opportunities there can be no change. Opposites struggle for position retrenchment so there is ever renewal, and the earth is forever reborn and refreshed.
> You have reached the pinnacle of wisdom, and so relax and protest no more. Farewell."

Morris passed away two months after completing his *Ode to Life*. His writings are his legacy.

Lester Dick Remembers

The move from California back to Montreal was made in 1928 when Lester was only 2 and already motherless. His father was forced to move in with his extended family so he could try to eke out a living for himself and his only child. A grandmother, aunts and uncles cared for Lester for about five years before being forced to put him in the Montefiore Home in 1933, aged 6. Only a short while later, Lester was transferred over to the Montreal Home on Claremont.

Trying so hard to remember why, Lester reasons that his uncles must have quietly given his father some money so he could be sent to a 'better' home—where there was more activity.

One of Lester's fondest memories of those early years was waiting for the school bus after school (Berthelet); when he came out every day he found his father waiting to see him before the bus departed for the Home. With a smile on his face, he recalls running into a bear-hug of his father's arms who greeted him with love. Says Lester today, "It must have been love, because he had to walk miles to get to the school (from his apartment at 9 Rachel East), but it must have been closer than the Home because I never saw him there."

Lester remembers being a good kid, but being in the wrong place at the wrong time. He recalls getting the strap for mischief caused by other boys near him. When questioned about his memories of the Home, a look of puzzlement crossed his face as he related how he and other boys lined up to get 'a needle'—6-8 times a year. Upon reflection now, he wondered if perhaps they were some sort of guinea pigs.*

(*Ed's. Note: no-one else has mentioned this!)

He had a small group of friends; they spent time together doing homework at meals or just sitting around. Some of these included Charles Berman, Moishe Diner, Morris Miller, Sam Rasminsky, Harry Schwartz, Sylvia Savitsky, Eva Gottlieb, Annie Reisler. When Lester came to his first reunion in the mid-90s, he felt chills all over his body as he entered the room and recognized so many friends from his past.

A pleasant experience for Lester was singing in the *Shaar Hashomayim* Synagogue choir (for three years) with 'brother' Harvey Israel. He wonders if the other choir members were professional as he had been told there were payments made to sing in the choir. He doesn't remember if he ever was on the receiving end! What he does remember, with happiness, is singing with the choir upstairs on the day of his Bar Mitzvah, and going down to participate in his Bar Mitzvah Service, then going back up again to resume his singing. He was 12 at the time; he said that if one had no mother, they could be Bar Mitzvah at 12 instead of waiting until age 13.

Among the added activities at the Montreal Home was swimming. Interested youngsters, and Lester was very interested, could enroll at the new Mortimer B. Davis (Mt. Royal) Y for instruction and participation in swim meets. And indeed, once out of the Home and up at Sunshine Camp, one of the counsellors there helped him with his diving, resulting in his earning a Junior championship.

Lester left the Home shortly after his Bar Mitzvah—he had been there six years. He moved in with his father, still on Rachel Street. He finished public school at Mount Royal P.S., and attended Baron Byng High for grade 8. He left to go to work. His first job was in the cutting room at a children's wear manufacturer near Atwater Street. During his early working years, he showed an interest in pattern-making. So, at night, he went to a pattern-making school near St. Catherine and McGill—*The Fashion Arts Academy*. After two years, armed with his diploma, he went to work for *Independent Skirt,* bluffing along the way that he was experienced.

During the war, Lester worked in fashion. His father, a pacifist, arranged to keep him out of the service. By his third call-to-arms, the war was almost over. He married in 1947, fathered four children over 13 years, then divorced in the early 60s. Over the years Lester worked hard and made himself into a top-flight designer in the *schmata* trade, in which he worked for over 30 years until his retirement in 1995. His last few jobs assured him a most comfortable living, working or not.

He met Irma in 1967, married her in '74 and is living 'happily ever after', in Kirkland, Quebec (on Montreal's West Island). He is a member of a choir, *The Retreads,* composed mainly of seniors. While his diving days are over, he's happy with aquatics. And golf, don't ask! This love gave him and four friends the impetus to start the *Green Valley Golf Club* in the Laurentians. He plays many times a week at the *Dorval Golf Club,* still trying to break 100! Irma sends him out as often as possible!

At the time of writing, Lester had a physical setback and now requires kidney dialysis three times a week. His children and grandchildren have been invaluable supports for Lester during this time. While Irma fusses over him daily, and doggy Cindy is so glad to have him back at home!

There is a troubling postscript to Lester's story. Several months after his intitial interview, he phoned Judy Gordon with a new memory, brought to the surface by an episode of the Oprah Show. He vividly remembers being molested by a Home staff member when he was about 10 years old. It happened on a bench in the dimly lit gymnasium. Lester said he has held this incident deep in his heart and soul for 65 years...ashamed and embarrassed. His heart feels a bit lighter now.

Muriel Fishman

Muriel was put into the Westmount Home in 1934 at about the age of 10 when her mother was hospitalized with tuberculosis. Her father took her, her younger brother and sister by streetcar to "check into the Home." They got off the streetcar at Sherbrooke and Claremont, were getting ready to walk up the hill, when Muriel started to "cry a river." A policeman came over to ask what the problem was. "I must have been traumatized from that moment, the fact of going to the Home, that I ceased to have any memory of what followed or of my years in the Home. No memory as to activities, of school, of playmates—although I can remember summer camp...but only the swimming and singing the Bacarole in harmony."

Muriel does remember that her sister sleep-walked, and that she (Muriel) wet the bed. But she had wiped out the memory of being obliged to bring down her wet sheet and show everyone in the dining room what she had done. Another boy who did the same thing told her this story. Someone else told her that one of the Supervisors confronted her in the dining room with the words, "You have done it again."

Strange as it seems to Muriel, she remembers the names of a lot of people and children during that period, although she has no memory of playing with them or sharing activities with them. "But, as luck would have it, I was able to run into them later on in life and enjoy them as if I had known them all my life." The MHOH reunions granted the opportunity to see many of these 'old' friends, and Muriel was able to put faces to some of the names in her head. "The fact that I can remember names and have a good feeling, indicates not a hostile thought (of my time in the Home), but the opposite."

Muriel also remembers that once, upon returning to the city after summer camp, on the urging or counselling of Irving Layton (he was a counsellor there at that time), the children were organized to turn over the tables in the dining room in protest of the bad food. A fight ensued, and the Director, Mr. Bye, was punched in the stomach. The Home was disbanded soon after, perhaps "as a result of all that."

Muriel guesses that she was in the Home about two years, when she, about 12 years old, and her family were reunited at home. Although if that is the case, she didn't enter until about 1939/40...the Westmount Home closed in 1942. Muriel went to work right away in a hat factory—on a machine. She later became a legal secretary. And for the past several years she has been a care-giver for an elderly aunt.

Muriel has since become a great asset in assisting with the MHOH reunions, and enjoys the bonding that takes place there and is enjoyed in turn. She certainly smiles a lot!

Arnold Irving Golub

(The following is excerpted from the Rabbi's sermon at Arnold's funeral, late March 1998)

The *Chassidic* teaching of balancing the good and the evil in life, the experiences which exalt and depress us, is typical of the life of Arnold Golub. His daughter, Marilyn, recalled it as the way she best remembered her father's philosophy. When something good happened, he would calmly greet the occasion and lessen the unbridled joy which he might have expressed. When confronted by tragedy, he balanced the difficulty with the belief that things could have been worse. He looked for the positive side.

When you read Arnold's story, he was fortunate to have this disposition!

Arnold was born in Poland near the Russian border in 1912. One of five children of Mordechai and Perel Leah Golub, he lost both his parents to an influenza epidemic when he was two years old. Raised by relatives who lived next door, his family was attacked by Polish and Russian soldiers who looted their home. His youngest brother, a baby, was killed as was his eldest, Simchah. He was saved by his older sister, Chayah Brachah, who covered him in a feather bed and admonished him to be silent. Kind Jews in Montreal, rescuing orphans of a certain age. brought him and his sister Ann to Canada. He was about six. World War I was just ending. A beautiful child, he was adopted by the J. B. Miller family, while his sister, Ann, was sent to

Vancouver. After a few years and with the help of the very compassionate Mrs. Miller, Ann was adopted by her sister-in-law in Montreal and so Arnold had a real family member close by. He helped out in the Miller family department store and had some adventures as a boy that he would retell for years.

At about age nine, with family trouble in his adoptive home, he was sent to the Montefiore Orphanage where he embarked on a long time pattern of working days and studying at nights. Leaving the home in 1928, he was apprenticed to a plumber, Becker, acquiring his life trade. What a difference from the rabbinical family his father had come from and yet, Arnold embodied many of the fine qualities of that earlier generation: kindness, gentleness and sweetness. Arnold roomed with a family and pursued a living by day and knowledge by night. His contacts with the kind Miller family allowed him to aid the reuniting of his family. Mrs. Miller sponsored his older sister Clara and allowed her to pay back her passage from her salary. She was then able to do the same for a large portion of his extended family.

In 1926, at the height of the depression, work was scarce in Montreal and Arnold decided to go to Palestine and become a pioneer member of *Po'alei Tzion.* He worked in fields and orchards but wanted to live in the city. When all of the jobs there were given to family men, he took a job, as a British subject, doing road construction for the government. Those were dangerous times and his learning of Arabic and friendship with local Arabs saved his life. With war in Europe imminent, he decided to return to Canada. On his way he passed through Italy, France and England, reasoning that there would be little left to see after the war. His luggage went down with the *Athena,* the first ship sunk in the war, while he arrived safely on the *Antonia.*

In Montreal at just the right time in 1939, he met a former Montefiore orphanage friend, Gertrude Miretsky, who was home on vacation, visiting her family members. Smitten, he pursued her to New York and they attended the World's Fair. He worked as a plumber in Montreal, at one point hiring an orphanage Alumnus, Myer Gordon, as an apprentice. Then, on a visit, moved in with his mother's sister in Brooklyn and opened a garage.

He excelled at anything mechanical. By 1941 he was working as a plumber and was sent by his union to prepare the military camps in Virginia. By 1942 he was drafted into the American Army. His honesty about the number of languages he spoke led him to be passed over as suspicious by the Army. Instead, he at first became a medic, and then volunteered for construction duty. After a return to *Fort Dix* for basic training, he was sent to Iceland for the remainder of the war. In January 1946, discharged at last, he returned to New York and married Gertie in September. She saw in him an honest and sincere young man, while he knew her and her whole family.

Living near his Aunt and Uncle on Avenue A, he worked days as a plumber wherever his union sent him and at nights, with the help of the G.I. Bill, learned all there was to know about heating and cooling. Had he the money to open his own business, he might have become wealthy. Instead he settled into a lifelong pattern of hard work. As the children were born, Gilda in 1948 and Marilyn in 1951, he would often go away to work, returning to his family for the weekends. His job, as a master plumber, eventually included estimating. His job as a father included idolizing his daughters and taking them to the *World's Fairgrounds,* playgrounds and to the parks where his family of cousins and his Aunt and Uncle met.

In the summers, they embarked on an adventure trip by car to Montreal to see the extended family. On the way he would plot the sightseeing attractions of upstate New York so that each trip was a little different. This pattern continued until his retirement in 1976 with some time out for various injuries he had sustained on the job. Gertie expanded her comptometer work hours to help fill in. The family eventually moved from Brooklyn to Long Island City to Bayside.

Gertie and Arnold got to see their daughters marry people they took to as their own sons. During one of his recuperations from injury, Arnold spent Fridays babysitting grandchildren. Then the family would all come together for a traditional Shabbat dinner. As his family became more far flung, they continued to visit back and forth to Long Island and Milwaukee and later to Florida where they wintered for Arnold's last nine years. As the number of grandchildren increased, Arnold loved to take their pictures, one of his lasting hobbies was to take walks and play games with them.

After retirement, Gertie and Arnold traveled extensively. They revisited Israel forty years later, culminating his Zionist longings; they traveled to Vancouver for a family *simchah* and toured California and the National Parks. They maintained the social activities with their group of twelve close friends and others, and kept close ties, as always with their cherished families. In retirement he continued to show the intelligence he had always had. He read avidly on many topics, particularly photography and the stock market, which became a special hobby. He researched and worked out the genealogy of his entire family and became a fine bridge player. He watched sports on TV and, as Florida became a regular winter destination, expanded his Shabbat synagogue attendance to include lectures and discussion groups. For more than fifty years, Arnold was a member of the Odd Fellows and attended their yearly gathering in the Catskills.

In 1988, his health began to fail. Asthma kept him from telling stories (in game form) to his grandchildren. He underwent open-heart surgery.

Yet, Arnold was still able to reflect on, and balance his happy and sad occasions. He survived a life most difficult, yet derived comfort from having made a safe refuge for his family after his initial tragic beginning. He passed away in 1997.

Ben Gordon

After his one year in the Montefiore Home, Ben was taken by his mother to live with her in New York (brother Myer remained in the orphanage). He was 12 and a rather difficult child. So his mother put him into a military school to teach him some discipline. She returned to Montreal in 1938 after her sister Annie had passed away, and married her brother-in-law. So, Ben became part of his cousins' family of six boys, counting himself and Myer. He later served overseas in the Canadian Army.

After the war, Ben married Toby Schwartz and they had two children, Gail and Mordy and, later, five grandchildren. Most of his working life was spent at *Gelco Furniture* and *Berman Knitting Mills*. His hobby was movies—he went to see them as often as he could! Ben was a dedicated volunteer for the *Knights of Pythias*. His hard work earned him the prestigious title of Grand Chancellor and he spent many, many years working for the success of the organization's many projects, including visiting veterans at St. Anne de Bellevue Veterans' Hospital and patients at the Verdun / Douglas Psychiatric Hospital. He was always thinking of other people, and, like his brother Myer, he never forgot to send family cards for birthdays and anniversaries... there was always a card in the mail!

Ben enjoyed his children and his extended family—Toby had a lot of brothers and sisters. She died in the 70s. Ben remarried in the early '80s, but this wife, too, passed away—after only one year. Ben, himself, died in 1987.

Myer Gordon

Myer was born in 1921 in Montreal to Russian emigrees from New York. His brother Ben was 6 years older. When his father died from TB Myer was 2 1/2. His mother tried to manage with the help of family and friends. But at the age of five, Reva Gordon was forced to put the boys in the orphanage, the Montefiore Home, as it was in the neighbourhood. She then went back to New York City to work at *The May Company*.

The following year she returned to Montreal for the specific purpose of taking her boys back to New York with her. The Supervisor suggested that she take Bennie, a troublemaker, but leave Myer, "because he was such a nice boy" in the Home! For some reason, she took this advice and left with Ben, *sans* Myer. To this day, Myer swears he holds no regrets nor bitterness about this incident.

Myer's 'big brothers' when he entered the Home were Willie Label and Willie Morgenstern. They looked after him, saw that he was dressed properly, took him to school, and helped where possible. He was a quiet, skinny kid. His mother used to send him $2. every few months to buy a malted milkshake to fatten him up. By the age of 12, Myer had his own 'little brothers', Moishe Letnick and Moe Ticker.

Home staff also looked after him very well and he enjoyed the food and the clean clothing that was supplied (especially for the Holidays)...the boys would go to the factory for new suits...that was enough to make him happy. He was an average student at Bancroft Public School. His best school memory is of the now famous Weider boys—Ben and Joe—good school friends. He also remembers "We had to go to and from school on St. Urbain, north of Mount Royal, via Villeneuve to avoid the streetcars on Mount Royal. One day, I decided to take a chance and go home via Mount Royal. I remember that, when I reached Jeanne Mance, there was only a treed field where a few years later the Mortimer B. Davis Y was built."

About age 10, Myer (and the other boys) went daily to the *Talmud Torah* for Hebrew lessons. When they got back to the Home, Yiddish lessons awaited. Many were in the Home choir which sang for the weekly Shabbat Services. He was a soprano in those days!

In 1934, Myer was Bar Mitzvahed with four others, whose names he could not remember until 1989...55 years later at the first Toronto reunion! That was when Benny Garber arrived bearing a wonderful photo of the five Bar Mitzvah boys...Norman Bydoff, Earl Greenberg, Abe Sokoloff, and, of course, Benny and Myer. He was so thrilled to have the photo; it now stands in a prominent place on his grand piano!

It seems odd that Myer has so few real memories of being in the Montefiore Home. One memory is of the fun the boys had after a social function in the downstairs hall, when they would sneak down to grab leftover food. He does recall finding pennies! And he does remember that he was much of a 'loner' in those days. As a teenager in the Home, he would think nothing of walking miles, or taking streetcars, to get to some place of interest to him. He remembers occasionally being disciplined by Max Matt, with a yardstick. Max, being softhearted, forewarned him, giving him time to place a phonebook in his pants. As a result, his behind felt no pain! Max was like that to all the mischievous kids...warning them in plenty of time to run for the phone-books. Myer never saw any sign of abuse (of any kind) that seemed to have existed in other, church-run, institutions.

Myer wasn't a real athlete, but enjoyed soccer, boxing, and ice-skating in the small Home yard. He still wonders why he only had one skate while Sam Rasminsky had two! At the ripe age of 13—in 1934—Myer fought in the Golden Gloves...won one, lost one. That was also the year he had to go to work. No one ever asked if he wanted to go to high school, and no money was supplied to cover the minimal costs, so he was unable to attend. Instead, he went alone by streetcar to City Hall to obtain a working permit. Which he still has to this day!

His first job was pulling basting on vests in a men's clothing factory for the princely sum of $3.50 a week. And that was having a relative as foreman, his uncle Harry Vatch! His big promotion was to pull basting on coats for $7.00 a week.

In June 1936, there were rumours that the Montefiore Home was going to close. Myer, now 15 years old, took his fibre-glass basket (stored today with his original work permit!) and walked the three blocks to the home of his Aunt Annie (his mother's sister) and Uncle Harry, and said, "Here I am!" They took him in.

There were already three sons in the family—Joe, aged 16; Ruby, 14; and Bram 4. Another brother, Gordie, was born in February 1938. Aunt Annie passed away only six months later, in October. Myer's mother returned to Montreal with brother, Ben, and soon after, married Uncle Harry, so that the boys would have a mother, not a strange step-mother. So, Myer's four cousins also became his step-brothers...

His next job was at *Art Novelty,* a ladies' pleating and embroidery manufacturer...he can still embroider and sew! Then he went to work as a packer for *Marvel Dress,* owned by Mr. Louis Brisken, father to Julius who became one of the Home's benefactors. From there, he got work as a shipper at *Decklebaum and Korny Dress.*

In June 1941, Myer was 20 and decided to join the Canadian Air Force. He trained for three months in St. Thomas, Ontario, during which time he was playing lacrosse and was hit in an ear by the ball. Following training, in January 1942, he was shipped to Gander, Newfoundland, which at that point was considered overseas. He worked in Quartermaster Stores, dispensing uniforms and supplies. "Gander was a God-forsaken place, especially with no women on base for eight months!" That is also where doctors discovered Myer had a perforated ear drum as a result of his lacrosse accident. He had many hospital visits while stationed over the next 3 years across Canada, from Vancouver to Gander. He is proud even today that one of his Gander buddies, Douglas Lee, remains a good friend, even though he has lived in Australia for many years.

In December 1944 Myer was given a medical discharge. He held only odd jobs during 1945, but in 1946, his mother and uncle moved to Sherbrooke, Quebec...Uncle Harry was offered a job he couldn't refuse, with *Rubin Brothers,* men's clothing manufacturers. Ruby, Bram and Myer all worked at the factory. Myer later got a job assisting the photographer of *The Sherbrooke Record.* He was also photographer for the *Sherbrooke Castor Hockey Team,* for whom the now famous 'coloured line' played...Manny McIntyre, Ozzie & Herbie Carnegie. The latter has since become even more famous through his work with a Foundation he initiated in Toronto, working with children to make them future productive members of society.

The family returned to Montreal in 1949 where Myer worked at many more odd jobs. He became service manager of *Thor Washers* in 1951, the year he married for the first time! His wife had a young daughter, Carol (aged four) and they had three children together—Marilyne, Alan and Ian. Myer formally adopted Carol. In 1955, Myer went back to work in 'ladies' clothing' as a shipper. Given an opportunity to become a commissioned salesman, he hit the road for northern Ontario. By the early 60s, his marriage was in jeopardy, resulting in a move to Ottawa by himself, in 1964. After five years struggling to support his children, things fell apart...his divorce was finalized and his $300. car was on its last legs. "I was forced to move to Toronto 'C.O.D.'" His friend, Lenny Schechtman, shared his apartment with him for three months; then Lenny, also separated, reconciled with his wife. Myer stayed in the apartment.

Myer got lucky when he met Murray Kates who ran a ladies' wear sales agency. He bought him a car and gave him work—but six months later, his floundering began again and he suffered an emotional breakdown in December 1970. While still hospitalized and sedated, he received a call from an executive of *Variety Club,* offering him work. In February, he was hired as manager of the Club Rooms of the *Variety Club*....his boss was Sam Shopsowitz, Chief Barker, and "the sweetest man I ever knew." A year later, Myer refused to keep the Club open until 3 a.m. (after legal hours). He was fired, and floundered for a few years when he remarried in '74..."not a very good marriage." But it lasted seven years, during which time Myer was able to purchase a small business. The separation came in February 1981.

"On Labour Day weekend, at a singles' outing in Parry Sound, I met Judy, also separated since February. It was Friday night; we talked, we danced, we talked and talked. When we met for breakfast, we talked some more, and by noon, we knew we were in love and wanted to marry." It took six months for the divorces to come through and on May 16, 1982, Myer and Judy married.

Myer has continued to run several small businesses, had many surgeries (some call him the 'bionic man'), plays poker, golf, and joins Judy in a volunteer choir. Judy, in turn, joined him in his *B'nai Brith* Lodge, both rising to the lofty position of president. They were also clowns for 15 years...at children's parties, seniors and handicapped children's residences, parades, and walkathons. They babysit, do movie extra work and look after the MHOH reunions and *Mishpocha.*

Between them, they have 12 grandchildren and two great-grandchildren. Myer has celebrated his 81st birthday.

Eva Gottlieb Goldberg

Eva was born in 1929 in White Russia. Her parents immigrated to Montreal when she was 9 months old. Shortly after that her father passed away, leaving her mother with 6 children. As a single parent, she found it very difficult to raise all the children because of the Depression. She was forced to place Eva, her sister Freda, and brother Jackie into the Montreal Hebrew Orphans' Home.

"In the Home, there were good times along with memories that I would rather forget. Sunshine Camp was the best, and we all couldn't wait for school to close for the summer, so we would all go to camp."

Freda, Jackie and Eva were in the Home for 5 years, 1935-1940, when they went back to live with their mother who, at that time, was able to look after them with a careful budget.

Eva became a very successful hairdresser. In 1945 she met her husband Jack Goldberg. He was a jack of all trades, but enjoyed photography the most...it became his long lasting profession. He opened up his own photo business, known as *Vogue Studio* in Montreal. It was very popular, and that name is still not forgotten.

Eva and Jack had five children, three boys and two girls, "all happy, intelligent, good natured and successful." Because of the political situation, their children moved to Toronto. Jack and Eva followed soon after.

"Sadly I became a widow in 1994. Although heart-broken, I picked myself up and joined a couple of musical groups who go to entertain the sick in hospitals, senior homes, shopping centres, etc. I enjoy my life very much but always say a prayer to my beloved Jack who I know is always at my side."

Sister Freda married Harold Sperling in 1943. They had two children, both girls. Freda is now deceased. Brother Jackie's whereabouts are unknown.

Earl Greenberg

At the age of five, Earl Greenberg and four of his five brothers and sisters were put in the Montefiore Orphans' Home in 1925. Earl was the second youngest...his sister Helen was three. He had an older sister Ann and two older brothers, Harry & Joe. The eldest, Freda, did not go into the Home. The others went in because their mother had passed away and their father was very ill with ulcers and could not look after them by himself.

"My earliest recollection is getting on the train with a little woman...we lived in Ottawa...to go to the orphanage. I remember her because the smell of her wet fur coat is with me to this day. My general reaction to the Home was positive—I loved being there...until I was around 10 years old. About that time I remember feeling very lonely and jealous of the other kids because they all had visitors on the weekends. I wondered why I had none. Until one day, when I was 12, the kids all yelled at me that I had a visitor. I was in the basement at the time, looked up and saw a man at the top of the stairs. It was my father—the one time he could manage to visit me in seven years!"

Earl realized later in life that his father was so sick and so poor that he couldn't make the fare from Ottawa where he still lived. The only thing he recalls from that visit is that, when his father came down the stairs after greeting him, he asked for a glass of water so he could take his baking soda for his ulcers. Earl didn't see him again for years.

There was no closeness in the Home with his siblings either. The older boys were in a different group, while sisters Ann and Helen had their own group of playmates. As the older ones reached age 16, they were sent home to their father.

Earl created his own birthday. He never knew his actual birthdate. He chose August 8th because another friend in the Home, Abie (Avramel) Stoffmaker celebrated his birthday on August 7th. Years later, when Earl needed his official papers to join the army, he learned he was really born on February 12th!

Once a week was shower night, followed by a search for head lice by a female staff member. Earl remembers that she used the same comb for each child, dipping it first in coal oil for 'sanitation' purposes.

There seemed to be a lot of keys to various rooms in the Home, 'found' and hidden by the boys for their own purposes. Hy Jacobson had one for a room next to the boys' dorm—a room filled with donated, used clothing from which Earl and Hy used to select some extra pants and shirts.

"I have beautiful memories of the summer holidays, spent in country camps at many different locations. I was very aware of other kids on the street who envied me because they never left the city in the summer. We had mass birthday and masquerade parties, good swimming facilities and lots of fun. I remember Mr. Cooper, the camp supervisor, and his wife...on the odd occasion he went swimming in the lake and would let me tag along, watching me carefully."

Earl has a confession to make. In his public school days, about 65 years ago, he was afraid to show his report card to Max Matt. So he learned to forge his name. "Max, you never did sign my report cards."

Earl and the other boys went to *shul* every Saturday in the Home... the girls never went. He recalls singing in the choir, but trying to hide beforehand to get out of it. "The *Shamas* taught us our *mutter.*" He was Bar Mitzvahed with four other boys, one of them Benny Garber, one of his best friends. Another was Myer Gordon...the other two are mentioned in Myer's bio.

At the Home, Thursday night's meal was hated by all—"it was chopped herring which ended up in napkins in our pockets and...then to the toilets!" Ben Garber hated porridge. All the children can remember Max Matt standing behind him and pushing in his cheeks so he would swallow, saying, "Eat it, Benny; it's good for you!" (Benny's porridge ended up in packets on the street.) "I remember breaking into the food pantry with some of my friends, stealing fruit and prunes, which we ate on a walk outside the grounds, usually on a weekend." In spite of it all, there was really never any real physical punishment.

The children often helped with kitchen chores. Earl's fondest memory of his early teens is of a cute little girl named Sarah, very shy, who held hands with him in the dirty dish water (as mentioned earlier). In a 1991 conversation with Sarah's daughter, Earl learned that she had changed her name to Connie and she did remember Earl—he was very cute—but she preferred to forget about the dishwashing episode. Earl called Connie and told her, "I'm 71, my hair is grey, I have a pot belly and chicken legs. But my wife Sandy still thinks I'm cute!" In their conversation, Connie told Earl she had only been in the Home for 11 months and then lived with her aunt. She was bright and wanted to go to university, but her aunt didn't think that was necessary.

Earl and Connie met again over 60 years later at one of the reunions...which brought back the original memory! But they didn't even recognize each other at first! They talked some more and Connie told Earl "the rest of the story"...how at age 65 she did go to back to school, to university, and graduated with a degree in Science.

He has other memories of those early days and discovering girls. Under the stairs to the basement was a little cubby-hole. This became the hideaway for experimental trysts between some of the 12-13 year old boys and girls. Earl remembers one girl, who shall remain nameless, grabbing him by his hand and pulling him into this cubby-hole for a little 'hanky-panky'. Some called it 'meditating' others 'fooling around' but whatever it was called, it was one popular sport!

A popular basement sport was touch-football, played with a ball made out of rags. Earl played soccer (a game he loves to watch even today), hockey and sports, and made a lot of friends during his teens, even though he had started having stomach problems and spent a lot of time on the top floor of the Home, in the nurse's room being sick. While Earl was developing ulcers, others were sleepwalking!

Abe Senderoff was another good soccer player and fan, so he and Earl became friends. One of their games—Earl would stand on top of the tall stair posts, jump off and Abe would catch him. Never a complaint, so Abe must have been really trustworthy! Earl also recalls Abe getting up early in the morning, and sneaking down to the kitchen where the 10-gallon milk cans were kept. Using a ladle, he would scoop up and drink the cream from the top! Abe was well organized as well as thirsty...he and Willie Label would faithfully line up their shoes each night for polishing.

Earl ran away from the Home when he was about 15 years old...he had $21 in the bank from a part-time job. Without telling anybody, he took a train to Ottawa, longing to see how his family was. All his siblings were now living there, except for Helen. He was devastated to see the conditions in which his father was living. The house was like a lean-to, ready to collapse, without inside plumbing.

Max Matt came after Earl a couple of days later and took him back to the Home. (Max, you were probably happy to come get me as it gave you the day off!) He remained there until 1936 when he turned 16 and the Home closed. He had spent 11-12 years there; now he joined his family in an apartment. When his father died one year later, he moved in with his sister Freda and then to a boarding house with his brothers.

After a couple of years, he moved back to Montreal and worked for the Royal Air Force Ferry Command during the war years. He tried to join the Army but was rejected because of his ulcers. "The British pilots were forming a soccer team, and when Abe Shein (also from the Home) recommended me, I got a job there (as a civilian)—mainly because I played soccer. I never had the opportunity to further my education once I left the Home as I needed to be self-supporting."

Later, Earl spent a year in Halifax working in an aircraft factory for the war effort. Then he returned to Montreal and took a job on an iron ore freighter on Lake Superior for *Canadian Steamship Lines.* "I jumped ship after two weeks in the middle of the night without a penny's pay because of the anti-Semitic atmosphere...I was the only Jew on board. I hitch-hiked back to Ottawa, sleeping in fields at night. One night in the rain I found refuge on a house porch. The lady of the house saw me, took me in and fed me a beautiful breakfast in the morning. The kindness of strangers!"

In his early 20s, Earl looked up another friend from the Home, Louis Bloom, and they went to work on a farm picking fruit for several months. Earl was so poor that Louis bought him clothes at Eatons. Years later, at one the reunions when they met again in the early 90s, Earl slipped Louis an envelope containing $50. to repay him for his kindness.

Earl so much liked life on the farm that he spent one summer pitching hay at a farm in Pickering, and another working inside a quonset hut on a mushroom farm—he was never able to escape the dark, hot, moist, smelly atmosphere there!

Back to sister Freda's he went and sold shoes at *La Roque* Department Store in Ottawa. Searching and restless, Earl soon headed for Toronto where Mendel Raffalovitch, one of the older boys' group in the Home, helped him by letting him stay at his house until Earl was able to get organized and settled on his own. Earl also remembers that the older Alumni paid for his tuition at *Beaux Arts* for art lessons, though he didn't stay very long—he was young and didn't feel he had the talent to continue after seeing the other students' work.

He met his future wife, Sandy, in Toronto, and went back to selling shoes downtown. Three years later they married and moved to Chicago where two of his three children were born. They moved back to Toronto after five years. Earl has been self-employed for the last 35 years in the industrial surplus business. He and Sandy have three childen and seven grandchildren. "We are truly blessed."

Earl considers himself lucky to have been in the Home, considering his family's circumstances and the times. His regret is that he can never tell his parents that he knew how much they gave up to have their children cared for, without getting anything in return. "We are lucky compared to them. They didn't even have enough to eat. I think about them every night. My background has influenced the way I live my life and how I brought up my children. It has paid off. My children are fine human beings and bringing up their kids the same way."

Earl recalls an anecdote about his older sister Ann...she never really got over her poor beginnings. Though she married well, until the day she died, in 1988, she always left over food on her plate for her father.

Beatrice Sabbath Hock—Volunteer in the Montreal Home

"Many years ago (in the early 30's) I was asked to help children at the Montreal Hebrew Orphans' Home with their home-lessons. I was a young teenager and agreed to come once a week (after school)—and kept on coming for ten years!

At first, it was awkward! The children were shy and I was unsure of myself. But, as the months went by, the situation changed. We became friends! I greeted them with a hug; their faces lit up as they related the week's happenings. What happy times we shared before finally settling down to lessons!

At Holiday time (*Hanukah*) I invited them to my home. Such excitement! Some had never been inside a private house. We played games and the winners won prizes. Upon leaving, each one received a bag filled with goodies! This was repeated year after year.

When orphans became sixteen they had to find a job, leave the Home and be on their own. One of them, Sam Baker, wanted desperately to locate a job, and told me it was impossible! It was during the Depression years. One couldn't gain any working experience at all. I said I would try to help. My father, John Louis Sabbath, became my first target. He was owner of one of the largest wholesale jewelry companies in Canada. He eventually agreed to interview Sam Baker and ended up giving him his first job. He worked very hard, and dreamed of the day when he could open his own business and give jobs to his two younger brothers still in the Home.

It all came true! Many years later Sam became head of one of the most successful jewelry manufacturing companies in Canada. We lost touch with each other when I moved to Ottawa. Through the years my father was called upon to give more '1st jobs' to other orphans. He became an example for other business firms to follow...they did!

Another one of the orphans that I took a personal interest in was Mary. She became a journalist, married, and lived in San Francisco. She later became editor of a medical journal. We corresponded through the years and enjoyed a wonderful visit together! She had come such a long way; and I was very proud of her! She died some time later...and 'remembered' me in her will!

So many stories to tell! I recall one of the young girls telling me about a shipment of shoes that arrived at the Home...they were new and shiny. The girls all rushed forward to claim a pair. They didn't fit but it didn't matter...they were brand new!

I was completely out of touch with the Montreal Orphans' Home when that fateful phone call arrived! A complete stranger asking me if I knew Beatrice Sabbath. Yes, I knew her a very long time ago! And thus began a lovely friendship with Myer and Judy Gordon of Toronto! He explained that he was trying to contact former residents of the two Jewish Orphan Homes in Montreal and, evidently some had mentioned my name and asked about me. He invited me to attend the first Reunion in Toronto. It was such a great, heartwarming affair!

Thank you, dear Myer and Judy, for keeping us together ever since! And, for the excellent, delightful monthly *Mishpocha* that keeps us in touch during the year. May we all continue in good health, and meet every year for as long as we're permitted!"

... in a letter from Beatrice Sabbath Hock, Ottawa, October 10 2001

Harvey Israel

"About four years before I was born, my then young, single father was courting a certain lady for some time. I was told that his intentions to marry her were serious. Then, for some reason, he lost interest and soon after met 'my mother', Rose Diner. They married in 1927...I was born in 1928, followed two years later by my sister Shirley.

These were the Depression years and things were tough for most of the population. But my father prospered in his business and we lived rather comfortably, even though other families could hardly make a living. We lived in apartments, first on Sherbrooke Street West near Cote St. Antoine, then moved to Queen Mary and then on to Maplewood.

It was December 1935 when Shirley and I lost our mother...I was seven years old; Shirley five. It was later learned that, had mother lived one more year, with the discovery of the sulfa drug, her pneumonia could then have been cured. A devoted husband and father, our father was devastated at his loss. He found it difficult to ask some of our relations to take us in and look after us.

At this time, it was the practice, when one parent died and left children, to put them in an orphanage. So, three months later, that is what happened to us. On March 15, 1936, I was admitted into The Montreal Hebrew Orphanage (my sister followed later, sometime in

June as we were preparing to leave for Sunshine Camp). I spent two weeks in the isolation ward of the Home's hospital for observation... was I healthy or not. "Needless to say, I was very sad when I watched my father walking down the hill on Claremont Avenue, knowing I could only see him on Sundays, the only day visiting was allowed."

While still in isolation, two other children were admitted to the Home...one named Harvey, and his sister, Shirley Smith. Guess what? These two were the offspring of the woman my father had courted (as noted above). And, coincidentally, both the Smiths and my parents gave their son and daughter the same names!

When I entered the Home, there were about 106 kids (when they disbanded, there remained approximately 40 of us). During my seven years there, we were 'governed' by Superintendent Henry Bye whose job was the overall running of the orphanage. The boys were supervised by a Mr. Levitt, followed by Irving Layton, the well known poet. At the same time, Mr. Maurice Ogulnick was also hired. Both shared the supervision and responsibility. But they could not get along, and Layton was soon dismissed...possibly because they were poles apart in their political thoughts—Ogulnick was to the right, Layton to the far left. So, Ogulnick took over the whole responsibility of looking after the boys. But he had a "very heavy hand and was disliked by the majority of the boys."

The boys and girls were kept in separate quarters. The supervision for the girls was given over to Miss Ida Kaufman, and she was adored by all the girls, my sister said.

The Home was administered by the Baron de Hirsch Institute. We were provided with the basic necessities—food was ample, our clothing was provided for and laundered twice a week. All our clothing had to be numbered—I was assigned No.45. This was done to prevent loss when our laundry was done. We were well-clothed and well-fed. For schooling we travelled to Berthelet School on Ontario Street. For lunch we got back onto our bus and went back to the Home for our midday meal. We frequently ran into anti-Semitism and had fights with the Gentile kids—that was the norm.

"One of my regrets is that we were all under the tough hand of Ogulnick. He was a tyrant, and whenever one of us stepped out of line, he did not hesitate to use his fist. I still bear his lashes from the beatings he administered to me. For example, like eating your porridge in the morning. I must explain that this porridge was cooked the night before, so that, when it was served hot the next morning, it was very lumpy and thick. No milk or sugar was given to make it more appetizing. Should one refuse to eat this concoction, Mr. Ogulnick would be right there and issue an order that if you don't start eating by the count of ten, he would give you a karate chop on the back of your neck. This occurred a number of times to the children. We were affected in other ways as well...we had a courtyard to play in, but never did we venture outside of our building or go down to the corner to buy something.

He did not have any love for the children, although he did have his favourite pets, Oscar Roth and Frankie Baker who are long gone now. No one really liked to come close to him because he always reeked of stale cigar smoke.

I could not 'kowtow' to this dictator...he was a miserable person. Unfortunately, he remained as Home supervisor until the orphanage was closed. Later on he became principal of a *Talmud Torah* School, in which I am sure he did not play the same role as in the orphanage. All I can say is that he could not have liked his job looking after us Home kids.

Mrs. Weisbord gave us Hebrew lessons twice a week and there were daily morning prayer services. At the same time, I had the opportunity to say Kaddish for both my parents...I had the misfortune to also lose my father in 1940. My uncle stepped into the picture. He became our guardian, contributing to our support while in the Home. A bachelor at the time, he loved us two kids. He was a very good man and we loved him.

Every Saturday morning we went to *Shaar Hashomyim* for morning prayers...all the boys had their Bar Mitzvahs there. I had mine, I remember with the well known Rabbi Abramowitz and Cantor Mendelson who officiated. I was Bar Mitzvahed along with Abie Shmoiser who now lives in Florida.

It was not the custom for the Home to throw a party to celebrate any boys' Bar Mitzvahs. No, this was never done. However, I still had family. It was my Auntie Ethel, Uncles Hymie and Isidore, Cousins Lionel, Philip, Harold and Sydney who saw that some fuss was made over me. I also remember Mr. Sam Bazer, from *B & B Banana Imports.* I was so innocent at the time that I never expected to get any gifts, so when Mr. Bazer handed over an envelope to me, I refused to take it until it was pushed into my hands!

We celebrated Passover in our dining hall with two *Seders.* Everybody recited part of the *Haggadah.*

We had some good times, too. The Finestones from the insurance business took an active part in providing extra-curricular activities. There was also Arthur Shalet, one of the top salesmen for the *Millionaire Sardine Company,* who had an 'in' with the movie houses...we got to see the latest features. He was a very generous man, and many a time we had ice cream and soda pop, all due to his generosity.

As school ended in June, we looked forward to going to our summer camp in Ste. Marguerite de Lac Masson, in a very secluded part of the Laurentians. There we had more freedom for ourselves. We were in our glory because Ogulnick was in the background, not given any active supervision. Different counsellors were assigned to the four bunks, all more 'sympatico' than the heavy hand of Ogulnick. Hy Welt was one of my counsellors, "...I was away from the clutches of Ogulnick." I remember counsellors like Gary Gleason, Jack Gross—who became a well known doctor in his field, Charlotte Garfinkle who later married Moe Steinberg—a friend of my cousin, Dr. Lionel Gordon, and many others whose names I can no longer recall.

These were good summers all around; we made life-long friends and participated in many activities. My favourite sport was swimming. I came first in a number of races.

In 1942, the "powers-that-be" decided to disband the entire orphanage and put all of us into foster homes. It was getting too uneconomical to keep such a huge building—one that held only some 40 kids—when it was built for over 100 or more residents. I believe at that time the decision made by the governing body to disband was their philosophy that institutional upbringing of an orphan was not very conducive to raising a child. Besides, I know from my own experience—it's a bit of a trauma, in every sense of the word.

I left the Home when it closed and was put into a foster home with the Kramers. I stayed with them for about a year...I was finishing public school at Edward VII. Then I went to live with the Goldenbergs...I lived with them for over four years, from 1944 to 1948 or '49 and attended Baron Byng High School for three years...I had the opportunity to complete high school, but got too distracted by friends who were not attending any school in any way. Consequently, they affected my studies, much to my regret.

My sister had gotten married by then and suggested that I come and live with her and her husband. I agreed. For the first time in some 12 years, I had a home to share with my own sister. After tenth grade, I found work with *L. Saloman & Sons* as a shipper. My wages were $22.00 per week. I did not take kindly to this job and moved on to hoped-for better fields...employment with *Bluestone Shirt Co.* Mr. Max Bluestone was a wonderful person to work for, and later on, when I told him that I had an opportunity to learn a trade, he wished me well and good luck.

The chance to learn to be a coat and suit cutter was with a firm called *Malber Inc.* owned by the Malkin Family—Lionel, Ben and their father Jack. All went well and I learned the cutting trade.

Soon after, my brother-in-law asked me to join him in his business—his partner was leaving, and he asked if I would be interested in taking his place. It was an opportunity to advance my career, and I accepted his offer. But this adventure did not last long, for business did not go very well. I handed my share of the business over to my brother-in-law and went back into the cutting trade.

Over the years I ventured into a number of things. I was happy to have learned the cutting trade, for when things did not turn out very well in my escapades, I could always fall back on it.

After working five years for the *Queenswear Childrens & Sportswear Co.*, I was approached by Don Walker, the owner; he propositioned me to buy out his Export & Import Division, which I did. The offer was too good to turn down. That got me into sales where I stayed for some 40 years, with no regret. As a salesperson, this endeavour was good to me, and it provided a secure future.

In 1965, I met my future wife. Shirley and I got married one year later, and in 1967 our first daughter Robyn was born...followed by second daughter Marla in 1969. At the beginning, we rented a four and a half room apartment. After five years, it got too small, and we moved to a four-plex where we lived for 11 years. Rents were increasing every year, so in 1983, we decided to buy our own home, self-contained, in a very nice part of town.

I have travelled a bit of the world and learned many things. I am still learning. Now retired, I find the days not long enough. I am busy with one thing or another—with no time to spare. I am into stamp collecting, computers, biking, walking, going to the Y and reading.

We now keep in touch with our old friends in the Home when some of the 'residents,' including me, get together at a once-a-year reunion where we have a chance to catch up on the latest gossip. For this we owe a vote of thanks to Myer Gordon who was a 'kid' in the Montefiore Home (which later merged with ours in 1936). Due to his efforts and organization, this event is held towards the end of each summer.

When I reflect on my past, the years that we stayed in the MHOH, I cannot say that I had many regrets. There were some bad moments, but there were some good ones, too. We survived."

Moses (Morris/Moe) Letnick

Moe was placed in the Montefiore Orphanage because his mother was a widow with two children and she was unable to care for both of them at the same time. It was 1929 and Moe was 5 years old.

While he still remembers crying for his mother, his memories of the Home are good ones. He was well treated by all the staff and never saw any signs of abuse.

At the beginning, he was too young to go to school and spent his time playing with the other children. He attended Bancroft School and remained in the Jeanne Mance Home until it closed in 1936 and he was sent to the Montreal Home on Claremont Avenue at age 12.

While he has good memories of the girls there, he also remembers the beatings at night by Ogulnick, "He was a bad man"...a feeling shared by several of the other boys under his care.

At the age of 14, Moe went to live with his mother and sister. He went to work delivering clothing until he joined the Navy at 17 1/2. His duties were on destroyers and frigates, escorting ship convoys overseas. He remained in the Navy until he was 23. Following this he became an electrician, working in construction and housing repairs.

Moe married Marie Claire in 1949 and they had five children, three girls and two boys. During those years he was a master electrician at *Christie Brown* (the bread company), the lead hand for 23 years. Then he worked in *Extended Care* in Montreal until he retired in 1990.

Moe enjoyed attending the MHOH reunions until he moved West, and still keeps in touch with the Gordons and through *The Mishpocha.*

With some of his children living in Western Canada, he and Marie Claire moved to Maple Ridge, B.C., then to White Rock in 2000. They now have 10 grandchildren.

Now in his late 70s, Moe still lives at home while suffering from Parkinsons and dementia...he goes to 'Care Share' twice a week. Though he can no longer read or write, he still sounds pretty good on the telephone, so reports Myer Gordon who keeps in touch with him!

He remembers the orphanage as, for the most part, "a very good place for me. I am very grateful that my growing up years were spent there."

Max Matt—a beloved Montefiore Supervisor
(Once one of the Montreal Home orphans himself)

Max was a mentor to many of the children, the catalyst who spurred them to meet, via the reunion route. Loved and admired by all his charges in the Montefiore Home, he was and still is, the number one person everyone wants to reminisce with, to hug, to share memories both happy and sad... the rush of adrenalin evident in all.

Max and his younger sister Hilda, spent their early years in a brutal orphanage in Romania. He came to 500 Claremont in 1921 at the age of 11 (Hilda was 5), having arrived only a few days earlier at the Port of Halifax ("...at times it feels like yesterday," he notes) with a group of Jewish Ukrainian orphans to be adopted. Among them was an Alper family, among them Max and Nat. Matt was first stripped of his old dirty clothes, deloused, bathed, embarrassed. He was given brand new clothes and never forgot the sight of his old clothes going down the chute... old clothes being destroyed, not passed on. This made a deep impression on his mind—save things, don't destroy.

Those youngsters who weren't chosen for adoption, for whatever reason—Max among them, went into the Montreal orphanage. Sister Hilda, who came with him by ship, was chosen for adoption by a wealthy family right away. Max yelled loudly when he learned that Hilda was not in the orphanage with him. And Hilda raised such a 'ruckus' at her new home when she knew Max was not nearby, that she was sent back to the orphanage where she was reunited with her beloved Max. She was met there by a giant of a man (compared to her little size), a volunteer whose smiles and hugs made her feel safe for the first time.

Max had picked up a 'street mentality' from Romania...to survive, one had to rob and run. The worst experience was starving...having to find his own food. After several days in the Home, Max discovered the kitchen with a lot of goodies. He sneaked in in the middle of the night where he found a tub of apples. He took as many as he could carry, and hid some under his pillow for another day. But he was seen by the Supervisor who called him on the carpet by reminding him that he was depriving others of having an apple. Max was punished, but not by the beating he expected. He remembered this lesson, and used it in similar situations when he himself became a supervisor.

Max showed an aptitude for working with children, so, when he was 16, he became an assistant, and the Home sent him on a Social Work Course. He went to the Montefiore Home in 1929 at age 19 as Supervisor to the 60 children there. He remained until it closed in 1936. Living in the two Homes was a marvelous experience for Max. "The Garden of Eden suddenly opened up to me," he once said.

Alumni Hy Jacobson related this story...a Ladies' Auxiliary ran card games, complete with 'cake in big pans.' Hy pre-empted the cake and hid it in his locker. Max ruled, the cake was returned and Hy was told that depriving the other kids of their dessert was wrong... he had to eat it all!..."I hope you choke on it!" At that remark, Hy dumped the cake in the laneway and never stole again.

Considered strict but caring, Max "insisted that they eat up all their food, and we did have a lot of porridge, pea soup and chicken. But they knew it was for their own good, and because I was an orphan myself, I could understand and feel for them."

His memories of that place in that far-away country were horrendous. His new home in Canada was "wonderful." Max thrived in the caring environment. For the most part, the staff was warm and pleasant; the food was good, and the activities were plentiful. As a facility in Westmount, the local Jewish community, including the Bronfmans, provided funding to add the extras that make a place more like a home.

When the home closed in 1936, Max moved to Connecticut to work with an uncle in his grocery store, and later on started his own business buying and selling grocery items himself. When he retired in 1979, he took up skiing, hiking and mountain climbing. He was forced to give up racquetball in 1988 after open heart surgery, but still went to New Zealand with a hiking club soon after. Following an accident which damaged his legs, he took up aerobics and became the darling of all his young 'classmates.'

Aged 91, he is a self-made man...'well-off' and living with his dear wife, Wanda, in a mountain-top home in Bloomfield, Connecticut. Even now, he makes it his business to attend every reunion.

Solly Mayoff and Family

Mrs. Mayoff passed away in 1924 leaving four children: Moe 15, Myer 13, Fritzie 9 and Solly 4. Their father placed them in the MHOH as he could not care for them properly.

He remarried and brought his children home...they were only in the Home for six months. As he was still so young, he has few, if any, memories of the Home.

Solly went to Fairmont School and later to a technical school which didn't work out too well. So he went to work for a jewelry company. Following a three year stint in the Army, he became partners with another Alumnus, Sam Baker, also in the jewelry business. They worked together for over 50 years!

Solly married Zelda 59 years ago. They had five children who blessed them with nine grandchildren and six great-grandchildren. He is now 82 years young and still living in Montreal, in Hampstead.

Brothers Moe and Myer have passed away. Sister Fritzie Perel married and had two children. Now in her 90s, she resides in a retirement home in Montreal. While she doesn't remember any of the names in *The Mishpocha,* she enjoys reading it! And apologized for not getting out to reunions, writing "I don't go out to social activities any more."

Judge Irving Pfeffer

"Luck versus Brains"-his story relayed at our 1997 reunion...

"If you have to choose between luck and brains, pick luck although a combination of both would be even better. March 28, 1932, a social worker from Baron De Hirsch Institute came to pick me up and take me to the Montreal Hebrew Orphans' Home. I vividly remember the day because, at seven years of age, I knew it would be important to be able to find my way back home. At the orphanage, they took my clothes away and gave me a new set, and I was given storage space, #79, for my things. I remember wearing my first pair of pyjamas.

I was not very happy at the home and ran away a number of times. (Irv. later confirmed that he was not very happy at the orphanage at the time, but, in retrospect, he recognizes that "they did give me a healthy start"—though this was not apparent for some years!) But where could a kid run? Ultimately, I was expelled from the Home shortly after my Bar Mitzvah. Left to fend for myself, I got a job as a message boy working nights and sleeping in the back of the drug store from where I delivered condoms to brothels. I had a lot of short-term jobs, earning anywhere from $0.10 to $0.25 an hour. I flunked out of the tenth grade at Baron Byng and was told by my teachers that I should forget about continuing education because it would be a waste of time. I had no aptitude for math.

I joined the army as soon as I could...for food, clothing, shelter-and to learn a trade. When an opportunity came up to take a course as a surveyor, I applied and got in—in spite of not having an aptitude for math! I learned enough trigonometry in one weekend to qualify. I then realized that maybe my high school teachers were wrong. Maybe what was needed was motivation—and luck.

When the war ended, I applied for a crash course to get into McGill and passed. My grades got better year by year and, ultimately, I had a PhD. in Economics. I got a job as an Assistant Professor at UCLA (in

California) and my academic career took off. I studied law by correspondence and passed the California Bar Exam in 1975. I have been a lawyer ever since.

All through my career, luck has been an important factor. Being at the right place at the right time. In spite of my treatment at the orphanage, they did give me a healthy start. My most lucky point at the Home was learning from, and being inspired by, Irving Layton. He initiated debating teams, English contests, botany, discussion groups and poetry at the Home...activities which inspired and encouraged me, and stood me well in my later years of study and in my career. He had us debating, reading, and dreaming of what might be possible. If that wasn't luck, what is?" (World-renowned writer-poet, Irving Layton, was a counsellor at Sunshine Camp and also worked in the Montreal Home for one year while at McGill University.)

Irving talked about 'bumping' into Sam Smith (Smitty) in California. Sam was like a hobo, travelling across the country. In his travels, he met many people and heard talk about an orphanage reunion. Because of this meeting, Irv renewed his connections with MHOH and has been connected to its reunions for over 10 years.

Irving added, several months later, "Some years ago, on a Montreal visit, I decided to see what had happened to the MHOH property at 500 Claremont. Evidently it was taken over by the RCAF during World War II, and later used by a Catholic organization for a children's facility. One of the nuns showed me around. What surprised me was how my perceptions had changed. I remembered the yard as very large with a giant oak tree in the middle. Now the yard is quite small and the giant oak wasn't nearly as big as I remembered it.

I remember as a kid standing in the yard with some of the other kids, looking up to the top of the building where there was an infirmary; and learning that Issie Chart had died there, evidently from a ruptured appendix. Castor oil was blamed. That day was a sad one that is vividly in my memory. Some time later, I saw the gravestone marker where Issie had been buried."

Again, following the late August 2000 reunion, on his way back to the airport, Irv stopped off at '500' to see the old building. The place was well maintained and for some years now has been a residence for priests and seminarians who stay for short periods of time. It was up to date with a computer at the manager's desk. The layout has changed some, but the only thing he found missing was the big oak tree. And now the new business card reads: *Pension Reservee aux Ministres du Culte aux Seminaristes aux Religieux...Congregation de la Fraternite Sacerdotale.*

Irv, living in San Francisco, California, wrote "the reunion has become a very high priority for me...it, and *The Mishpocha,* is about the only way to keep track of people."

It is through stories like Irving Pfeffer's that an important era in Montreal can be preserved.

He wrote to the Gordons in December 2001 saying that "I have been admitted to practice before the U.S. Supreme Court, which is not bad for a kid who dropped out after flunking the tenth grade at Baron Byng High!"

Sam and Herbie Rasminsky

The Rasminsky family was made up of six sons—Bernard, Abe, Ancel, Harry, Herbie and Sam—and three daughters—Alice, Fanny and Rhoda. When their mother passed away in 1931, the youngest brothers were put into the Montefiore Home the following year. Their youngest sister, Rhoda, went to live with Aunt Sophie, their father's sister. Aunt Sophie was married to Abe Bronfman of *Seagrams.*

Herbie left the Home when it closed in 1936, and joined the Army in 1941...discharged in '45 in Toronto where he met and married Ruby. They had two sons and a daughter. He went into the automotive business. Ruby passed away in the early 80s, Herbie 15 years later.

While still in the Home, Sam, who was an excellent athlete, fought in the Golden Gloves, becoming a 147 pound champion.

Sam came to the Montreal Home in 1936. He lived there until 1938 when he moved in with his older sister. Two older brothers had also been on their own, old enough to manage when their mother died.

Sam worked in the clothing trade until 1941 when he joined the Canadian Air Force. He played hockey, baseball and boxed while in the Service. When he was discharged in 1945, he continued playing hockey...good enough to tryout with the *Montreal Canadians*...and was sent to play in Baltimore in a semi-pro league.

Sam originally met Sylvia Savitsky in the Montreal Home. Ten years later, he started to see her again, and they married in 1946. Now living in Toronto, they have four daughters, eight grandsons, and three great-grandchildren who all live in different cities. The only surviving siblings (out of nine) are Sam and Rhoda.

Annie Reisler's story

When Annie Reisler Thomas was 3 1/2 years old, her mother became ill and remained in hospital for several years until her death. Annie's father was left with three small children: Annie, 7 year old brother Reuben and 9 month old baby sister Etta. Unable to care for them, Annie and Reuben were put into the Montreal Hebrew Orphans' Home in 1935-1942 (7 1/2 years).

Annie had longed for her freedom throughout her years in the Home, and when it closed in 1942, she was so happy. The three children were placed in separate foster homes. Baby Etta was also put in a foster home where she was raised as one of the family, remaining there until she married.

Annie spent the next seven years in 12 different foster homes until her marriage in 1951 at age 20. When she was 13 (in the foster home), she composed her first song, with lyrics, on the piano there. She played by ear, but soon her foster mother refused to let her use the piano because "she said I was making too much noise."

She continued to write songs for amusement. Without a piano, musical training or background, she jotted down what she called polka dots for notes. She memorized all her tunes, and also took up other artistic hobbies, such as sketching and writing plays. But she found raising children was a full time job that left her no time for hobbies.

After her children graduated from college, they moved to Toronto. In 1988, her husband Syd's skills as a freelance writer and translator of French to English were needed in Toronto...Annie joined her children there. On her 60th birthday, Syd gave her a small keyboard, and she began composing music...resuming her song-writing and resurrecting her old music from her younger years. Only one year later, she signed a contract with *Music Box Dance Publications* to include six of her compositions in an upcoming compact disc compilation.

"I play music by ear; using only my right hand. The music comes from my heart and there is a story behind every one of my compositions." Her first big hit, "Solitude" sprang from her time in the orphanage and years' experiences after.

Her experiences in the orphanage echo as well in some of her other melodies, such as "Just Your Smile." The inspiration for this tune came after meeting up with a former orphan some years later—Bernard Turowitz. He told me that, when he was left at the Montreal Home at only 5 years of age, he was in such despair that he wanted to escape by jumping out a 3rd floor window. He happened to turn his head and saw a little blonde girl smiling at him (that was Annie, also aged 5). Even in his young mind, Bernard said to himself that "If she's smiling in a place like this, it can't be that bad in here." So, he didn't jump, and years later, he excitedly told me, "It was your smile that saved my life!"

Annie has since become a composer of easy-listening melodies played on the radio from coast to coast in North America, Europe, Asia and the Far East. They are also being used on some 'soaps,' ice-skating shows, commercials and some movie tracks. She has been interviewed for TV, radio, magazines and newspapers. In 1997, Annie was named a Canadian Achiever.

Her instrumental music even impressed Frank Mills who wrote an arrangement of "Solitude" entitling it "Reminiscing With You" for his new albums. He also plays this melody in concerts worldwide.

Ruby (Reuben) Reisler

Ruby was born January 22, 1927 in Montreal, Quebec. His sister Annie has already described how and why the Reisler children went into the Montreal Hebrew Orphans' Home in Westmount.

"I didn't like the Home at all. Mr. Ogulnik, our Supervisor and known as Ogie, was a very cruel, vicious man. He was a bully who picked on and beat the little children. I had plenty of beatings by Ogie. He dared not lay a hand on the bigger boys.

I was very happy when the Home closed down in 1942. I went into a foster home with my sister Annie, but soon we were separated, both going somewhere else. I lived in 3 foster homes but the last one was the best, and remained there till I got married. I met my wife Barbara Bagelman in 1952—she was originally from England, but was living in Montreal with her parents. We married and had 2 daughters, Sheryl and Carolyn. In 1963, we all moved to England with Barbara's parents. I went into the Amusement Business with my father-in-law, until he sold me his share and I became sole owner. I am now retired. For those who are interested, my address is: #1 Riverside Gardens, London, England N3 3GR.Telephone: 011-44-208-343-0163."

Edes Sarner—Another Valued Volunteer

Edes Sarner was not a child in either of the two Jewish orphanages, but was one of the valued volunteers as a teenager more than 70 years ago! She organized a rhythm band at the Montreal Home, inspiring many a child to enjoy and make music.

The Alumni learned about Edes from an article in a seniors' magazine honouring her as the 'volunteer of the month.' When it briefly mentioned her love of helping others began in the Home, Myer Gordon called her and invited her to the upcoming MHOH reunion slated for Toronto that year, 1999. She came, told her story and was applauded for her work 'way back then.' Now in her 80s and living in Toronto, she continues with volunteer work at many organizations.

Jack Senderoff

Jack was placed in the Montefiore Home at the age of six, with his older brother Abe (age 9), when his father died in 1928. As young as he was, he remembers being well treated, and, in his mind, he found the living conditions were good.

He remained there for nine years, leaving at age 13 in 1935. He went to live with his mother and sisters. He was old enough and ambitious enough, and so went to work in Montreal to help out his family. Jack served in Wales, Abe in North Africa during World War II. He met, wooed and wed his dear Gertrude in 1945, to whom he was happily married for 53 years. They moved to New York City in 1947, where he worked as a transit clerk for the N.Y. Subway System for 23 years, after which he retired. Upon Gert's passing in May 1998, Jack moved to Florida to be near his two daughters.

While there, he was entranced by a lovely lady from Halifax and is now married to his Rose! They enjoy weekly boat trips for a little gambling and the dance nights at their condo complex in Deerfield.

Jack keeps in touch with his brother Abe who lives in New York and is single. "It looks like he'll never marry—he's going to be 82!"

Issie Shamovitch/Issac Shamai

Issie's mother was hired as a Hebrew teacher for the Montefiore Home around 1929. Issie, aged seven, came to live there at that same time. His father had passed away two years earlier. Issie remained in the orphanage until 1935, then lived with his mother until she, too, passed away in 1938.

Issie joined the Canadian Air Force in '39, and was sent overseas for five years. On his return, he went to McGill University, graduating in 1949. He met and married his wife the following year. They moved to Israel for two years, then settled in Toronto where he changed his name to Issac Shamai.

Issie had a wholesale hardware store and four daughters! Rebecca is a prominent Judge, Lisa runs a successful café and catering business. The others are Ruth and Sally (and we don't know what they do!). When their mother died in 1966, Issie moved to Michigan and opened a building supply warehouse. He married Katie in 1967.

Earl Greenberg remembers Issie as a kind fellow when he lived in the orphanage. He would help anyone whenever he could, as he did in later life. When Earl went to visit with Issie in his Toronto store, he asked him if he could pick up (buy) an item or two so that he could sell it and make a few bucks to pay his rent. Issie's reply was, "Take whatever you want, and you can pay me later." Earl took a case of flashlights and sold them at a profit. It took a while to repay Issie because he always said, "There's no hurry." He was one swell brother!

Myer Gordon's comments...Issie was a diabetic for many years, and around 1999 complications set in. A few years later, he lost both legs below the knees.

"When Issie's mail (*Mishpocha*) came back, I hunted him down by locating one of his Toronto daughters. So it was that in 1998, I learned of his medical problem, and that he and Katie had moved into a retirement home. I started calling every few weeks and felt he was truly a brother because I felt his pain when I spoke with him. He was very disillusioned at the beginning, which is easy to understand. The last time I spoke to him (at time of writing this) was February 17, 2002, and his outlook on life has much improved, to a point where, though he still feels the pain, he now accepts life in a different way."

Nettie Avrith Shragie

Nettie was put into the Montreal Home in 1924 when she was only 7 years old. Her mother had died and her father could not care for her and her three brothers, Harry, 8; Sammy, 6; and Mickey, 4.

She clearly remembers entering the Home through the basement and hearing music. However, she had been told by family she couldn't listen to music because her mother had only recently died and so she wanted to leave. One of the ladies in attendance told her it was o.k. for a child to listen to music, and it was quite alright for her to stay. She was separated from her brothers because, as boys, they lived on the other side of the building. Even they weren't together—they were all different ages and lived with their own age group.

While Nettie was quite happy in the Home, she was unhappy that her father left her there and then remarried and raised another family. What made her most unhappy was that, because she was not at her mother's funeral, she didn't believe that her mother had died. She spent eight years dreaming about searching for her mother and burying something in the back yard. When she awoke, she rushed to the Home's yard to look for her mother, certain she had buried a clue to her whereabouts there. She so badly needed proof that her mother was still alive and in an asylum as she believed.

Mostly, she needed her mother's love. Her father would visit 'every now and then' and give Nettie a quarter. She remembers that and the fact that the other girls envied her. He also brought her roller skates—"he felt guilty over leaving."

Nettie slept badly in the early years at the Home and had bags under her eyes; she ate little, earning the nickname of Broomstick, she was so skinny.

Supervisor Irving Gerdy had just left and the new Supervisors were a Mr. & Mrs. Rosen who were wonderful to Nettie, and everybody. It was Mrs. Rosen who took Romanian orphan Max Matt under her wing and over the years helped him, so that he, too, gained an interest in Social Work, took a course and became Supervisor in the Montefiore Home. Nettie also remembers Mrs. Rosen 'adopting' another young Home resident, Ida Kaufman. Ida had a limp and was dearly in need of such a friend.

Says Nettie, "I learned my culture from the Rosens. They encouraged us to put on plays, listen to opera, and the best and latest music. I learned a lot about, and an appreciation for, music this way." At the other end of the activities spectrum, the Rosens allowed the boys and girls to swim together at summer camp. Nettie was rather upset when the next Supervisors, The Byes, changed those rules.

Nettie recalls the daily routine in the orphanage. The children all got up by 6:00 a.m. They had to strip their beds and turn the mattress before breakfast. Each mattress had a large 'X' on one side, an 'O' on the other...one day the 'X' side was up, the next day, the 'O's were up. This clearly showed who did not turn over the mattress and who had wet the bed. The latter had their faces rubbed on the dirty sheet. "It broke my heart when I thought about that in later years."

After breakfast, they made their beds and left for school by streetcar. Tickets were 12 for 25 cents. It was a long ride to school from the Home...from Claremont in Westmount, to Ontario Street near Bleury. Lunch was served at the Baron de Hirsch Institute on Bleury by Board ladies. One of these played an important part in Nettie's life; Mrs. Hart saw that she ate. If Nettie didn't like what was served for lunch, Mrs.Hart went into the kitchen and made her an egg.

She also remembers that another Board member, Charlie Fisher and his wife, used to visit the children in the Home all the time. He had a ladies' wear store on Guy Street at the time.

After school there were Hebrew lessons at the Home three days a week. And the children had duties as well. One week two boys and two girls set tables; the following week, they washed the dishes. Says Nettie, "I wasn't unhappy about these duties because I was working with the other kids which made it a social thing, like a family."

While the children went to the *Shaar Hashomayim* on Saturdays for Shabbat Services—the Brumer boys were all in the choir, Sunday School was held in the Home. One of the teachers for a short while was A.M. Klein, the noted poet and author; he lectured there several times. A regular teacher was Mrs. Zunenshine.

But Rabbi Stern, of Temple Emanuel, who also spoke on Sunday at the Home, impressed Nettie the most; he imparted lifelong lessons—"I lived my life according to him." To illustrate, she related the story of a man who went to a Rabbi asking him to teach him how to be a good Jew while the man stood on one leg. The Rabbi told him it takes too long, and, taking him for a fool, he threw him out. The man went to several Rabbis asking the same question, with the same results. Then, he went to Rabbi Hillel, who told him it was easy to be a good Jew... "Do unto others as you would have them do unto you and you will be the best Jew."

One experience proved to be a bad one. Nettie and five other younger children were taken to the Herzl Clinic, on St. Urbain at the time, to have their tonsils out. A Dr. Tanenbaum picked them up in his car, and as he was putting their things in the trunk, Nettie noticed toys there. He told her that, as the eldest, if she was good during the entire procedure, she could have a toy. Concentrating only on the toys, Nettie was the only one who did not cry...she remembers counting down before the anaesthetic and eating everything offered afterwards. But she never got to see the toys again. She shed tears of disappointment.

Nettie liked the Home as all the kids were in the 'same position,' none better than the other. She does remember feeling isolated from childen outside the orphanage except at school. There just didn't seem to be enough time to make other friends. She was best friends with Mary Boxenbaum and Minnie Kushner. Nettie used to dream how she and Mary would live after they left the Home... they would earn $5.00 a week and share an apartment for $28.00 a month. A good part of her dream was spent on figuring out their finances! As it happened, Nettie left the orphanage first in 1932 to live with her father and stepmother. When she returned to see Mary, she learned she had left for New York. She regrets now that she did not pursue her search for Mary after she had moved to New York.

Nettie remembers that her brother Harry's best friend was Lou Raven and that she was very friendly with the Brumer family. She kept up this relationship over the years, and at one point, when former Home friend Goldie Velter passed away, and there was no one to look after a headstone, Nettie, her brother Sammy, and Sam Brumer made all the necessary arrangements.

Moving in with her father and his new family proved to be another painful experience. Nettie felt she was better treated at the orphanage than by her stepmother. She worked for her father in his factory, learning how to be a bookkeeper, for $2.00 a week. Her stepmother demanded all her pay or she couldn't eat at home...her parents fought a lot over this issue. Nettie was also called on to help with the children; a new one seemed to be born every year! Then, one day, she realized she did this to earn her father's love, and so started to like herself. This gave her the courage to manage without her father. So, after several months, when her stepmother's sister advised her to leave and find a room in which to live, she did so.

Nettie had learned never to depend on anyone.

Her brothers also moved back home at different times, living in one room. Mickey married at age 18 just to get out of the house.

Nettie worked for many years as a bookkeeper, spending six months a year in New York with her late mother's sister, then back to her room in Montreal. She married Al Shragie when she was 34.They had two sons, Alan, now a top corporate lawyer with Goodman, Phillips &Vineberg; the other, Michael, a successful realtor. There are four grandchildren.

But that is not even the end of Nettie's story!

When her boys were young, she wanted to adopt a similar-age girl to show the boys that there was no difference between boys and girls.

This thinking stemmed from her experiences in the Home, where everyone was treated the same...she felt that if kids fell into the wrong foster care, they could be treated very badly.

Because they already had a family of their own, the only girl they were eventually offered was 11 years old. After some soul-searching, they agreed to foster her...and after some years, also took in her sister. The sister was hard to manage as she was always testing them. So, when she became a teenager, Nettie, feeling she was not happy with them, suggested she go into a Jewish foster home for teens. It was interesting that the only way the youngster would go was knowing that she could always come home to the Shragies. Apparently, some of their loving care had rubbed off, in spite of the problems!

This loving care in the early years included singing lessons and beautiful clothes. And when the time came, it included giving both girls weddings, providing for their children and keeping in touch, even today. Nettie wants them independent, but they know they can still turn to her when they need her.

And the difficult sister told her that she learned only good from her. What a testimony!

At this writing, Nettie is 85 years young (with a fantastic memory!) and her husband Al is 87. Myer Gordon, who interviewed Nettie over the phone for this bio, says, "Bless them both for many more years."

The Stolovs

Meyer Stolov contacted the Gordons as a result of the *CJN* article seen by his twin brother Ben. As a youngster, Ben was in the Julius Richardson Convalescent Hospital in Chateauguay with his other brothers, Nathan and Matthew, while sister Judith and Meyer were in the Montreal Home. "I think the reason was that Judith and I were healthier and needed less attention. I am not totally certain of that fact, but I present it anyway."

Meyer and sister Judith entered the Montreal Home in 1934 when their mother was seriously ill. Upon her recovery about one year later, they rejoined both parents at home.

Judith Stolov Kazdan's life might have started in adversity, but as years went by, she discovered running and soon became a marathoner. Her walls are filled with ribbons, awards and trophies from world-wide competitions which have continued for almost 50 years. One can still see her jogging around her Toronto neighbourhood, now well into her 80s.

The Gordons visited with Meyer in the spring of 2001 in Ithaca. He was only in the Montreal Home for one year, aged 3-4, so doesn't know anyone. "He's a gentle, talented, unassuming man, still enjoying playing first violin in local orchestras." His twin, Ben, lives in Montreal with his wife Bluma. Ben is also a violinist and a member of the Montreal Symphony Orchestra—for the past 40 years!

Meyer's story is an interesting one, and obviously tells of a life far removed from the orphanage of his youth. He has been a professional violinist most of his life and is, at present, semi-retired and living in up-state New York in Ithaca. Born in Montreal, Meyer began his training with a Viennese teacher, Dr. Josef Berliawsky, and left for London to study at the Royal Academy of Music: 1953-56. There, he was awarded the highest honour, the Dove Prize, for most outstanding student, and soon after was elected Fellow (FRAM) for his achievements in music. In 1957, he was awarded a Diploma from the *Conservatoire Royale de Bruxelles,* Belgium. Performances during many years in England included Concertos, Recitals, String Quartets and other combinations of Chamber Music. Many of these were broadcast on the BBC. In addition, there were numerous occasions for teaching, both private and in institutions.

Meyer has had the good fortune to work with outstanding conductors and soloists over the years which undoubtedly contributed to an ongoing musical education of unparalled value. His experience at Covent Garden was of great musical value as he was exposed to singing and dancing of the highest order. Of particular note, too, was his association with Yehudi Menuhin when he played in the *Menuhin Chamber Orchestra* for two years, and a season with Pablo Casals in 1979 at Prades in Perpignan, France, in a chamber orchestra engaged for the *Casals Festival.*

In 1982, Meyer left England for New York City and freelanced for five years before deciding to settle in Ithaca, where he is now an active performer and teacher in the Finger Lakes region of New York State.

"Here is my musical history; so to speak"...

1994 to present	Member of Glimmerglass Opera Orchestra, Cooperstown, NY.
1987 to present	Concertmaster of the Orchestra of the Southern Finger Lakes, NY.
1989 to present	Member of the Binghamton Philharmonic Orchestra, NY.
1981-1985	Freelance work with American Symphony Orchestra, NYC Opera, American Ballet Theater, Harlem Dance Theater, New York City.
1972-1981	Concertmaster, Royal Opera House, Covent Garden, London, England.
1971 -1972	Assistant Concertmaster, Vancouver Symphony Orchestra, Canada.
1968-1971	Concertmaster and Soloist, Ulster Chamber Orchestra, Belfast, Ireland.
1965 -1968	Concertmaster, London Mozart Players, England
1960 -1963	Concertmaster, City of Birmingham Symphony Orchestra, England.
1962-1965	Leader of Voces Intimae Quartet, Delphos Ensemble, Birmingham, England

The Tolmasky Family—Abe, Claire and Saul

When their father passed away in 1920 in Russia, Saul, the youngest, was only six months old. Their mother came to Canada, via Italy, in 1924 and put the children into the Montefiore Home in 1925. Claire left the Home in 1928, Abe and Saul in '29.

During those years, Mrs. Tolmasky looked after the provisions (fruit, meat and vegetables) for the orphanage, for three years. Everyone knew her as a lovely woman. And even after her children had left the Home, she continued to be involved.

Some of the Alumni boarded at her home, namely Harry Ostrofsky and Harry Zelfin. She also assisted Nurse Milstein when some of the children were quarantined with chicken pox. For *Chanukah*, she organized a little party at her home for some of the little girls. Vita Shein Seidler remembers going there several times for delicious *latkas*!

Meanwhile, Saul went to Mt. Royal School and then on to Baron Byng High School. They all went to work...Claire for *Raginsky Bedding*, Abe 'went into' men's wear, while Saul worked for a ladies' hat firm called *Nadelle Hats*.

Saul went into the Canadian Air Force in 1941 and was sent overseas the following year. He was discharged in 1946 and married Gertrude soon after. He returned to the ladies' hat business, and then into an automobile dealership with his brother-in-law. Saul had one daughter.

Abe was also called for service, but was rejected because of flat feet! He became a cutter in the dress industry and was involved in its union. Abe married Esther in 1939, and they remained married for about 60 years. They had one daughter and now three grandsons. Both Abe and Esther passed away within the last three years.

Claire and Sam Margolian have one son.

Montefiore Home Reunion, 1957

Montefiore Home Alumni, 1989

Montreal Home Alumni, 1989

First combined MHOH Reunion, 1989. The Spouses.

L-R: Manny & Mary Cohen, Lester & Irma Dick, Hannah & Nathan Cohen

L-R (Bk. Row): Myer Gordon, Louis Brumer, Saul Tolmasky, John Brownston, Manny Cohen, Earl Greenberg, Harry Schwartz, Joe Miller
L-R (Seated): Harry Lenetsky, Sam Rasminsky, Max Matt, Nathan Cohen.

L-R: Sam Rasminsky, Myer Gordon, Max Matt.
(With the original basket issued by the Home
to Myer Gordon.)

L-R: Myer Gordon, Irving Pfeffer, author Judy Gordon

APPENDIX

Montreal Hebrew Orphans' Home Alumni
The women are listed by maiden names,
their married names are in brackets.

Albert, Henry
Albert, Julius
Alper, Max
Alper, Nat
Avrith, Michael
Avrith, Nettie (Shragie)
Avrith, Sam
Axman, Charlie
Baker, Harry
Berman, Ann (Alexander)
Berman, Sam
Bye, Abe
Bye, Edie
Chart, Ruth (Littlefield)
Cohen, Herbie
Cohen, Manny
Cohen, Nathan
Cohen, Yetta (Novak)
Dick, Lester
Dubin, Celia (Altrows)
Epstein, Sally Ann (Kerman)
Fishman, Lionel
Fishman, Muriel
Fishman, Ruth (Tobin)
Florian, Sam
Freedman, Sam
Goldsmith, Bessie (Grossner)
Goldsmith, Nathan
Gottlieb, Eva (Goldberg)
Greene, Harry
Gross, Dr. Jack
Israel, Harvey
Israel, Shirley (Thau)
Kushner, Alex
Lang, Lou
Levy, Lionel
Lieberman, Michael
Lipson, David
Matt, Hilda (Brownstone)
Melnick, Martin
Nachbar, Mildred (n/a)
Novak, Yetta (Cohen)
Pfeffer, Judge Irving
Randolph, Moss
Randolph, Sylvia (Rich)
Reider, Ernestine (Justitz)
Reisler, Annie (Thomas)
Reisler, Reuben
Sandell, Joseph
Savitsky, Reva (Schuman)
Savitsky, Rose (Manzi)
Savitsky, Sylvia (Rasminsky)
Schwartz, Harry
Schwartz, Libby (Kashenberg)
Schwartz, Samuel
Shenker, Ann (Hershon)
Smilovitch, Ruth (Furman)
Smith, Rachel (Raub)
Solomon, Aaron (Shmoiser)
Spielman, Sara (Frenkel)
Stolov, Ben*
Stolov, Judith (Kazdan)

Stolov, Matthew *
Stolov, Meyer
Turowetz, Allan
Turowetz, Jerry
Wener, Ella (Wilbourne)
Yanovitch, Vivienne (Urman)
Yanovitch, Cecil Young
Zimmerman, Sherry (Grossman)

* Ben and Matthew Stolov were not placed with Judith and Meyer...they were put in the Julius Richardson Convalescent Hospital in Chateauguay.

Montefiore Hebrew Orphans' Home Alumni

The women are listed by maiden names,
their married names are in brackets

Adelstein, Minnie (Leibo)
Adelstein, Moe
Bercusson, Sara (Connie Gore)
Cherry, Dave
Frankel, Hymie
Frankel, Ruth (Margolese)
Garber, Ben
Greenberg, Earl
Greenberg, Helen (Zawalsky)
Hoffman, Tillie
Label, Willie
Letnick, Morris
Matt, Max
Miller, Harry
Miretsky, Edith (Landen)
Miretsky, Gert (Golub)
Miretsky, Ruth (Gorelik)
Newton, Jeannie (Lichtenstein)
Rasminsky, Sam
Schwartz, Hymie
Senderoff, Abe
Senderoff, Jack
Shamai, Issac (Shamovitch)
Shaner, Dr. Sydney M.
Shein, Vita (Seidler)
Sheiner, Albert
Sklar, Ida (Lewis)
Steinberg, Issie
Ticker, Moe
Ticker, Shirley (Brothman)
Ticker, Sydney
Tolmalsky, Abe
Tolmasky, Claire (Margolian)
Tolmasky, Saul
Wagon, Anita (Bercovitch)
Weisman, Celia (Tina Rosen)
White, Saul
Zukerman, Jack

The names included in the lists of living and deceased Alumni are only those of whom we are aware. It is likely that many names, unknown to us, are missing...for this, we apologize.

Those MHOH Alumni known to us who have passed away
and the year, where known

Prior to 1992

Bill Aaron
Ann (Jacobson) Aaronson
Rose (Cherry) Abrams
Frances Appel
Charlie Axman (1990)

Frankie Baker
Johnnie Baker
Ralph Belkin
Hilda Benjamin
Oscar Black
Seymour Black (1975)
Charlie Bloom
Lily (Feldman) Braverman
Surie Broitman
Ben Brumer (1991
Harry Brumer
Hymie Brumer
Sam Brumer
Moe Burke
Norman Bydoff
Mr. & Mrs. Henry Bye

Issie Chart
Lynn Cohen
Moishe Cohen

Charlie Davies

Minnie Engel
Philip Epstein

Sam Feldman

Hymie Fine
Evelyn (Shano) Furlong (1992)
Dr. Gisella Freedman
Issie Freedman

Sarah (Umansky) Gatis
Ann (Greenberg) Gluzman
Jennie Gold
Ben Gordon (1987)
Joe Greenberg

Harry Kaminsky
Mary Kantor
Rosie (Bercovitch) Kaufman
Milton Kramer
Solly Kravitz

Eli Linetsky

Esther (Gold) Mann
Leon Markson
Mike Mendelson (1992)
Eli Miller
Dave Milstein
Fanny Milstein
Max Milstein
Saul Milstein
Bessie Muchnick

Dennis Newton (1992)

Dr. Maurice Ogulnick
Louis Ostrovsky

Oscar Plotnick
Mendel Raffalovitch
Lou Raven (1990)
Moe Resnick (1989)
Josephine (Cohen) Romisher
Mollie Rosenberg

Oscar Roth
Mollie Rubin
Sollie Rubin

Dave Schacter
Arthur Shalat
Abie Shein
Dora (Goldstein) Sheinker
Mrs. Shenker
Abie Sokoloff
Jack Sokoloff
Mary Sokoloff

Phyllis Sokoloff/Felicia Sotell, 1992
Eddie Spielman
Nathan Spielman
Jack Spinner
Issie Steinberg
Avrum Stoffmaker

Mrs. Ticker
Gert Tolmasky (wife of Saul)

Goldie Velter
Tillie Velter
Maurice Vineberg

Leah Wener
Sara Wener
Ben Wiseman (1992)

Agnes Zukerman (Jack's wife))
Morris Zukerman (1988)

1993-1995

Toby Frankel
Jack Gross
Arnold Greene
Ida Label (wife of Willie)

Herbie Rasminsky
Leo Schwartz
Doris Smilovitch

Federation of Jewish Philanthropies of Montreal, 1919
Montreal Hebrew Orphans' & Sheltering Home
18 Evans Street
Miss Rose Myers, Superintendent
(from Annual Report)

Board of Directors

A. M. Vineberg, Sol Kellert, Honourary Presidents
A. Lesser, President
M. Rittenberg, Treasurer
H. H. Cohen, Hon.Secretary

Wm. Albert
J. Goldstein
Alan J. Hart
Philip Glickman
Charles Samit
Charles Fisher
David Chorlton
M. Marcus
A. Kellnor
Harry Gordon

Medical Board

Dr. S. Ortenberg, Chairman
Dr. J. Rosenbaum, Secretary

Dr. L. Mendel
Dr. A. R. Illievitz
Dr. J. Kolber
Dr. D. H. Ballon
Dr. S. F. Stein
Dr. D. Tannenbaum
Dr. E. C. Levine

Dental Board

Dr. A.S. Solomon Vice-Chairman
(Joint Board)

Dr. J. Rubin, Dr. E. Elkan, Dr. N. Titleman,
Dr. M. N. Fineberg, Dr. S. Mendel, Dr. H. S. Gross,
Dr. M. Gold

Montreal Hebrew Orphans' Home
Expenditures for the Twelve-Month Period.
January 1st to December 31st, 1925

Physical Maintenance of Bldgs. and Equipment		
Repair/ Repl. to Bldgs. and Equipment	$ 2,388.79	
Rep./Repl. to Furniture	106.25	
Materials for Repair	150.07	
Deco System	500.00	
		$ 3,645.14
Physical Operation of Plant		
Janitorial Service	$ 1,110.50	
Laundry, Cl. and Dis. Supplies	1,536.13	
Janitorial Equipment	148.17	
Light, Heat and Power	453.76	
Fuel	1,737.32	
		$ 4,985.88
Cost of Administration		
Salaries of Officers, Clerks, etc.	$ 3,350.39	
Printing, Postage and Stationery	74.31	
Repairs on Office Equipment	3.24	
Telephone Service	101.41	
Telegrams	5.62	
		$ 3,354.97
Institutional Operation		
Meat	$ 1,285.40	
Groceries	2,833.60	
Milk	1,486.00	
Bread	1,883.33	
Fish	564.39	
Eggs	1,178.79	
Butter	635.63	
Refrigerating Supplies	64.70	
Household Supplies and Equipment	902.61	
Linens and Bedding	472.11	
Wages, Cooks, etc.	2,277.60	
Wearing Apparel	3,087.66	
Medical Supplies and Equipment	471.04	

Salaries of Nurses, etc.	$ 862.90	
Professional Services	253.00	
Educational Costs	925.13	
Text and Reference Books	467.17	
Optical Supplies	28.00	
Dental Supplies	25.81	
Barber	51.75	
Water Supplies	257.05	
		$ 20,014.56
Fixed Charges		
Interest	$ 192.50	
Taxes	117.33	
Insurance	258.12	
		$ 567.95

A Depression Shopping List; 1932

Automobiles

New:

Pontiac coupe	585.00
Chrysler sedan	995.00
Dodge	595.00
Studebaker	840.00
Packard	2,150.00
Chevrolet pickup truck	650.00

Used:

Lincoln '27	125.00
Studebaker '30	200.00
Ford '29	57.50

Clothing

Women's

Mink coat	585.00
Leopard coat	92.00
Cloth coat	6.98
Raincoat	2.69
Wool dress	1.95
Wool suit	3.98
Wool sweater	1.69
Silk stocking	.69
Leather shoes	1.79

Men's

Men's Overcoat	11.00
Wool suit	10.50
Trousers	2.00
Shirt	.47
Pullover sweater	1.95
Silk necktie	1.95
Golf suit	20.00
Tuxedo	5.00
Shoes	3.98

Household Items

Silver-plate, 26 piece	4.98
Double-bed sheets	.67
Bath towel	.24
Wool blanket	1.00
Linen tablecloth	1.00
Wool rug (9' x 12')	5.85

Appliances

Electric iron	2.00
Electric percolator	1.39
Electric mixer	9.95
Vacuum cleaner	18.75
Electric washer	47.95
Gas stove	23.95

Furniture

Dining room set, 8 piece	46.50
Bedroom set, 3 piece	49.95
Lounge chair	19.95
Double bed/Spring mattress	14.95
Bridge table	1.00
Mahogany coffee table	10.75
Wing chair	39.00
Grand piano	395.00

Toys

Doll carriage	4.98
Sled	1.45
Tricycle	3.98
Bicycle	10.95
Catcher's mitt	1.19
Leather basketball	1.00
BB air rifle	.79

Food

Sirloin steak (per lb.)	.29
Rib roast	.22
Chicken (per lb.)	.22
Salmon (16 oz. can)	.19
Milk (per qt.)	.10
Butter (per lb.)	.28
Eggs (per dozen)	.29
Cheese (per lb.)	.24
Bread (20 oz. loaf)	.05
Coffee (per lb.)	.26
Sugar (per lb.)	.05
Rice (per lb.)	.06
Potatoes (per lb.)	.02
Tomatoes (16 oz. can)	.09
Bananas (per lb.)	.07
Onions (per lb.)	.03
Cornflakes (8 oz. pkg.)	.08

Real Estate

Modern house, 6 rooms, 2-car garage (Detroit)	$ 2,800.00
Italian Villa, 12 rooms (Westchester, NY)	17,000.00
Spanish Studio, 7 rooms (Beverly Hills, CA)	5,000.00

Travel

Air:

New York to Chicago, round trip	86.31
Chicago to Los Angeles, round trip	207.00

Rail:

Chicago to San Francisco, round trip, 15 days	80.50
NYC to Scarsdale, NY, monthly commuter tkt.	10.39

Sea:

Tour of Europe, 60 days, 11 countries	495.00.
Bermuda-Havana-Nassau cruise, 10 days	110.00
N.Y. to California via Panama Canal	120.00
San Francisco to Hawaii, round trip	220.00

Miscellaneous

Dental filling	1.00
Toothpaste (large)	.25
Coty face powder	1.50
L'Aimant perfume (1/4 oz.)	1.00
Cultivated oriental pearls	35.00
Razor blades (10)	.49
Cigarettes	.15
Lighter	.39
Pipe	.83
Alarm clock	2.00
Briefcase	1.00
Console radio	49.95
Typewriter	19.75
Moviecamera, 8 mm	29.50
Kodak Box Brownie	2.50
Car tire	6.20
Gasoline (per gallon)	.18

(From: *Journey Through the Lean Years,* p. 29 by The Editors of Time-Life Books)

Women's Division
Montreal Hebrew Orphans' Home -1934

Officers

Mrs. Samuel Bronfman, Honorary President
Mrs. Bernard Gardner, Hon. Vice-President
Mrs. S. Jaffe, Hon. Vice-President

Mrs. Julius Block, President
Mrs. C. B. Fainer, Vice-President
Mrs. C. J. Gross, Vice-President
Mrs. S. Leopold, Vice-President
Mrs. D. Raff, Vice-President
Mrs. D. M. Notkin, Recording Secretary
Mrs. E. Lazare, Corresponding Secretary
Mrs. H. Singer, Publicity Manager

Board of Directors

Mrs. Barney Aaron
Mrs. Philip Abbey
Mrs. A. Z. Cohen
Mrs. Adolphe Gardner
Mrs. Jacob Kellert
Mrs. Joseph Kruger
Mrs. L. Klineberg
Mrs. J. Lewinson
Mrs. E. P. Van Geun
Mrs. H. Levine
Mrs. M.A. Michaels
Mrs. Adolphe Pesner
Mrs. A. Raginsky, Sr.
Mrs. L. A. Shapiro
Miss A. Silverstone
Mrs. Martin Simon
Mrs. Edward Solomon

COMMITTEES
(Montefiore Home 18th Annual Report - 1935)

ADMISSION
M. ABRAMOWITZ, Chairman

Mrs. R. BERNSTEIN
M. H. COHEN
Mrs. B. GIBSON
M. HANDMAN
S. LERNER
Mrs. M. ROSOVITCH
Mrs. H. SCHAFER

BAZAAR
MOE FELDMAN, Chairman

I. BRISKIN
M. DESKIN
Mrs. M. CRELINSTEN
Mrs. M. DESKIN
H. ROSEMAN, M. SCHNEIDERMAN, Co-Chairmen
Mrs H ROSEMAN, Mrs. B. VOSKO, Convenors

TAG-DAY
Alderman MAX SEIGLER, Chairman

SUNSHINE CAMP
Alderman MAX SEIGLER, Chairman

ANNUAL CAMPAIGN
J. BRODIE, Chairman
BEN GOLDENBERG, J. BLOCK

EDUCATION
S. LERNER, M. ABRAMOWITZ

BUILDING AND MAINTENANCE
M. DESKIN, M. HANDMAN, Co-Chairmen

HOUSE COMMITTEE
Mrs. M. DESKIN, Chairman
Mrs. R. BERNSTEIN, MRS. M. ROSOVITCH
Mrs. D. COHEN, MRS. B. VOSKO

WAYS & MEANS COMMITTEE

I. BRISKIN, J. BRODIE, Co-Chairmen
M. H. COHEN, M. DESKIN, A. RAGINSKY, Sr.
M. COOPERBERG, BEN GOLDENBERG,
Alderman MAX SEIGLER

CLOTHING

Boys - M. COOPERBERG
Girls - L. BRISKIN

CONSTITUTION & BY-LAWS

I. BRODIE, M. DESKINICH,
I. POPLIGER, I. M. RUBINOVITCH

ENTERTAINMENT

I. LIEBMAN

CHRONOLOGY OF DEVELOPMENTS FEDERATION OF JEWISH PHILANTHROPIES and CONSTITUENT AGENCIES

1863	Founding of Young Men's Hebrew Benevolent Society (YMHBS).
1891	Elizabeth Street building of YMHBS opens. This building was the location of the BHI school as well as a sheltering home for new immigrants.
1900	Name change to Baron de Hirsch Institute (BHI).
1901	Opening of 2040 Bleury Street BHI building, named the Baron de Hirsch Institute Building.
1907	The BHI School ceases teaching English classes and becomes a Hebrew Free School.
1907	The Jewish Colonization Association (JCA) becomes an independent body from the BHI.
1909	Founding of Montreal Hebrew Orphans' and Sheltering Home, later Montreal Hebrew Orphans' Home (MHOH) and Hebrew Old People's Sheltering Home (HOPSH).
1912	Opening of Jewish Public Library (JPL).
1912	Opening of Herzl Dispensary.
1912	Opening of Mount Sinai Sanatarium (MSS).
1913	Founding at BHI of the Friendly League of Jewish Women and Welcome Club for Jewish working girls.
1914	Hebrew Maternity Hospital opens.
1916	Incorporation of the Federation of Jewish Philanthropies.
1917	Closing of Beth Israel Day Nursery and Infants' Home.
1919	Amalgamation of the Friendly League Welcome Club and Young Women's Hebrew Association (YWHA).
1920	Founding of Camp B'nai Brith.
1920	YWHA opens a branch in the Papineau district of Montreal.
1923	Founding of Businessmen's Council (a fundraising body).
1926	Founding of Neighbourhood House (a settlement house/ socialization centre for Jewish children and youths).
1929	Closing of Hebrew Maternity Hospital.
1934	Opening of the Jewish General Hospital (JGH).
1934	The YMHA takes over the administration of the YWHA although still provides YWHA's financial support.

1935	Opening of the Jewish Sunshine Camp.
1935	Closing of BHI Library.
1938	Juvenile Aid Dept. of BHI ceases its operations.
1941	CJC, FJP, JGH and UJRA merge to form Combined Jewish Appeal (CJA).
1943	MHOH and Montefiore Orphans' Home close and the Jewish Child Welfare Bureau (JCWB) is created.
1943	United Jewish Council Camps (UJCC) become beneficiaries of CJA
1945	Precursor to Jewish Vocational Service (JVS) created.
1946	Publication of *Your Community* begins.
1947	BHI merges with Family Welfare Dept.
1948	FJP moves to Sherbrooke Street building.
1950	BHI merges with JCWB.
1951	Name change from FJP to Federation of Jewish Community Services (FJCS).
1952	Jewish Convalescent Hospital opens.
1952	Jewish Camping Service created, opening of Camp Wooden Acres
1952	Closing of Jewish Sunshine Camp.
1962	Jewish Convalescent Hospital joins FJCS, later to be called Jewish Rehabilitation Hospital.
1963	BHI moves to Van Horne Ave.
1963	Golden Age Association (for senior citizens) enters Federation
1964	Miriam Home for the Exceptional becomes associated with (but not a constituent agency of) FJCS.

INDEX

About the Author

Judy Gordon was born and raised in Montreal,Quebec and had her first writing assigments as a student at McGill University in the early 1950s, when she worked for its newspaper *The McGill Daily*. She moved to Toronto with her husband and three children in 1969. Judy wrote a community column for a local newspaper, worked as a guide-demonstrator at the 1850-period Gibson House, then returned to finish her B.A. degree...graduating from York University in 1980 with a B.A. in Psychology and Recreation.

Judy has been writing poetry since her early teens, and for the past 30 years has entertained family and friends with humourous poems for their 'special' occasions. She wrote her first book (unpublished) about the true experiences of her young family moving to (and from) B.C. in 1966-67.

Her children's book of poetry, *The Body Book*, was written and published in 1990 as a fundraiser for The Canadian Shaare Zedek Hospital Foundation—Judy was its public relations director from 1988-1999.

Divorced in 1982, she married Myer Gordon, from whom she first learned of the Jewish orphanages in Montreal. Following 12 years of Alumni reunions, she saw an opportunity to educate the Montreal community about these two institutions and decided to write a book describing life in Montreal between 1909 and 1942, containing anecdotes about the children's experiences in the Homes and biographies and photographs where possible. Her assiduous research has resulted in a serious contribution to the history of North American Jews by shedding light on a hitherto little known segment of the important Montreal community.

Judy still resides in Toronto with Myer and enjoys a relationship with their blended family of seven children and 12 grandchildren—Adam and Tristan, Randy, Marshall and Jordana, Melissa, Brooke, Alex, Pam and Robbie, and Paul and Liz. Liz has since presented Myer with two great-grandchildren, Michael and Mackenzie. Unfortunately, none of the original four-legged family members are with them.